Murderous Tyneside

Murderous Tyneside

The executed of the Twentieth Century

John J. Eddleston

The Breedon Books
Publishing Company
Derby

First published in Great Britain by
The Breedon Books Publishing Company Limited
Breedon House, 44 Friar Gate, Derby, DE1 1DA.
1997

ISBN 1 85983 082 X

Printed and bound by Butler & Tanner Ltd., Selwood Printing Works, Caxton Road, Frome, Somerset.

Front cover photograph by W.W. Winter Ltd., Derby.

Colour separations by RPS, Leicester.

Jackets printed by Lawrence-Allen, Weston-super-Mare, Avon.

CONTENTS

Acknowledgements

THERE are a number of people who greatly assisted me in the production of this book. First and foremost I must thank Yvonne Berger who helped with the research at the Public Record Office and the newspaper library at Colindale in London. She also proof read the book, advised on changes and assisted in the tracing of illustrations. I would also like to thank the staff of the PRO at both Kew and the now sadly closed office at Chancery Lane. I would also like to express my appreciation of the efforts of the staff at the Colindale newspaper library, especially Mr Fred Harwood.

Finally, I must mention Barbara Heathcote of the Local Studies Section of the Newcastle City Library, for her assistance with some of the stories.

INTRODUCTION

THE city of Newcastle and its immediate environs of Jarrow, North and South Shields and the outlying towns, have seen some most intriguing murder cases. Perhaps the most famous of all is that of the murder of John Innes Nisbet by John Alexander Dickman, for which the latter was hanged in August 1910. Yet there are others in the pages of this book whose stories are equally fascinating.

You will read of the two Millers, hanged 90 minutes apart on the same day for what was a senseless crime. Or consider Thomas Craig, a man determined to avenge himself on the woman who had spurned him; of William Ambrose Collins who brutally murdered a WAAF during the war years.

Capital punishment is a very emotive subject and this book is not intended to argue the case either for, or against. The facts are told and it is up to the reader to decide for themselves whether the hanging of these killers served any purpose beyond judicial revenge.

John J. Eddleston
Brighton, 1997

A FAMILY AFFAIR

T HE MILLER family of Cullercoats had some rather complex relationships. John Miller, who was 67 years of age, was the stepson of Mary Ferguson, who in turn had been the second wife of Miller's father. John Miller's father had died seven years before, leaving his widow, Mary, financially secure. Originally the family had been hawkers with no fixed abode but by sheer hard work they had amassed enough money to move to Cullercoats and buy property in the area. Mary had herself remarried, this time to John Ferguson, and he was in fact a few years younger than his new stepson. That marriage had taken place some four and a half years before.

John Miller was well known in the area. He owned round-abouts on Tynemouth Sands and was quite close to his nephew, a 31-year-old musician named John Robert Miller. They were often seen together.

John Ferguson, who was about 60 years of age, had been a joiner by trade but had not worked for some time. In fact, Ferguson had no real need to work since Mary was, after all, a woman of property and, for a resident of Cullercoats in 1901, was quite comfortably off. Together with his son, Ferguson had originally been a lodger in the Miller household after old Mr Miller had died. After a while, a relationship had blossomed between him and Mary, culminating in their marriage two and a half years later. Ferguson's son had moved on long ago and now Mary, much to the anger of her family, had made a new will leaving all her property to John Ferguson in the event of her death.

At 2.30pm on Friday, September 20th, 1901, John Miller and his nephew entered a shop at 70 Saville Street, North Shields. The shop was owned by George Purvis who knew the older man as he had had dealings with him many times over the previous 20 years.

It was the older Miller who said, "We want to look at some knives." He went on to explain that his nephew was going to sea as a cook and needed a special kind of knife. After looking at various blades, John Robert Miller selected a type of sheath knife and the sheath to go with it. Mr Purvis, ever a salesman, also tried to sell him a belt to hold the sheath but this was declined. As the two men left the shop, George Purvis saw John Robert Miller put the knife inside his topcoat pocket. He had paid over the 11d, which was the cost of the knife, and as they left the shop, he handed some coppers to his uncle.

One hour later, at 3.30pm, both the Millers were leaning over the railings at the top of the cliffs at Cullercoats. They were seen there by Zeppaniah Miller, a cab driver who was no relation. Zeppaniah saw the two men walk away from the railings and enter the Bay Hotel where they stayed for no more than a couple of minutes. The cab driver was still there when they left and he saw them as they walked down Dove Street where the younger man vanished around a corner, leaving his older companion standing in the street. Just a few minutes more passed until the younger man reappeared, joined his companion and the two then walked off in the direction of Hudleston Street. Zeppaniah thought that both men were drunk.

Indeed, the younger man was staggering along the pavement. At the same time, Robert Stephenson Oliver, a 13-

year-old boy, also saw the two Millers, heading for 55 Hudleston Street.

When they arrived at that address, young Oliver saw the younger man knock on the door while the elder concealed himself in the doorway of the next house. The door was soon opened, whereupon both of the men appeared to rush inside and the door was slammed shut behind them.

James Melvin was a grocer who ran a shop in Hudleston Street, almost directly opposite to number 55, the house occupied by Mary and John Ferguson.

He looked out of his shop window at some time around 3.30pm and saw John Robert Miller standing outside the front door of the Fergusons' house. Melvin also noticed that Miller's uncle had positioned himself against the outside wall of the house next door so that anyone opening the door of number 55 would be unable to see him.

Melvin watched the younger Miller knock on the front door. Almost immediately it was opened by John Ferguson who kept his left hand on the door lock. John Robert Miller rushed into the house. From his position, Melvin could see Miller pushing Ferguson before him, with his uncle quickly following into the house. Melvin saw the door close and heard the sound of a dog barking coming from within.

Such behaviour was unusual, to say the least, so, for two or three minutes James Melvin watched the front door of the house opposite. Suddenly he saw Mary Ferguson appear at the upstairs front window, from where she attracted the attention of a young boy who happened to be passing and asked him to knock next door. He did as he was asked and when the neighbour appeared, Mary asked her to contact the police.

The first officer on the scene was Police Constable White-head, who was on duty in the village. He dashed to number 55, only to find that the front door was bolted against him. Once he had identified himself Mary Ferguson opened the door and upon entering Constable Whitehead found the body of John

Ferguson lying at the foot of the stairs which led up to his flat. Later he found the bloodstained knife inside the flat.

Constable Whitehead did not have to look far for the two men who had committed this crime. Going around the back of the house he found a crowd of people guarding both the Millers. They were taken into custody and removed to the Central police station in North Shields, where both were charged with murder.

The inquest on John Ferguson opened at the Bay Hotel, Cullercoats, on the day after the murder. The proceedings were before the deputy coroner for South Northumberland, Mr H.T. Rutherford and only evidence of identification was called, the matter then being adjourned until October 2nd.

The first court appearance was at North Shields police court on September 21st, before Mr A.O. Carr and Mr F.R.N. Haswell. The proceedings were very brief, John Miller telling the clerk of the court, "I am entirely innocent of it." Then, pointing to his nephew he added, "He told me he was going to sea and wanted a knife." When it came to his turn, John Robert Miller would only mutter, "I have nothing to say, Sir." The pair were remanded for one week.

On September 28th, the prosecution asked for a further remand, which was granted, the third appearance taking place on October 2nd. By now, Mr Whitehorn had been instructed to handle the prosecution but he pointed out that the inquest on John Ferguson would be held that afternoon and further evidence would come from that. For that reason he asked for another remand. Neither of the accused men objected, but John Miller asked if his spectacles could be returned to him. He was told that the matter would be attended to.

In fact, there were two more police court appearances, one on October 9th and the last on October 16th. The two men were then committed for trial at the next assizes. That trial took place at the Moot Hall, Newcastle, on November 15th, 1901, before Mr Justice Grantham. The prosecution case was put by Mr J.E. Joel and Mr E. Meynell. The elder Miller was represented by Mr Mitchell Innes while his nephew's case was put by Mr Horace Marshall. Both men pleaded not guilty although John Robert Miller put it somewhat differently by saying, "I can't say I'm guilty."

Mary Ferguson gave evidence that at the time the two Millers arrived at her house, she was in the kitchen cooking a meal for John Ferguson and herself. Before any knock came to the door, she heard raised voices outside. Someone then hammered on the door and her husband went downstairs. Mary had tried to stop him because of the noise she had heard but even as she spoke, John was opening the door.

It all happened so quickly that Mary couldn't be sure exactly what took place next. She seemed to remember that the older Miller had bolted the front door while John Robert Miller engaged in some sort of scuffle with her husband and at the end of this, John Ferguson lay dead at the foot of the stairs. The two Millers then came up the stairs and into her flat, leaving the front door bolted. As they approached Mary, one of the men shouted, "Do you see that?" Mary nodded and cried, "Yes you villain, you have murdered my husband." The knife was then thrown down upon the floor and both men then walked down a second set of stairs which led to the back of the flats and left the building.

Mary Ferguson told the court that she knew of no reason for the attack. There was no bad feeling that she knew about and John Miller had certainly made no objections when she had announced that she was to marry Ferguson. She could only assume that if there was any reason it was jealousy over her money, although she had always given her relatives money whenever they asked for it. She ended by describing her dead husband as a 'quiet lamb of a man, who was always good to everybody'.

Robert Oliver told the court that when John Robert Miller had knocked on the door he had used the flat of his hand, although the door had a knocker. Some ten minutes after both men had rushed into the house, Oliver saw a crowd of people gathering at the back of the house. These people were guarding both men, although the elder man certainly looked unperturbed. He was busily trying to light his pipe and asked people in the crowd if they had a match.

James Melvin told the court that after Mary Ferguson had shouted for someone to fetch a policeman, he, too, went around the back of the house and saw the two Millers amongst a crowd of people. It was Melvin who told the crowd that they should not let the men go as the police were on their way.

Mrs Isabella Mason was another who had seen the crowd guarding the two men, but by the time she arrived, it was common knowledge that John Ferguson had been attacked. Not realising who was responsible she had told the Millers that Ferguson had been stabbed. The elder man replied, "Yes, four or five times," whereupon his nephew turned to him and said, "You have tantalised me; you have irritated me; you gave me drink; you gave me the knife."

Zeppaniah Miller told the court that after watching the two men head from the Bay Hotel to Hudleston Street, he had remained with his cab in the same position. Some ten minutes later, he heard of the attack and went over to the back of Hudleston Street himself. According to his evidence, John Miller had a patch of blood upon his face, although no one else had mentioned this. He went on to say that the door of the yard which led to number 55 was wide open and the back door to the house was half open. Zeppaniah went inside the house and up the back stairs where he was stopped in his tracks by a rather large dog. Mary Ferguson appeared, quietened the dog and told Zeppaniah to come up. He saw John Ferguson lying on the ground and took a lighted candle to examine him. Ferguson was on his right side with his face up against the lobby door and his legs against the stairs. It was Zeppaniah who then went outside and told the assembled crowd that

Ferguson was dead. At the time, John Miller was leaning against the wall while his nephew was walking up and down, 'all of a tremble'.

Sergeant Proud gave evidence of the two men being examined by Dr Brumwell, the police surgeon, in the warrant office at the station. As the doctor was doing his work, John Robert Miller had been heard to say, "I done it doctor; I done it; take me and hang me; I have murdered my uncle." At this point, Proud had cautioned him and told him that anything he said would be taken down and given in evidence. The young man had continued, "It's alright. I'm going to die. I have done something to make me die. It's the truth. I have committed murder. I will die a coward. Never before God had I any intention of doing it. I will go to the scaffold and die. I feel miserable to think that I had no provocation to do it." Meanwhile, the elder Miller had only said, "I have nothing to do with the affair. I tried to prevent the affair, but could not. I have as little to do with it as you have."

Inspector H. McQueen had been the officer who charged both the Millers in the office of the chief constable. The elder Miller had replied, "I know nothing about it. I'm as innocent as a babe unborn. I believe if I had my eyesight, I could have stopped it, at least to a great extent." John Robert Miller had said, "I simply say I deserve all I get for being such a fool. I was mad with drink or I would not have done such a thing. That is all I have to say. I am very sorry. God bless everybody."

Dr Brumwell and the assistant police surgeon, Dr Phillips, gave details of the injuries the dead man had sustained. He had been stabbed a total of six times about the face and neck and had also received two wounds to his left hand, implying that he had tried to defend himself from the onslaught.

The defences of the two men were somewhat different. John Miller simply denied that he had anything to do with the death of John Ferguson. It had been his nephew who wielded the knife and he had actually tried to stop it. John Robert Miller said that he was drunk at the time of the attack, had been enticed into it by his uncle and added that he had been kicked in the head by a horse when he was a boy and had suffered from severe headaches ever since. As a result of all this, he was not responsible for his actions at the time of the killing.

In due course, the jury returned a guilty verdict on both men and Mr Justice Grantham sentenced them to death. Eight days later, on November 23rd, Victor Grunhut, the South Shields solicitor who had acted for John Robert Miller, applied to the Home Secretary for mitigation of the sentence on his client. The request was refused and the death sentence confirmed.

Originally it had been planned to hang both men at the same time but as the appointed day grew ever closer, John Robert Miller became hysterical. Given his state, the authorities decided to stagger the executions, to spare the younger man the sight of his uncle on the scaffold, although they would still both be hanged on the same day.

There was a large crowd gathered outside the prison on the morning of the executions. A canvas had been erected from the condemned cell to the scaffold to prevent the men being seen as they walked their final journey. The previous night had been very windy but Saturday, December 7th, 1901, dawned clear and calm.

At a few minutes to 8.00am William and John Billington entered the condemned cell at Newcastle jail and began to pinion John Miller's hands behind his back. Miller then announced, "Gentlemen, I die an innocent man." He was marched to the scaffold where death was reported to be instantaneous. Soon afterwards, his nephew was moved to that same condemned cell, so that he would be nearer to the scaffold.

After John Miller's body had hung for the statutory hour, the execution room was prepared for its second victim of the day. At 9.30am the same two executioners once again marched into the cell, this time to escort John Robert Miller to his fate. The young man looked very nervous and as he was positioned over the trap he looked around the room at the various witnesses and asked, "What are all these people doing here?" He was never to receive a reply. The hood was placed over his head, the noose positioned and John Robert Miller was launched into eternity. Once again, death was said to be instantaneous.

CHAPTER ONE

A LOVER SPURNED

CHARLES WILLIAM Atkinson managed one of the shops owned by Mr Mendelssohn. This particular branch, in Blackett Street, Newcastle, was a general dealers which also sold revolvers. Early on the afternoon of Monday, September 16th, 1901, a man entered the shop and purchased one of those revolvers. The customer seemed to be in a hurry and was in the shop for only a few minutes and didn't haggle over the price of 10s 6d.

Charles Watson was a gunmaker and ran his establishment from Clayton Street, which was situated close to Blackett Street. At 1.00pm that day, he served a customer who purchased a box of 50 cartridges. The man did not seem too clear about what sort of cartridges his gun took, for he brought the weapon out of his right-hand coat pocket and showed it to Watson who saw that the gun had been made in Belgium.

Earlier that same day, at around 10.30am, 33-year-old Maggie Ann Lieutand, who was known to her friends as 'May,' went with her friend, Ivy Dawson, to post a letter at a box in Askew Road, close to where they lived. While they were there, they were approached by John George Thompson, who had, until June 1901, been living with Maggie in Teams, but she had left him when the relationship broke down. He had found the

17

subsequent split impossible to accept and had seen her on a number of occasions since and had tried to get her to return to him. Now he told Maggie once more that he wished to speak to her but she simply told him to go away.

Thompson became abusive and threatening but the women finally managed to evade him and then went on to Byker, where they visited Maggie's sister, Elizabeth Mary Sample.

It was around 2.00pm, when Ivy and Maggie were on their way back to 121 Milling Street, Gateshead, and the three-bedroomed upstairs flat that they shared. The women were travelling on a tramcar and as they approached their stop, Ivy saw Thompson standing near the Redheugh Hotel. Maggie lowered her head in an attempt to avoid being seen and the two women stayed on the tram past their usual stop. They finally alighted close by the Teams police station, although it had meant them travelling some 200 yards further than they had needed to. They did this to avoid Thompson but the attempt had been in vain, for when they walked back towards their home they found him waiting at the corner of Milling Street.

Once more Thompson tried to speak to Maggie but she made it clear that she wanted nothing to do with him. Ivy now decided to intervene and turning to Thompson said, "Go away man, the girl does not want you." Thompson, though, was not to be deterred and as the women continued down Milling Street, he followed close behind.

Ivy and Maggie arrived at the house first. Ivy unlocked the door and tried to pull Maggie inside but Thompson, seeing his chance, pushed his way in and had gone up three or four steps before the women turned on him and, using their combined strength, managed to force him back into the street. The door was still open, though, and now Thompson grabbed Maggie with his left hand and tried to pull her back outside. With his right hand he took a revolver out of his pocket and fired it once at his former lover.

Thompson then put the revolver to Maggie's neck, whereupon Ivy shouted for her to run. Maggie fled across the road, to number 122, a house occupied by Mrs Boyle, who had seen something of the scuffle and opened her front door. As Maggie ran towards her house, Mrs Boyle held the door open but saw to her horror that Thompson was also heading in the same direction.

Maggie got inside Mrs Boyle's house and tried to slam the door shut, but Thompson managed to squeeze his foot inside and for a few moments, a stalemate existed. Maggie could not get the door closed, but Thompson could not force it open either. Thompson, however, still had the gun in his hand and he slowly managed to force his arm through the gap between the door and the frame. He lifted the weapon and pointed it in Maggie's general direction, firing twice more. One of the bullets hit Maggie in the arm but the second struck her in the head and she collapsed to the floor.

Seeing that she was hit, Thompson was now apparently overcome with remorse. He picked her up, lifted her on to the step and sat down beside her. Maggie managed to gasp, "Oh, don't Jack. I love you." Thompson put his arm around the injured woman and tried to support her. He was still in this same position when Sergeant William Cockburn arrived and told Thompson he was under arrest. John Thompson made no attempt to escape and calmly handed over the revolver he had used. Maggie Lieutand was badly injured. Indeed, the police surgeon, Dr Abraham, felt that she was too ill to be taken to hospital and instead she was taken gently to her home and when she died there the following day. John Thompson was charged with murder.

Thompson's first appearance at the police court came on September 18th when the basic details of the case were given by Sergeant Cockburn and the Chief Constable James Trotter asked for a remand until September 22nd. Throughout the hearing, Thompson appeared dazed and forlorn as a police inspector held him by the wrist.

The inquest on Maggie Lieutand opened on September 19th before Mr John Graham. Here Maggie's sister, Elizabeth Sample, explained that Maggie had married in 1898. Her husband, Lazarre Lieutand, was a ship's cook. However, it had not been a happy marriage and they had lived apart on several occasions since their wedding. They had been separated for some while and the last time Lazarre had been heard of, he had been living somewhere in Gateshead.

Elizabeth also stated that Maggie's maiden name had been Whistton, but she had continued to be known by her married name after she had split from her husband. The inquest finally came to a close on September 21st when Mr Graham, in his summing up, said that there was no justification for a manslaughter charge and that he wished to send Thompson to the assizes on a capital murder charge. The jury did not even bother to retire and after a brief discussion amongst themselves, returned the verdict of wilful murder against Thompson, who was then committed for trial.

John Thompson's trial took place at Durham on November 23rd, 1901, before Mr Justice Grantham. The case for the Crown was led by Mr Luck, assisted by Mr Simey, while Thompson's defence was handled by Mr Edward Shortt.

Ivy Dawson was the wife of a ship's steward and had known Maggie since before her marriage to Lazarre. At that time, Maggie lived in Addison Road, Heaton, and she stayed there for a time even after the marriage. After splitting with her husband, she had lived with Thompson in Victoria Street, Teams, but when she left him in June she moved to Milling Street. Ivy told the court that she had not seen Maggie for quite some time and did not know of her situation since she had moved out of the area soon after Maggie's marriage. They had bumped into each other in Newcastle, two weeks before Maggie's death, and at that time Maggie asked Ivy to move in with her at number 121, as she did not wish to live alone.

Ivy first saw Thompson at around 9.00pm on the evening of

September 13th, when he called to visit Maggie. He appeared to be sober at the time but Maggie was cool towards him. Thompson wanted Maggie to stay in and talk to him but she had said that she and Ivy had arranged to go out together. To emphasis this, Maggie had then started to get ready and Thompson had followed her about the flat as she did so. It was only when Maggie put her hat on that he finally said goodnight and rather reluctantly left. Maggie had been badly shaken by Thompson's visit, had needed a brandy to steady her nerves and was unable to leave the flat for a full 15 minutes.

When the two women finally left for their evening out, Thompson appeared to be following them around, for later that night, at around 10.00pm, they saw him in Grainger Street, Newcastle. They passed him without speaking but Thompson fell in behind them and wherever they went, he seemed to be there. They last saw him at around midnight. Only when they were absolutely sure he had gone did Maggie have the nerve to return home.

Ivy next saw Thompson at around 10.30am on Monday September 16th, when she and Maggie were posting a letter at the box in Askew Road. Thompson did not appreciate being rebuffed and called Maggie 'a drunken liar who only spoke the truth by accident'. He ended his tirade by threatening to 'knock her head through the wall'.

Referring to the shooting, Ivy related how, after the first shot had been fired, she noticed that Mrs Boyle was at the door of her house, number 122, opposite to her own. Ivy saw Maggie running for the open door and slammed her own door shut. Going into her front room, she heard two more shots fired. She then ran to the police station and reported the matter to Sergeant Cockburn.

Mrs Boyle told the court that she had seen Ivy and Maggie coming home. She had also seen Thompson. After the initial scuffle she saw Thompson draw something shiny out of his pocket and at the time, thought it might be a knife. Only when the first shot was fired did Mrs Boyle realise that Thompson was holding a gun. Maggie now screamed, "Help. Mercy. Mercy," and ran as fast as she could towards Mrs Boyle's front door which she held open for her. Both she and Maggie then tried to slam it shut and keep Thompson at bay, but he had his foot in the way. To her horror, Mrs Boyle saw that Thompson's hand had slowly snaked around the door. She ran upstairs and on the way, heard two further shots.

It was when the court heard the evidence of Henry Alder Smith, that the trial judge, Mr Justice William Grantham, who had been appointed to the bench back in January 1886, showed how out of touch with real life he was.

Henry Smith, who was a 20-year-old draper's traveller, was in Milling Street at 2.20pm on September 16th, on his way to pay a call at number 102. He, too, saw Maggie and Ivy approaching from the direction of Askew Road, with Thompson close behind, arguing with Maggie. Smith saw Ivy open her front door, the scuffle when Thompson tried to force his way in and then Thompson draw something out of his pocket with his left hand. At the same time, Thompson pulled Maggie out with his right hand. He appeared to be dragging her by her coat collar and when they were within a yard or so of the front door, he fired the first shot, which Smith did not think had hit the woman.

Henry now saw Maggie break away and dash into Mrs Boyle's, only for Thompson to almost force his way in. He also watched Thompson force his right arm through the gap and heard two more shots fired. Smith stayed in the street, uncertain what to do. He was still there when Sergeant Cockburn appeared and Smith then directed the officer to where Thompson now cradled Maggie in his arms.

Upon hearing this evidence, Justice Grantham berated Smith for not stopping Thompson after the first shot had been fired. The judge went on to say, "If you only had a little courage, you might have saved this woman's life. If you had

had the blood of an Englishman, you would have saved this woman's life and saved the man's life probably. You deliberately walked away. I should think there is not another man in Durham who would have done it. It was a little bit risky but a man doesn't care for the risk. If he is bold, he practically invariably saves the person who has been run after. You might have tripped the man or knocked him down." Such were the men who had the power of life and death over their fellows.

Dr Abraham had conducted the post-mortem and he told the court that Maggie Lieutand had been a healthy young woman. He had removed three bullets from her body and one, which was flattened, was the one responsible for her death. Two of the bullets had passed into the cerebellum and death was due to laceration of the brain, haemorrhage and shock. The third bullet was found lodged in Maggie's arm.

Sergeant William Cockburn said that when he came upon the scene, Thompson had his right arm underneath Maggie Lieutand's head. Thompson seemed to be overcome with remorse and had willingly handed the revolver over, saying, "I've done it." Having ensured that Maggie was being taken care of, Cockburn took Thompson into custody. At the police station, Thompson also handed over a box of cartridges. As for the gun, it had five chambers. Three were empty, two were still loaded. Of the original 50 cartridges in the box, 45 still remained.

The only hope for the defence was to show that Thompson was insane at the time he had shot Maggie. However, Dr Gilbert, the prison medical officer at Durham, stated that Thompson was perfectly sane, as did Dr Steele, the medical superintendent of the Durham County Asylum, who had examined Thompson after his arrest. For that reason, the jury had no difficulty in deciding that Thompson was guilty as charged and he was sentenced to death.

Held in the condemned cell back at Durham prison, John Thompson began to fret in his final days. He did not talk much to his jailers and when he did, it was never about the crime. He was allowed to smoke his pipe and took pleasure from his daily exercise periods. He never expected a reprieve and so took it well when he heard that none had been granted.

On the night before he was due to hang, Thompson retired at 9.00pm. He rose at 5.00am on the morning of Tuesday, December 10th, 1901, to face a breakfast of tea, bread and butter. He drank the tea but ate only sparingly. At 7.45am two dozen prisoners who had served their time were released from the prison. Fifteen minutes later, at 8.00am, William and Thomas Billington entered the condemned cell and pinioned Thompson's arms behind his back. John George Thompson then walked with a firm military step towards the gallows where he was launched into eternity.

CHAPTER THREE

CHAPTER THREE

IN THE LONG GRASS

ALTHOUGH there was a four-year age difference between them, Johanna Geraldine Scott and Mary Ina Stewart were close friends. In fact, it was more than mere friendship because their two families had now been linked by marriage. Mary, a pretty seven-year-old with a mass of golden hair, lived at 16 Joel Terrace in Bill Quay. Her uncle, Frederick Stewart, lived at 8 Gosforth Terrace, Pelaw, and Frederick was married to 11-year-old Johanna Scott's sister.

On the morning of Saturday, August 16th, 1902, Johanna left her house at 12 Grange Terrace, Heworth High Lane, and called for her friend. The two girls spent the rest of that day in each other's company and at around 6.45pm, announced that they intended visiting Frederick Stewart's house at Pelaw. Having been given permission by Mary's mother, the two set off to walk across the fields from Bill Quay, to Pelaw, over an area known as the Hilly Fields.

It was just a few minutes later, at 6.50pm, that the girls met Christina Storey, who lived at 33 Cromwell Road, Bill Quay. Christina lived in the house opposite to Mary and knew the child well. The girls stayed with her for a few minutes before Mary told Christina of their plan to visit her uncle at Gosforth Terrace.

Mary and Johanna arrived at Frederick Stewart's house

some time around 7.00pm. They stayed for about half an hour and as they left, Frederick stood at his door to see them off. Johanna turned one way, to walk towards Heworth, and Mary turned the other, towards Bill Quay. Her uncle watched Mary as she walked to the top of Hilly Fields where she disappeared into a hollow. He believed that she would be home within minutes.

James Stewart, Mary's father, was a brickmaker by trade. He had left his home at 10.00am on that Saturday and had travelled first to Pelaw and then on to Hexham, arriving there at around 1.00pm. It was 10.30pm, after a long, hard day's work, before he arrived back home and was surprised to hear that Mary had not returned from his brother's house. He assumed that that she was still there but was annoyed that Frederick — and, indeed, Mary herself — hadn't thought the family would be worried.

He waited another half-hour but when there was still no sign of Mary, he walked over to his brother's house, to collect the girl himself and no doubt give her a piece of his mind for being out so late. When Frederick confirmed that Mary had left at 7.30pm and should have been home some time ago, James Stewart became concerned for his daughter's safety.

Returning home, he contacted a number of his friends and neighbours and a search party was organised. Using torches to light their way, men combed the surrounding countryside, including Cat Dene Quarry. Although they searched through-out the night, no sign of Mary Stewart could be found. The search continued all day on August 17th, and on into the next day. It was not until some time around 3.00pm on Monday, August 18th, that Mary was finally discovered and her father's worst fears were realised.

Her body lay in long grass in a disused brickyard once owned by Wood, Skinner & Co. The yard had in fact already been searched but Mary's body had been well hidden and covered by grass. James Stewart was called and it was he who gently picked up the bloody body of his daughter and carried her home.

The police investigation lay in the hands of Inspector Thompson. He interviewed as many local people as he could and the things he heard led him to the conclusion that the person he was looking for was 24-year-old Thomas Nicholson, a farmer's carter, who lived at Ann Street, Bill Quay. At 1.00am on the morning of August 19th, Inspector Thompson arrived at Nicholson's house and took him into custody.

That same day, the inquest on Mary Stewart opened at the Wardley Hotel, before the deputy coroner, Mr Shepherd. Only evidence of identification was given before the proceedings were adjourned for two weeks. Two days later, on August 21st, Nicholson appeared before Mr Claude Bowes Palmer, at the Felling police station where evidence of arrest was given and Nicholson was remanded.

On August 23rd, the funeral of Mary Stewart took place at the Heworth cemetery, the ceremony being conducted by the Reverend Dr Steel. The entire village apparently turned out and many floral tributes were sent. Mary's father had five brothers and three sisters and all of them were present, as were Mary's four brothers and her sister. Mary's coffin bore a small brass plaque on which was engraved, "Mary Ina Stewart. Departed this life August 16th, 1902, aged 7 years."

Nicholson made his second appearance at the Felling police station on September 3rd, when he was again remanded, this time pending the outcome of the inquest which reopened on September 9th, now at the Wesleyan School Room, Bill Quay. Johanna Scott described the journey she and Mary had made on the day that her friend was murdered.

Other witnesses were also heard and at the end of the day, the evidence pointed to Nicholson being the culprit and so it was no surprise that the verdict was one of murder against Thomas Nicholson.

The following day, September 10th, Nicholson was brought before the magistrates at Gateshead. The case for the Director of Public Prosecutions was put by Mr Frederick Harle, while Nicholson was represented by Mr Wynn Parry. The hearing continued on September 19th when the magistrate, Mr Robert Affleck, sent Nicholson for trial.

The case opened at the assizes on November 26th, 1902, at Durham before Mr Justice Channell. Nicholson was defended by Mr Mitchell Innes while the prosecution was led by Mr J.E. Joel, assisted by Mr Simey. A great deal of evidence was heard, most of it circumstantial, but it built up a very strong case against the accused man.

James Dinning was a miner at the Wardley colliery and lived at 4 Swinburne Terrace, Bill Quay. The back of his house looked on to the rear of Nicholson's house and the two men, who were friends, often went drinking together. At 4.30pm on the day of the murder, Nicholson had called at Dinning's house and asked him to go with him to the Mason's Arms. On the way they called in at Nicholson's brother's house but he wasn't at home so they went on to the pub, arriving there at about 5.00pm.

Dinning and Nicholson stayed in the Mason's Arms until 6.30pm. From there they visited the house of a Mr Holmes and while there, Nicholson went to get a glass of whisky for an old woman in the house, who was ill. Leaving there, Nicholson said he wanted to go to Felling but Dinning did not want to and instead, the pair crossed the fields, walked down Hanningwood Terrace and arrived at Dinning's house. They stayed there together for a few minutes after which Nicholson announced that he was going home. By then it was around 7.30pm and after Nicholson had been gone for a few minutes, Dinning decided to join him and walked across to his friend's house.

It was then that something rather curious happened. Nicholson said that he was going to get something to eat, and left the room. Dinning watched his friend go into his kitchen, but he never reappeared. After waiting some time, Dinning went into the kitchen but seeing that Nicholson was not there, returned to his own house. It was then about 7.45pm and Dinning stayed at home until 8.30pm, when he decided to find out what had happened to Nicholson and went out to look for him. Dinning checked the Ship Inn, the Cricketer's Arms and the Mason's Arms but still there was no sign of Thomas Nicholson. Finally giving up on his friend, Dinning walked to Pelaw across the fields, went on to Heworth and had a couple of drinks in the Swan Inn there. He left the Swan at 9.30pm and walked directly home. Dinning did not see Nicholson again until the following afternoon when he asked his friend where he had vanished to. Nicholson mumbled a reply, but Dinning failed to catch what he had said.

Dinning's wife, Christina, backed up the early part of her husband's story, but she was able to give some extra information because after Dinning had followed Nicholson into his house, she had been working in her kitchen and she saw Nicholson come out of the house, carrying a piece of bread in his hand. She saw him walk off up Brack Terrace, taking an occasional bite from the bread. He was heading in the direction of Hilly Fields.

At 9.30pm Christina was standing at her back door, talking to her neighbour, Mrs Morton. They saw Nicholson walking back up the lane. He was wearing a dark suit and without speaking to them, went into his house, only to reappear a few minutes later. Nicholson walked over to Christina and asked, "Is Jim in?" As Christina was replying in the negative, Nicholson's mother and father came up and took their son back inside the house.

Some of this timetable was backed up by other witnesses. Edward Shell was the innkeeper of the Mason's Arms and he confirmed that Dinning and Nicholson had come into his establishment at 5.00pm. He put the time of their departure at

closer to 6.15pm than 6.30pm and from what he had over-
heard, believed that Nicholson wanted to go into Newcastle.
Shell confirmed that at the time, Nicholson was wearing a dark
jacket suit and a dark cap.

Robert Felton, a miner, was in Brack Terrace at around
7.30pm and he saw Nicholson going down Back Ann Street
towards his house. Perhaps five minutes later, Nicholson
reappeared and headed off along Hanningwood Terrace
towards Hilly Fields. Nicholson was also seen at about the
same time by Martin Mackay. Martin was also a carter and he
knew Nicholson very well so he stopped Nicholson and asked
him where he was off to. Nicholson replied that he was going
to walk to Felling and buy himself a new suit of clothes.
Mackay thought his friend was rather the worse for drink and
advised him to turn around and go home but Nicholson said
he felt fine and then struck the wall with his fist as if to tell
Mackay to mind his own business.

Two days later, on August 18th, the day Mary's body was
found, Mackay had seen Nicholson again when both men
watered their horses at the village trough. Nicholson was the
first to refer to the murder when he said, "That's an awful job
that has happened here." Mackay agreed and added, "Someone will get to know about it."

The evidence of three men caused a few problems for the
prosecution. William Dunnett, Robert Stewart and William
Taylor had all been to Pelaw to get a shave. Walking back to Bill
Quay, all three men reported that they had seen Nicholson
with James Dinning, about 100 yards from the Mason's Arms.
All three put the time of this meeting at around 8.00pm or just
afterwards. By this time of course, other witnesses said that
Dinning was at home and that Nicholson had gone off towards
Hilly Fields. One of those three men was to give other, more
harrowing evidence, for it was William Taylor who found the
brutalised body of Mary Stewart in the brickyard.

Margaret Ann Dempsey lived in Brack Terrace and she had

been sitting on her doorstep at 7.30pm. Some time after this, she too saw Nicholson, carrying his piece of bread, heading towards Hilly Fields. None of these witnesses put Nicholson at the murder scene, but other witnesses did.

Thomas Henry Douglas was only 12 years old and he lived at Gosforth Terrace, Pelaw, close to Mary's uncle's house. On the evening of August 16th, Thomas' mother was baking and noticed that she was running low on flour. Thomas was asked to go to the shop at Bill Quay to buy some more and on his way, he ran over Hilly Fields. Near the top of the quarry, Thomas saw Nicholson, a man he knew, walking backwards and forwards.

Even more telling was the evidence of Alice Nichols, who lived in Heworth. She had left her home at about 7.20pm and walked over Hilly Fields. As she approached Bill Quay she saw a young man coming from the direction of the Mason's Arms. Alice also saw a young girl with beautiful golden hair, walking towards Bill Quay but some way behind her. When the two met, the young man stopped the little girl and said something to her. Alice took a keen interest in this as the man appeared to be rather the worse for drink. She saw the young man take the girl by the hand and, as Alice watched them over her shoulder, the couple walked off towards the quarry. Alice Nichols could not positively identify the young man as Thomas Nicholson but she could say that the man wore dark clothes and a dark cap. Later, Alice was taken to view the body of Mary Ina Stewart and she was certain that this was the little girl she had seen on the pathway.

Joseph Lightfoot was a pawnbroker of Tyne Street, Felling Shore. After the police had arrested Nicholson, the prisoner's mother had told Inspector Thompson that the dark blue suit her son had worn on the evening of the murder had now been pawned for 6s, something she had done many times before. Thompson collected the suit from Mr Lightfoot on August 19th. The clothing was handed over to Sergeant William

Watson and he in turn delivered the items to William Frederick Keating Stock, the county analyst.

Mr Stock examined not just Nicholson's clothes, but also those taken from the body of Mary Stewart. Of the male items, Stock was able to report that he had found traces of blood on the right hand side of the coat, just below the pocket and also on the left side, above the pocket. There was also blood on the trousers. As for the child's clothing, detailed analysis was impossible because it had rained heavily before the body was found and the clothes were saturated with water. Stock did, however, find extensive bloodstains on the chemise, drawers and on two petticoats. Finally, Mr Stock had examined a pocket knife found amongst Nicholson's property. This too showed a positive reaction for blood, on the blade, close to the shaft.

Dr John W. Mackay had examined Mary's body three times, first at the location where it was found, again at her home after it had been removed there and finally when he and Dr Prentice performed the post-mortem. There was evidence of extensive subcutaneous bleeding over Mary's skull, and Dr Mackay believed that these had been caused by sharply struck blows during life and these would almost certainly have produced unconsciousness.

There were puncture wounds on Mary's arm and body, caused by some blunt instrument being brought into violent contact with the flesh. Around the mouth and nostrils were marks of fingers and a thumb where a hand had been held over the mouth, possibly to stifle any cries. It was this that had in fact caused Mary's death, from suffocation. Finally, the doctor had to describe how the genital area had been badly mutilated by means of a sharp knife so that the assailant could complete his rape of the child. The loss of blood these injuries caused, also contributed to the death of Mary Stewart.

The jury were out for only 35 minutes before returning their guilty verdict. Nicholson showed no emotion and made no comment as the sentence of death was passed. There was no appeal court at this time, so Nicholson's only chance was that he would be reprieved but even that faint hope was dashed when the Home Secretary confirmed that the sentence would be carried out.

During his days in the condemned cell, although he made no full confession, Nicholson made statements and comments to the warders which confirmed that he was indeed the man who had murdered Mary Ina Stewart. He retired early on the night before he was to die, apparently slept well, and rose soon after 6.00am on the appointed day. He ate sparingly of a light breakfast of tea, bread and butter and was then attended by the prison chaplain, the Reverend E.F. Jackson.

At 8.00am on Tuesday, December 16th, 1902, William and John Billington entered two cells at Durham prison. The execution was to be a double one and Nicholson was to hang alongside Samuel Walton of Spennymoor, who had killed his wife, mother-in-law and child. As a crowd of 50 or more gathered outside the walls of Durham prison, the two men were taken into the execution chamber where they stood upon chalk marks of their initials. Thomas Nicholson, who looked as though he had been crying, took his place upon the initials TN and as both men had their ankles strapped, Walton remarked to Nicholson, "Good morning lad. Keep thy heart up." Seconds later, both men were dead.

CHAPTER FOUR

A PARTICULARLY
SENSELESS MURDER

IT SEEMED to be an argument over nothing. At 6.30pm on the evening of Wednesday, July 12th, 1905, Annie Jackson, who worked as a charwoman at a lodging house at 94 Newgate Street, Newcastle upon Tyne, had heard two of the residents shouting at each other. Forty-year-old Henry Perkins had claimed that he had £4,000 to his name — and his friend, Patrick Durkin had called him a liar.

Annie had seen the two men fighting earlier in the day. They had fought in the downstairs lavatory and Annie had later seen Perkins strike Durkin in the lane outside. When they came inside, a brief struggle had followed on the staircase and Durkin had lashed out at Perkins. Perkins in turn now grabbed Patrick by the throat and said he would, "...do for him". The lodging house keeper, William Harris had had to intervene. He had grabbed Henry Perkins by the arm just as he drew out a knife and prepared to stab his fellow lodger. The knife fell to the ground.

No further action was taken on this occasion because it was well known that both Henry Perkins and Patrick Durkin were rather fond of drink and it seemed that both were heavily under the influence at the time. Unfortunately, both men were in exactly the same condition on the following night.

It was some time after 7.00pm on July 13th when Patrick Durkin walked into 94 Newgate Street. Although it was still quite early, Durkin was much the worse for drink, and fell asleep on a long wooden bench in the kitchen. At the time, Annie Jackson was busying herself in that same room, carrying out her household duties. She noted that it was at about 7.30pm when Perkins came into that same kitchen and he, too, was very drunk and was making a lot of noise.

Yet for all the unpleasantness there appeared to be no reason for what had happened next. Annie Jackson had asked Perkins to be quiet, pointing out to him that Durkin was asleep. Perkins did not make any reply to Annie's request, so she had turned around to see what he was doing and now noticed that he carried a knife in his hand. Perkins had walked purposely over to where his fellow lodger lay asleep, placed his knee on his chest and made a movement as if to slash his throat.

Bravely, Annie Jackson had rushed forward and pulled Perkins away from his intended victim. Then, realising that she would need help to get Perkins under control, she had run to fetch Mr Harris but by the time they had returned to the kitchen, Henry Perkins was making his escape out of the door at the far side of the room and Patrick Durkin was trying to pull himself to his feet, bleeding heavily from a wound in his neck.

Henry Perkins did not run very far. He was a cobbler by trade, and for the past two years or so had worked for John Proctor who had premises in Church Street, Walker. Perkins had not turned up for work on the morning of July 13th, but now, after the attack upon Durkin, he went to Mr Proctor's shop and although he was very drunk, managed to say, "I have stabbed a man, Mr Proctor. I am sorry."

Proctor, probably not taking Perkins seriously, suggested that he should have a wash and sit down to some food but

Perkins had declined the offer and said he was "…off to the mountains". He then left the shop but John Proctor called the police and Perkins had been found in the city centre in the early hours of July 14th, when he had been taken into custody by Constable Walter Wood.

On July 14th, 1905, Perkins appeared at the police court where he was charged with unlawfully wounding Patrick Durkin. The wounded man had been rushed to the infirmary where he had been visited by Superintendent Koch who had taken a deposition from him. Apparently Durkin had two wounds in his throat and one of these had severed a small artery. After hearing evidence of arrest, the magistrates remanded Henry Perkins for one week.

On Wednesday, July 19th, Patrick Durkin succumbed to his wounds and died in hospital. That same night, an inquest opened at Newcastle Royal Infirmary where evidence of identification was given by Michael Durkin, the dead man's brother.

Michael stated that Patrick had been 29 years of age, a mason's labourer, and to his knowledge had lived in the lodging house at Newgate Street for only five or six weeks. Michael also stated that he thought Patrick was fairly temperate in his habits but that when he was drunk, he went quiet rather than turning argumentative. Michael said he had visited his brother in the hospital and he had managed to state that it had been Perkins who attacked him.

Two days later, Perkins was back in court, now charged with wilful murder, and received another remand for a week. On July 28th, he was back in court again, when the case for the prosecution was led by Mr Herbert Lee. Perkins was still undefended but this was due to a mix-up more than anything else. Superintendent Koch explained to the court that Perkins had said he did not want anything done for him. At this point, Perkins interjected and said, "Beg pardon, sir. I did not understand you that way. You asked me if I had any money for a solicitor to represent me. I told you I had not. I have no means whatsoever."

Perkins was admitting that his claim to have £4,000 was nothing more than a tall story and it was now explained to him that the court would provide him with legal representation if he could not afford to pay for it himself. The clerk of the court patiently explained the procedure to Perkins and told him that he would do everything he could to assist him. Perkins' final police court appearance took place a week later, on August 5th, when he was finally sent for trial.

The trial of 40-year-old Henry Perkins took place at Newcastle on November 16th, 1905, before Mr Justice Darling. He was defended by Mr Hedley, while the case for the Crown was led by Mr J.E. Joel, who was assisted by Mr E. Meynell.

One of the most vital witnesses, of course, was Annie Jackson. She testified that after Durkin had come into the lodging house, he had washed first and then laid himself down on the long bench in the kitchen. He was very drunk at the time and within minutes, she could see that he was sound asleep.

When Perkins came in, he too was rather drunk but she did not think he was as drunk as Durkin. He sat down at the end of the same bench and Annie could see that he held what looked like a shoemaker's knife in his hand. She went on to describe the initial attack upon Durkin, after which she managed to pull Perkins away and tell him that she was going for Mr Harris. As she left the room, she heard a single cry of, "Oh!" and when she and Mr Harris returned, Durkin was bleeding from the neck.

William Harris agreed that Annie Jackson had come to him for help. He, too, had heard Durkin cry out and, seeing that he was wounded, had bandaged his throat rather than chase after Perkins. Mr Harris went on to say that Durkin and Perkins had shared a bedroom with two other men and they also confirmed that there had been bad feeling between the two for some time. After the argument of July 12th, Harris had suggested to Perkins that it might be better if he was moved to another room. Perkins had declined the offer by saying that he did not think he would be there the following day.

James Healey was a riveter and he had met up with Perkins on July 13th, before the stabbing had taken place. He reported that Perkins had been talking about Durkin when he pulled a knife out of his pocket and said, "I am going for the Irish heifer."

Medical evidence was given by Dr H.E. Featherstone. He described two wounds in Durkin's neck. One was in the lower jaw, one inch long, and rather superficial. The other was in the left side of the neck, and some two to three inches deep. When Durkin was admitted to hospital, he was semi-conscious and was never able to give a clear and concise account of what had happened to him. The cause of death was given as pericarditis, pleurisy and blood poisoning, due to the larger of the wounds in the neck.

Perkins went into the witness box and claimed that he had been sitting on the bench for some time when Durkin sat up. Durkin then moved as if to strike him, as he had done the previous evening, and so he had struck out himself and since his hand had a knife in it, Durkin was stabbed. The killing was therefore accidental and Perkins was only guilty of man-slaughter, not murder.

The jury were out for just ten minutes before deciding that Perkins was guilty as charged. Asked if he had anything to say before sentence was passed, he said in a loud voice, "Nothing, my Lord." The death sentence was passed and after hearing it, Perkins said, "Thank you, my Lord" turned on his heel and was taken to the cells below the court.

On Sunday, December 3rd, the governor of Newcastle prison received notification that there would be no reprieve and the sentence would be carried out. Perkins had already resigned himself to this fact and admitted that the sentence was a just one and added that he deserved to pay the full penalty of the law.

At 8.00am on Wednesday, December 6th, 1905, Henry Perkins was hanged at Newcastle by Henry Pierrepoint, who was assisted by John Ellis. Perkins' name had been linked with another murder, 19 years previously, at Kettering. Perkins had admitted that he was a Nottinghamshire man, and had been in Kettering at the time, but said that he had no part in that crime.

Other killers were more fortunate than Perkins. Robert Cummings had been sentenced to death at the same assizes for the murder of his sweetheart, Hannah Walls, and was in Durham prison awaiting his execution set for December 13th. At the same time, Philip Edward Mee was awaiting execution in Leicester for the killing of Annie Elizabeth Smith. Both men were reprieved on the day that Perkins lost his life.

CHAPTER FIVE

MURDER AT
WINDY NOOK

JAMES Robson Melville was rather concerned. As the general manager of the Co-operative store which stood on the corner of Union Street and Howard Street in Windy Nook, he had become aware that someone was stealing from his shop.

It was in October, 1907, that, on three separate occasions in as many weeks, footprints had been found in the sawdust which was spread on the floor of the butchery department. After the stock had been checked, a shortage in the meat had been noted. There were no signs of a forced entry so it appeared that the thief, whoever he was, had a key. The thefts had to be stopped so the committee of the Co-op called a special meeting, on October 29th, where possible courses of action were discussed.

Eventually, the members decided that it would be a good idea to keep a special watch on certain nights in the hope of catching the thief red-handed. A rota was drawn up and so it was that just two days after the meeting, on the night of Thursday, October 31st, three of the committee, plus a young apprentice from the butchery department, agreed to stay in the store overnight. At around 10.00pm the manager of the branch, Mr Sutton, went through the motions of locking the main door as usual, but in reality, the door was locked from the inside, and the four men settled down for what might prove to be a long and fruitless night.

George Ather, John Patterson and Christopher Carr were all positioned around the meat-mincing room and office, while the apprentice, John Joseph Cowell, was positioned in the office close to a long string which would enable the gas light to be switched on from a distance if anyone came in to the premises. For some hours, the men spoke to each other in low whispers, waiting for something to happen.

For three hours, everything was uneventful. Then, at a few minutes after 1.00am on November 1st, someone tried the front door. At first the four men thought that their quarry might have put in an appearance but the shape in the doorway was that of the local policeman, Constable John James Thompson, who was on his rounds, checking that all the shops were securely locked for the night. More hours passed and still there was no sign of any intruder. But then, shortly after 4.00am, something very curious happened.

Outside, in Howard Street, was a gas-lamp which shed a little light into the slaughter room of the store. Now, although no footsteps had been heard, someone was turning that light off. Christopher Carr realised immediately that this might well be the man they were waiting for and that he was about to gain entry under cover of pitch darkness.

Carr whispered to his companions, "Now lads, get ready, he's coming."

The thief was indeed coming. All four men heard the turning of a key inside the lock and then slowly, the door to the butchery department swung open. For a few seconds there was nothing but silence and then a figure, crouching low and treading without making a sound, crept into the room. Cowell made ready to turn up the light and the other three men watched the hunched figure as he walked slowly around the room and entered the back part of the shop. On his return, the watchers sprang into action.

The first two men who threw themselves on to the figure were Patterson and Carr. Ather was slightly further away but in seconds he too was upon him as Cowell pulled the string, flooding the room with light. Cowell, who held the key to the premises, rushed to lock the door. Upon his return, he saw the well-built, bearded intruder was fighting like a tiger and all of the three men who were attempting to overcome him were struggling hard to keep him pinned to the floor.

John Patterson had hold of the man's left side while Ather held him by the right wrist. Carr was on his back, having grabbed the man by the collar, but still the intruder was holding his own in the fracas. It was not until Christopher Carr saw a butcher's steel on the counter that they finally began to get the better of him. Carr picked up the steel and gave the man two sharp blows on the back of the head. This seemed to subdue him somewhat and as Carr raised the steel to inflict a third blow, Patterson called out, "For God's sake, don't badly use him." Carr stayed his hand but that turned out to be a critical mistake for, from the doorway, Cowell saw that the intruder was drawing something from his pocket.

Cowell saw what was happening and shouted, "Look out! He's got a revolver." It was too late, though. As Cowell ran to unlock the door, a shot rang out and Patterson fell to the floor, a bullet in his head. A second shot hit Carr in the upper leg but still he managed to hobble out of the room. Believing now that the man was trapped inside, Carr and Ather held the shop door shut as Cowell tried to call for help. The commotion brought Ather's wife from their house, 1 Union Street. It was she who spotted that the intruder was trying to make good his escape out of a window into the street, and raised the alarm. Cowell, who had a hammer with him, now passed this weapon to George Ather, who dashed around the corner and gave the man a hard blow on the right leg. Despite all the injuries he had sustained, though, the man managed to run off towards the nearby quarries. Mrs Ather bravely gave chase but he was faster than her and finally managed to lose her.

It wasn't long before Constable Thompson was on the scene, and medical assistance was summoned. Carr was not badly wounded, but John Patterson had slipped into unconsciousness and was in a critical condition. A cart was brought to the store and Patterson was put on it to be taken to hospital, but within two or three minutes he died, making this a case of murder.

The first thing for the police to do was to make a careful search of the Co-operative premises. A number of clues were found. The man who had shot Patterson and Carr had been wearing a false beard and this had been torn off by Carr in the struggle. He had also left behind a hazel stick, a slouch cap, a lamp and the skeleton key which he had used to gain entry. He had made his escape through the window of a room where fat was rendered down and in his hurry to get out, had stepped into a pan in which a little fat remained, leaving a clear footprint behind. Finally, of course, there was evidence that the killer had been injured, perhaps badly, by means of the butcher's steel and the hammer.

The three men who had been inside the room with Patterson were interviewed and each told much the same story. John Cowell said that he believed the killer had been wearing india-rubber soles, as he had made no noise as he crept about the room. Cowell had not been involved in the actual fight but had seen Carr hit the man with the steel and felt that he must have been injured as later he had found blood on one of the panels of the doorway into the rendering room.

Cowell went on to say, "I saw the man draw the revolver and fire it at Patterson; and then fire a second shot at Carr and I am confident that when he escaped by the window, he fired a third shot."

In fact, there was no evidence that more than two shots had been fired and none of the other witnesses ever made this

claim. Cowell, though, had no doubt that after the first shot
had been fired, Ather had shouted for him to run for the
police. Cowell had already picked up a butcher's hammer and
was about to use this on the assailant but, at Ather's words, he
had run out into the street and began to shout for help.
Outside, Cowell had seen another man who he believed was an
accomplice of the first, so he cried out, "Here's another one,
where's the chopper?" at which this second man had run away.

Cowell had been outside just a minute or so when Ather
and Carr came out. Ather now held the door shut and at one
point the man trapped inside must have tried to force the door
because Ather called out for the hammer which Cowell was
still holding. Cowell passed the hammer to him when suddenly
Mrs Ather shouted to them, "It's no use fastening the door, he
is coming out of the window." Ather had immediately run
around the corner, into Union Street, and struck the man with
the hammer. Cowell saw the man hobble off and then he
returned to where Patterson lay on the shop floor.

George Ather told the police that when the man had first
come into the store, he had been carrying his lamp in his left
hand and shading the light with his right. The man was
dressed in a dark coat and although he kept his head down
somewhat, Ather could plainly see that he sported a full beard
and moustache. Ather told much the same story as Cowell had
about the fight itself but added that at the time the first shot
was fired, he still had a firm hold of the man's right hand. He
must, therefore, have drawn the gun out with his left hand,
and fired with that same hand.

Continuing his evidence, Ather confirmed that he had seen
the man coming out of the window in Union Street and being
on his right-hand side, had struck him a severe blow on the
lower right leg, just below the knee. The man had cried out in
pain. Indeed, he had also spoken once or twice during the fight
itself although Ather made no comment as to recognising his
voice. He went on to relate how his wife had chased after the

man until she had been told that he was carrying a gun. Ather
and his wife had then returned to the store and tried to offer
whatever assistance they could to Patterson.

Christopher Carr told the police that in his opinion, the
man he had fought with was about 5ft 8ins tall, 30 to 40 years
old and had a very powerful build. After he had struck out with
the butcher's steel, Carr had heard the man cry out, "Don't
behave badly to a man" and described his accent as being a
local one. Carr confirmed that he had only hit the man twice.
He had prepared to hit him for a third time when Patterson
had intervened and soon afterwards, he had himself been hit
by a bullet and managed to limp outside. Carr was later treated
at the Newcastle Royal Infirmary where a bullet was removed
from his hip and he was allowed to go home on Saturday,
November 2nd.

There were two other witnesses to what had happened in
the early hours of November 1st. Mrs Ather had been asleep
in bed when she was awakened by someone knocking on her
door, shouting, "Come on. We've got him." When she went
out into the street she heard the commotion from the store.
She knew, of course, that her husband was one of the men on
watch inside, so rushed down to see what was going on. She
heard her husband calling for a hammer and so dashed back
home to fetch a chopping axe. Although she was gone less
than a minute, by the time she got back the man's legs were
already out of the window and she called out that he was
getting away. She saw her husband hit out at the man's legs
and heard him cry out in pain. He must have been quite badly
hurt for, as he ran off up the street, he stumbled before
regaining his balance and dashing off. She began to give chase,
still brandishing the axe, until her husband called out, "Mind,
he's got a firearm."

The other witness was John Richard Stoker, a coal miner
who lived at 8 Howard Street and was just arriving home from
work when the fight began inside the store. He, too, saw the

man's legs coming out of the window in Union Street and after the intruder had run off, Stoker went to Constable Thompson's house and told him what had happened.

On Saturday, November 2nd, the inquest on the body of John Patterson opened at the Felling police station, before the deputy coroner, Mr Shepherd. The only witness was Mr John Dance, the uncle of the dead man, who gave evidence of identification. He said that Patterson had been 33 years old and was a married man with two children, a boy and a girl, twins who were seven years old. The inquest was then adjourned until November 8th.

The police had come to believe that the man they were looking for was local. Those who had heard him speak had said that he spoke with a local accent and since this was, in all probability, the fourth time he had paid a visit to the same premises, he almost certainly lived close by. Their investigation then concentrated on powerfully-built men, living in the area, who may well now be injured. It was this course of inquiry which led officers to Joseph William Noble, a 50-year-old blacksmith.

Joseph Noble worked at the Park Lane premises of the North Eastern Railway Company, at Gateshead but he lived in an area known as the Blue Quarries, between Sheriff Hill and Windy Nook and this was no more than five minutes walk from the scene of the crime.

Five minutes before he was due to leave work on Monday, November 4th, Noble was called to the time office at Park Lane and there he was greeted by three men he had never seen before. One of these identified himself as Inspector Thomas McDonald, who introduced his colleague, Sergeant Nesbit. The other man was a sergeant from the railway police, but it was McDonald who did all the talking.

McDonald said, "I won't waste any words, but ask you to take off your cap, and let me examine your head." Noble did as the policeman asked and upon checking, McDonald saw that there were two wounds on the back of Noble's head, and a third behind his ear. Asked to explain this injury, Noble said that he had been lifting some iron bars at work and these had fallen on to him. McDonald then asked to see Noble's legs. Noble bared his left leg, which was seen to be free of marks, but once his right leg had been revealed, McDonald saw a bruise, the size of a sixpence, on the inside. Noble said that he had suffered this particular injury when he walked into a wheelbarrow on the Saturday morning but had to admit that neither this, nor the iron bars incident, had been reported to his employers. Satisfied that they had their man, the police officers took Noble to the police station and charged him with the murder of John Patterson and the attempted murder of Christopher Carr.

On November 5th, the funeral of John Patterson took place at St Alban's Church in Windy Nook. The same day, Noble made his first appearance before Mr Claude Bowes Palmer at Felling police station where evidence of arrest was given and Noble was remanded until November 7th. There were other remands to follow, both in the police court proceedings and the inquest. The latter came to a conclusion on November 28th when the coroner said that the jury had to decide whether this was murder or manslaughter. He went on to say that it could only be manslaughter if the jury considered that the shooting was an accident. They, in turn, took only three minutes to decide that this was a case of murder and that Noble was responsible. The last appearance before the magistrates opened on December 3rd, and continued over into the following day when Noble was sent for trial.

Joseph William Noble appeared in the courtroom at Durham on March 2nd, 1908, before Mr Justice Channell. He was defended by Mr Edward Shortt and Mr Morgan Griffith Jones while the prosecution case was led by Mr J. Scott-Fox who was assisted by Mr Bruce Williamson and Mr Walter Hedley. The jury was all male and one, a Quaker, chose to affirm rather than take the oath. The trial lasted for two days and overnight, the jury were ensconced in the Three Tuns Hotel at New Elvet.

One of the more contentious parts of the trial, was the identification of Noble by the men who had been involved in the affray at the Co-operative stores in Windy Nook. On November 5th, an identification parade had taken place and Cowell, Carr and Ather had all picked out Noble, without hesitation. All three had known Noble for many years, indeed Carr had known him for more than 30 years. Curiously, Carr and Ather were now both saying that at the time of the attack, when the killer spoke, they both believed that the man they were struggling with was Joseph Noble. If that was the case it was then most surprising that neither they, nor Cowell, had mentioned Noble's name in their statements or depositions. In fact, Noble's name had been specifically mentioned to Carr and he had stated that he knew Noble well and did not think he was the man. This subject was returned to when the time came for Mr Shortt to outline Noble's defence.

Matthew Kay worked at Heworth colliery and lived at 13 Clayton Street, in Windy Nook. He arrived home from work at about 3.20am on the morning of November 1st, and went up to his bed. It was perhaps half an hour later when he heard what sounded like a shot. Kay got out of bed but before he got to the window, he heard a second shot. Seeing the lights were on at the Co-operative store, Kay made his way there and going inside, saw Patterson lying on the floor. Constable Thompson was already on the scene, and at his instigation, Kay, along with Carr, Ather and Stoker, went in the direction of the quarry. The men went as far as White House Farm and then turned back. Constable Thompson now asked Kay and Stoker to report the matter to Felling police station and on the way back, they saw Noble coming down from Windy Nook. By this time it was 5.30am.

Constable John James Thompson testified that after being

called to the scene of the crime, he and others had, once it was daylight, traced a line of footprints from the store up to the quarry area. Various plaster casts of these prints had been taken and these were shown to be size 9, the same as Noble's. Further, the last footprint had been found in mud close to White House Farm and this pointed directly towards Noble's house. It was true that there was a quicker way from the store to Noble's house but the footprints traced a quieter and more deserted route, one which the killer of Patterson may well have thought was a safer way home.

Inspector Lambert was stationed at Felling and had played a major part in the investigation. On the day that Noble had been arrested, he, Constable Thompson and other officers had conducted a search of Noble's house at 11 Store Street, Windy Nook. In a back room upstairs, they had found a jemmy, skeleton keys and 40 cartridges inside a box. There were many kinds of cartridge, but two were the same as those used by the killer of John Patterson. In other parts of the house, Inspector Lambert found 114 pairs of boots, shoes and slippers, and large quantities of items such as drapery goods, blankets and sheets. In boxes under the bed, the police found tea, mustard, boot polish and bars of soap. These boxes were labelled, "The Co-operative Wholesale Society".

Continuing his search, Inspector Lambert also found a work-bench and tools and a number of gun barrels. He also found hazel sticks similar to the one left at the store, and letterheads marked, "Bought of J.W. Noble — gun maker." There was a shed behind the house and here the police found a tub of water in which a coat floated. This and other items of clothing were taken, and handed over to the county analyst.

The lamp left at the scene of the crime was traced to a company in London, Messrs Dolan & Co of Vauxhall, and the court now heard of two letters sent by Noble to this manufacturer. The first of these was dated October 1st, and read, "Dear Sir — Please send me prices of your Crescent patent lamps and other dark lamps, if you have any that is used by the police and night watchmen; nett price, or subject to the usual cash discount for cash with order." The second letter was an order and contained the confirmation that Noble wanted a lamp which did not emit any smoke.

One mystery was cleared up in court. Cowell had reported that when he went outside, he had seen another man whom he assumed was an accomplice of the robber. Now Robert Carter was called to give evidence. He testified that he was a morning caller who got other people up for work. He usually began work at 1.40am and finished at around 5.00am. At around 4.30am on November 1st, he was near the Windy Nook store, on his rounds, when he heard the sound of a scuffle and shouts from within. Looking through the window he saw a number of men, including Ather, who he recognised, fighting on the floor. In due course, Cowell came out and accused him of being an accomplice. Carter had pointed out his error, said he was, "the caller" and had then walked away, not run as Cowell had suggested.

Robert Carter also had other evidence to give. He reported that on his nightly walks around Windy Nook he had previously noticed that certain gas lights had been turned out by someone. Amongst those he had seen extinguished were the ones in front of and behind Joseph Noble's house in Store Street. Under cross-examination though, Mr Carter admitted that many other lights throughout the area had been extinguished from time to time.

Thomas Yeldar Nicholson was a gardener and had known Joseph Noble for eight or nine years. He told the court that about a year before the incident at the store, he had seen Noble in Leam Drive. At the time, Noble had for some reason been wearing a false beard. Nicholson had greeted Noble by saying, "I know you, Joe." Noble had not replied, but had smiled at him.

James Robson Melville, the general manager of the Co-operative store, identified 120 separate articles, collected by the police from Noble's house, as items which had come from his store. He estimated the total value at £11 but admitted under cross-examination that there was no evidence these items had been stolen.

Dr Samuel Vernon Robinson had conducted a medical examination of Noble, at the police station at Gateshead, on November 4th. He described two lacerated wounds towards the right side of Noble's head, at the back. One was one and a half inches long and the other, just below it, was slightly shorter at about one inch. There was a third wound behind the left ear and all of these were recent wounds. Dr Robinson also found a small abrasion and a larger, contused bruise on the inside of Noble's right leg.

Dr Patterson had conducted the post-mortem on John Patterson. A bullet had penetrated Patterson's head, hitting him just above the left eyebrow and then entering his brain. The cause of death was laceration and haemorrhage of the brain, caused by that bullet. He had removed the bullet from the body and handed it over to the police. That bullet had since been examined by Thomas Simpson who was the manager of W.R. Pape & Sons, gunsmiths of Collingwood Street. The bullet had been fired from a UMC cartridge case and was of .32 calibre. This was the same type as the bullet removed from Christopher Carr's hip and the police had found two such cartridges at Noble's house.

One of the final witnesses for the prosecution was William Frederick Keating Stock, the analyst for the county of Durham. He had examined seven articles of Noble's clothing including the coat found soaking in the tub. He found no signs of blood on that coat but said that this was not surprising as it had been given a thorough wetting. There were, however, spots of blood on Noble's vest and trousers. More importantly there were grease spots on the coat. He had tested this grease and found that it was animal fat melting at 31 degrees Centigrade. This was the melting point of fat from a hog's back and two pig's carcasses had been hanging in the butchery department of the store on the night of the incident in which Patterson died.

The time came for Mr Shortt to outline the case for the defence and he began by trying to demolish much of the circumstantial evidence against his client. To begin with, he argued, there was no certainty this was in fact murder at all. If a shot was fired by a man in his own defence, and under great provocation, and this ended in death that it would be up to the jury to decide if he was not justified in defending himself, making it manslaughter rather than murder.

Mr Shortt now turned to Noble's injuries. Christopher Carr had sworn throughout that he gave the killer two blows with the butcher's steel. The killer therefore should have two wounds upon his head. Noble, though, had three wounds, not two and he saw no way that two blows could cause three wounds. In addition, Ather had testified that he came upon the man from the right while he was climbing out of the window, and immediately struck him on the right leg. If Noble was the killer then he should have a bruise or mark on the outside of his right leg, but Noble sported one on the inside. In addition, this wound was relatively minor and surely a hard blow from a hammer would have caused a much more severe wound.

Mr Shortt referred to the grease stains on Noble's coat. The witnesses had testified that the two pig's carcasses were hanging belly out. If these had been brushed against in the fight, then the killer would have had grease from the belly of a pig on his clothing. Mr Stock had sworn that the fat was from a hog's back. This could only be reconciled if the carcasses had been turned completely around during the fight and there was no evidence of this.

The man seen by Thomas Nicholson wearing the beard had made no reply to him and there was no proof that this had been Noble. Much of the other evidence could also be explained away. The lamp was needed for the innocent purpose of feeding animals that Noble kept, before he went to work and there was no proof that the one found at the scene of the crime was his. The hazel sticks were used to build nets to catch sparrows; the 'jemmy' the police had found was an iron bar and since Noble was a blacksmith, there was nothing suspicious in that. The gun barrels were not an unusual things to find on the premises of a man who made and repaired guns and no revolver had been found at Noble's house. Finally, Noble was right handed and the shot had been fired by a man who drew out the revolver with his left hand, and fired it with his left hand, with some degree of accuracy.

Joseph Noble stepped into the witness box to give evidence on his own behalf. He said he was a married man, with three children. He had been at home at the time John Patterson was shot dead, had never owned a revolver and was not guilty of this crime. He went on to try to explain away other sections of the evidence by saying that he had been given the so-called skeleton keys by his father, many years before, and as for the cartridges, they were a mixed box which a gun maker might be expected to have. He had had them for many years and some were so corroded as to be unusable. The police were claiming that he had disposed of the murder weapon. Why then had he not also had the common sense to dispose of the cartridges which the police found so incriminating? As for the injuries he claimed to have sustained at work, Noble had not reported these as anyone who did was termed 'soft' by his workmates.

On the second day of the trial, the jury found Noble guilty as charged. Asked if he had anything to say before the sentence of death was passed, Noble replied, "You may break my neck, but you won't break my heart."

For a few days after the death sentence, Noble was, not unnaturally, upset and paced his cell. He then settled down and appeared to become resigned to his fate although as the fateful day approached, he began to have difficulty sleeping and became restless again.

Despite a petition with close to 5,000 signatures, there was no reprieve. On the morning of Tuesday, March 24th, 1908, Noble ate a light breakfast of tea, bread and butter and waited for the executioners to come for him. As his shirt was loosened, prior to his arms being pinioned, Noble muttered, "Don't hurt my neck." They were the last words he was ever to utter. He marched unflinchingly to the scaffold where he took his position next to Robert Lawman, the subject of the next chapter. Both men were then launched into eternity by the Pierrepoint brothers, Henry and Thomas.

Later that same morning, Noble's wife received a last letter penned by her husband. In that note he said that he had never had any belief that a reprieve would come but declared once again that he was innocent of the crime which had claimed his life.

CHAPTER SIX

MURDER FOR LOVE

AMELIA BELL WOOD hailed from Newcastle and until
1901, lived with her parents at Heaton. In that year, the
family moved to Burnopfield and when the time came
for Amelia to earn her own living, she served an apprenticeship
as a tailoress, again in Newcastle. Amelia, though, never used
her new-found skills and instead took a position as a barmaid.
Then, in 1904, she met Robert Lawman, a miner, who was
eight years her senior.

Although Lawman was a married man he had been
separated from his wife for some considerable time, she having
left him and their two sons. He and Amelia were attracted to
each other from the very beginning and eventually they began
living together. They first set up home in Byker, later moving
to Carlisle and finally returning to Newcastle where they took
lodgings in Joseph Street, Elswick. On January 22nd, 1908,
though, the couple parted and just over a week later, on
January 30th, Amelia took fresh lodgings with Elizabeth Senior
at 1 Hyde Park Street, Gateshead.

On Friday, January 31st, Amelia went out for a few drinks at
around 7.30pm, but when she returned that night, at 11.30pm,
Robert Lawman was with her. Lawman was introduced to Mrs
Senior and she consented to him staying the night. After all,

Amelia had already told her about her circumstances and had explained to Mrs Senior that she had been living with a married man, but that they had argued and she had left him.

At about 11.50pm Amelia came into the kitchen where Elizabeth Senior was sitting, and asked if she could have some bread. Elizabeth gave her the bread, and Amelia returned to her own room. Elizabeth did not see her again that night.

Next morning, Saturday, February 1st, at 11.00am, Amelia called Elizabeth Senior into the front room she had shared with Lawman. The young couple were in bed together and Mrs Senior asked them what they wanted for breakfast. Lawman was the first to reply and he said, "Anything will do for me." He asked Mrs Senior to pass him his trousers, which she did, and he reached into the pocket and handed over a 2s piece. Amelia told Elizabeth that she should use it to get something for breakfast for them and added that Lawman had already been up and about once. Apparently he had risen at 5.00am and gone out to buy some beer and whisky, but now he wanted more. It was now suggested that perhaps Mrs Senior could use some of the money she had been given to buy 8d-worth of whisky.

Elizabeth Senior did as she had been asked and in due course returned with the whisky. When she handed it over, Amelia and Lawman were still in bed together and were looking at some pictures in a locket. They showed Mrs Senior the locket and Amelia asked her if she thought the picture looked like her. Elizabeth Senior told her that it did and then went back to the kitchen to make their breakfast.

Not long afterwards, Amelia, who was still not fully dressed, came into the kitchen and gave Elizabeth Senior 3d to get her some beer as she did not like whisky. She was still holding the pendant which she put it on to the mantelpiece for safety. As the women talked, they heard Lawman call from the bedroom, "Come here Millie." Amelia returned to her bedroom and Elizabeth Senior returned to the shop to buy the beer for Amelia.

Mrs Senior took the beer into the bedroom and poured it into glasses for the couple, both of whom were now back in bed. Once again she returned to the kitchen, and breakfast. When the meal was finally ready, Mrs Senior went back to the bedroom, knocked on the door and asked if she should bring it in. The reply was the sound of the bolt being shot. Elizabeth knocked again and heard Amelia say, "Oh!...Oh!" Once again she tried the door, but it was locked against her, so she returned to the kitchen.

Elizabeth Senior had been in her kitchen for only a minute or so when a bloodcurdling scream shattered the quiet of the house. Rushing back to the bedroom, Mrs Senior knocked again and demanded to be let in. From within, Lawman called that he would open the door when he was ready. Elizabeth now ran outside to see if she could look in through the window. She could see nothing but still there were screams coming from within the room. Elizabeth tried the door once more and then, still unable to gain entrance, ran for assistance.

Police Constable Patrick Kelly was on duty nearby and returned with Elizabeth Senior to her house. He called out for Lawman to open the door. Again Lawman called out that he would open it soon. Kelly tried to force open the door with a poker, but without success.

Constable Kelly stayed at the scene while Elizabeth Senior went to get more help and in due course Inspector Grey and Constable Cairns arrived and they, too, shouted for Lawman to let them in. Lawman was heard to say, "I cannot open it. I am too weak." The three officers now used their combined strength to break down the door. Inside they found Amelia Bell Wood lying on the bed wearing her chemise and a light blouse. She had been stabbed in the throat and was already dead. Lawman, who was kneeling over Amelia, also had a wound in his throat and Dr Robinson was summoned to attend to him. He was rushed to the Royal Infirmary where he made a full recovery, eventually being discharged on Thursday, February 6th.

The inquest on Amelia Bell Wood opened at Gateshead Town Hall on February 4th, before the coroner Mr John Graham. The first witness was Matthew Ellison Wood, a journeyman baker of 188 Shipley Street, Byker, who testified that the dead woman was his sister. He had not seen her for a considerable time until one day she turned up at his house with a man she introduced as 'Bob' and said that he was her husband. That was the last time he had seen her alive. At that point the inquest was adjourned, until February 18th.

After he had been discharged from hospital, Lawman made his first appearance at the Gateshead Borough police court. He had no legal representation at this time and as he stood in the dock he had a thick bandage around his throat.

The first witness was Chief Constable James Trotter, who gave evidence on behalf of the police officers involved in the case. He explained Lawman's background and stated that while they had lived at Joseph Street, there had been frequent violent quarrels between Lawman and the dead woman. No one knew where Amelia had gone when she left Joseph Street on January 22nd, but she arrived at Mrs Senior's house at 10.00pm on January 30th, asking for lodgings.

On January 31st, Lawman had not gone to work. He had told his son that he was going to shave off his moustache and was then going to look for 'Melia' and if he found her, he would hit her. Lawman had evidently found Amelia for that night they returned to her lodgings where he was introduced by Amelia as, "her boy" and at that time, he was clean shaven. Details of the events of the following morning were then related and Mr Trotter explained that a small silver table knife had been found at the scene of the crime. This had been slipped into some curtains and was smeared with wet blood. There was also a long hair adhering to the blade and this matched Amelia's.

Constable Robert Cairns was called to prove details of the arrest and told the court that at the time, Lawman had said, "I loved her. I killed her. I will swing for her." At this point, Mr Trotter requested a remand until February 17th. This was granted and when Lawman was asked if he wished to attend the inquest when it re-opened, he replied that he would.

By the time the police court reconvened, on February 17th, Lawman no longer had a bandage around his throat, although he did have his coat collar turned up. This hearing was very brief indeed, Mr Trotter asking for a further remand. Lawman made no objection.

The following day, the inquest resumed. Police Sergeant Topping testified that he was on duty in the police station at Gateshead at 11.30pm on January 24th, when Amelia Bell Wood and Robert Lawman came in. Both appeared to be sober, but were involved in some kind of dispute. Amelia told the sergeant that she wanted protection from Lawman. She explained that they were not married but had been living together for several years. To this, Lawman had replied that he was not happy with the way Amelia was living and wanted her to come back to him. Amelia said that in the last two weeks, Lawman had given her only 8s 0d and as a result, she had had to go 'on the streets'. Sergeant Topping ended by saying that at the time he had told Lawman that as Amelia was not his wife, he had no claim upon her. She had then said she was not going back with Lawman but would stay with her sister instead. At the time, Robert Lawman was sporting a moustache.

Elizabeth Senior said that she was the wife of Alfred Senior, a carpenter, and they lived together in two back rooms at 1 Hyde Park Street. The single front room was a large, bedsitting room, and this was let out to paying guests. Amelia had arrived on the night of January 30th and the following morning had enjoyed breakfast in the kitchen. Mrs Senior related what she had seen and heard since the arrival of Robert Lawman in her house. She ended by saying that the knife used to kill Amelia was not one that belonged to her household.

At this point the coroner took the opportunity of examining

the knife and noted that it had been recently sharpened. Lawman was given the opportunity to cross-examine witnesses and now began to ask Elizabeth Senior about who had opened the door on the night he and Amelia had come in together. The coroner ruled that these questions were irrelevant, and Mrs Senior was dismissed.

Eleven-year-old William Lawman was the son of the accused man and as he took the oath, his father began to show signs of emotional distress. He said that he had lived with his father and 'Millie' until February 1st, and identified the locket as one that belonged to Millie. The pictures inside it were of his father and the dead woman.

William reported that his father and Millie often argued, especially after Lawman had been paid and had spent rather too much money on drink. William went on to say that the knife shown in court was one from their house at Joseph Street. Asked if he wanted to ask his son any questions, Robert Lawman, his voice tinged with emotion, said, "It's alright. I will not ask him anything."

Constable Patrick Kelly told of his attempts to break into the room on February 1st. Once he had gained admission he noticed that in addition to the wound in her throat, Amelia also had one over her right eye. Lawman, who was wearing a night-shirt and socks, also had a wound to his jaw and there appeared to have been some kind of struggle as there were broken bottles and bits of broken glass littered about the room.

Dr Samuel Vernon Robinson had performed the post-mortem on Amelia's body and he said that there were five or six superficial lacerations on the front of her throat and also small wounds on her right cheekbone and on the left of her chin. A large bruise above her right eyebrow and two more on the back of her head were probably caused by a bottle and the minor cuts had been caused by broken glass.

Although Amelia had a severe wound in her throat, the

blood vessels of the neck had not been severed. Death was due to asphyxia due to the blood from that wound interfering with her respiration, and from shock caused by loss of blood. Finally, the doctor stated that the wounds could not possibly have been self inflicted.

The coroner summed up the evidence, describing it as, "...a wretched, sordid story of what might be called a low-lived amour — a story the result of lust, jealousy and drink." The jury took only five minutes to return a verdict of wilful murder against Lawman.

The police court hearing resumed the following day, February 19th. In addition to the witnesses already mentioned, Dorothy Cook was called to give evidence. She lived in Elswick, close to Lawman, and knew the couple well. She testified that Lawman was often the worse for drink when he got paid and during his periods of bad temper, Amelia often came to her for protection. As for Amelia, Dorothy had only seen her drinking when she was in the company of Robert Lawman. Robert's youngest son, George, was also called and he confirmed that he had seen his father strike Millie.

The trial of Robert Lawman took place on February 28th, 1908, at Durham, before Mr Justice Channell. The case for the prosecution was put by Mr C.F. Lowenthal and Mr H.S. Mundahl, while Lawman was defended by Mr Morgan Griffith Jones.

All the evidence already described was given again but now witnesses agreed that Amelia, too, had something of a temper. Dorothy Cook said she thought that Amelia was very quick tempered and both William and George Lawman said they had seen her throw pots and pans at their father. Of more interest, though, was the location of the weapon which had been used to kill Amelia.

When the police had broken into the room, no knife had been found. The weapon had been discovered in the hallway, outside the bedroom, after the police had broken down the door. The prosecution explained this by saying that after stabbing Amelia, Lawman must have opened the door and hidden the knife, while Elizabeth Senior was out seeking help. He had then cut his own throat with some of the broken glass in the room in an attempt to show that both he and Amelia had been injured during the course of a fight.

In the event, the jury had no trouble in returning a guilty verdict but the story of the ill-fated lovers had so affected the trial judge that as he passed the death sentence, there were tears in his eyes. Lawman listened quietly to the dread words and after the judge had finished, he stood to attention, saluted the judge and in a firm voice cried, "I thank you, my Lord."

Lawman was a model prisoner while in the condemned cell and passed away much of his time by copying out his favourite hymns. He spent a relatively quiet last night and apparently slept well. At 9.00am on the morning of Tuesday, March 24th, 1908, Robert Lawman was hanged by the Pierrepoint brothers at Durham prison, alongside Joseph William Noble, the subject of the last chapter. It was just seven and a half weeks since the death of Amelia Bell Wood.

CHAPTER SEVEN

FOR THE LOVE
OF FRANCES

T HERE WERE a number of people living in the house at 20 Thames Street, Chopwell, in 1909. The head of the house was Jacob Patrick, a miner, and he lived with his wife, Elizabeth Ann, and their four children, Frances, Maggie, Joseph and George Robert. In addition, there also lived at number 20 a lodger, 29-year-old Abel Atherton, who was also a miner and worked with Jacob at the Chopwell Colliery.

Abel Atherton, a native of Wigan in Lancashire, had lodged with the Patrick family for some two years but towards the end of that time, he had grown rather too fond of Frances Patrick, who was by then 15 years old. Atherton made advances towards Frances and when these were rejected, he was asked to leave the house, which he did on July 24th, 1909, when he moved into new lodgings with Mr and Mrs Forster at Mercy Street.

Atherton was not happy about leaving Thames Street and began to spread rumours that there was some very strange behaviour going on in the Patrick household, including, he alleged, that Jacob was sleeping with his own daughter. Despite these comments, he still visited his old lodgings almost every day. Things were, however, coming to a head and on Wednesday, August 11th, 1909, Abel Atherton finally embarked on a course of action that would cost both him and his former landlady their lives.

Early that day, Atherton had said to his landlady, Mrs Forster, that it was a good job he left the Patrick's before he did some mischief. He told her, "I have carried these about all day," and then produced three cartridges from his pocket, adding, "One was meant for Frances, one for Patrick and one for myself."

At around 6.00pm Atherton was back at Thames Street where he made further allegations against Jacob Patrick. Elizabeth said she was sick of hearing these comments and suggested that he come back when her husband was there and challenge him to his face. Atherton returned to his new lodgings and asked Mrs Forster for his gun, saying, "I'm going to have a bit of sport." As he took the weapon Mrs Forster saw that there were tears in his eyes. So concerned was Mrs Forster that she tried to get Atherton to leave the gun behind but to this he had shouted, "Stand back or I will shoot you." Then he went out of the back door as Mrs Forster ran out of the front in order to summon help.

It was 6.30pm when Abel Atherton arrived at the back door of 20 Thames Street. Inside the kitchen were Elizabeth Ann Patrick, her daughter Frances, her son, Joseph, and a neighbour, Mrs Marley. As soon as Atherton walked in the door, Elizabeth saw that he was carrying a gun under one arm. She got up from her seat by the fire, saying, "You are not going to use that gun." She ran at Atherton and a brief struggle followed, during which a shot was fired. The pellets passed harmlessly into the street but as the struggle continued between Elizabeth and Atherton, a second shot was heard and Elizabeth Patrick fell to the floor, wounded in her thigh. Unfortunately, the shot had severed her femoral artery and she bled to death within minutes.

Seeing that Elizabeth was badly wounded, Atherton discarded the gun and, apparently overcome by remorse, knelt down and made as if to kiss her. Then he stood up again, took a knife from his pocket and proceeded to cut his own throat. Atherton then walked outside where he was met by Constable John Coulson at the top of Blyth Street. Atherton announced, "I am the man you want. She is quite dead. It's a pity I didn't manage myself as well. It is a bad job for me." He was taken into custody and, seeing that Atherton's throat wound was not serious, Coulson escorted the prisoner to his house where he told him that he was under arrest for murder. To this Atherton replied, "I think she shot herself, but I have been the instigator of it. I wish I had finished myself at the same time." Later still, Atherton was escorted to Blaydon police station where he was formally charged, and claimed that the shooting was, "a pure accident".

The first police court hearing took place on August 12th, at Gateshead. The formal proceedings lasted only a few minutes and only evidence of arrest was given. Atherton, a short, stoutly-built man with a florid complexion, was asked if there was anything he wished to say as to why he should not be remanded in custody. Atherton began, "I never shot the woman. I went to the house…" At this point, the chairman of the magistrates, Mr Robert Middleton, interrupted and told him that he had better reserve his defence. To this Atherton again stated, "I am not guilty of shooting the woman." He was then remanded for eight days.

The inquest on Elizabeth Ann Patrick opened at the Workmen's Institute at Chopwell, before Mr John Graham, on August 13th. Joseph Patrick, Elizabeth's 14-year-old son, was the first witness to describe the events of August 11th and after hearing his testimony, and that of others, the proceedings were adjourned until August 17th. On that date, Frances Patrick was one of the witnesses and although Atherton himself was not present, he was represented by Mr W.N. Armstrong. Medical evidence was also called concerning the injuries the dead woman had suffered.

Meanwhile, the funeral of Elizabeth Patrick had taken place at Tow Law Cemetery on Saturday, August 14th. The funeral cortège left her home at noon, watched by a large crowd of people. A short service was led by the Reverend T.W. Hanson, the curate of Chopwell, and the choir of St John's Church then sang, *Lead Kindly Light*. All Elizabeth's family, including her mother, Mrs Caygill, were present to pay their last respects.

The final hearing before the magistrates took place on August 27th, when Atherton was committed for trial. He finally appeared before Mr Justice Walton at Durham, on November 10th, 1909, when the case for the prosecution was led by Mr C.F. Lowenthal, assisted by Mr A.J. Lawrie, while Atherton was defended by Mr Morgan Griffith Jones. The proceedings lasted for two days.

Constable Coulson repeated his earlier evidence and added that when he had searched Atherton at the police station, he had found on him 12 ball cartridges as well as a pocket knife. Atherton had complained at the time that his knife was not sharp enough, presumably referring to his unsuccessful suicide attempt. Coulson went on to describe how, on May 12th, Atherton had made a further statement in which he claimed he had taken the gun with him only to frighten the people in the house.

Jacob Patrick described how he had gone to work at 3.45pm on the day his wife was killed. As a result of a message he received at work, he rushed home, arriving there at about 7.00pm, by which time, of course, Elizabeth was dead. Jacob went on to describe some of the problems the family had had with Atherton over his infatuation with Frances and stated that he had been the one who told Atherton to find somewhere else to live. The prisoner had visited his house a number of times since but Jacob had never heard him issue any threats, although he had come to hear of the rumours Atherton was spreading about.

Frances Mary Patrick was a most important witness. She

described how several times before July 1909, Atherton had
put his arms around her and kissed her. She had thought
nothing about it at the time but one day her father had taken
her to one side and warned her what might happen if she
allowed such behaviour to continue. From that time onwards,
she was not happy for Atherton to touch her in such an
affectionate way.

On Easter Monday, Atherton had been ill in bed at 8.30pm.
Elizabeth was out of the house at the time and Atherton had
asked Frances to bring him some tea. The girl took him up a
drink and also some cakes and put them down on a chair by
his bed. She was about to leave the room when he sat up,
grabbed her around the waist and pulled her towards him. He
kissed her and then made a suggestion which she did not like.
Frances had then pushed him away saying, "I will tell if you
don't let me go." Atherton had done as she asked and Frances
went back downstairs but did not mention what had been said
to her parents.

About a month after this incident, Frances' parents had
gone out together leaving her alone in the kitchen with
Atherton. Once again he grabbed at her and made an improper
suggestion. Frances shouted for her mother, whereupon
Atherton immediately let her go and then went out of the
house. Again, Frances did not report this to her parents.

Half an hour later, Atherton came back to the house. By
now, Elizabeth had returned and Atherton announced that he
wanted to leave and was giving a month's notice. Elizabeth
asked him what was wrong and Atherton said that he had no
fault to find with anyone there. Over the next couple of weeks,
Atherton made a few more passes at Frances, all of which were
rejected, and then one day he handed her a note which suggested that she was 'carrying on' with her own father. Frances
did not show the letter to anyone but did write back to Atherton, saying that his accusations were untrue. Further notes
of a similar nature followed but Frances destroyed them all.

On July 24th, Frances was in the kitchen by the fire when Atherton came in at 11.30am. Yet again he threw his arms around her and kissed her and again made suggestions as to what he would like to do to her. Frances was so upset that she walked out of the house and went to a neighbour's where her mother called for her a few minutes later. When her father came home from work that night, Frances finally told her parents what had been going on and said that if Atherton did not leave the house, she would. It was then that Jacob spoke to Atherton and he moved out that same night.

Atherton continued to visit Thames Street and most of those visits ended in some kind of argument. Frances was there when, on August 8th, Atherton had shouted to her, "It was through you I had to leave the house. You have done your worst for me and I will do my worst for you." The following night, Atherton was there again, repeating his allegations of misconduct between Frances and her father and pointing out that if he made an official complaint, the courts would take it very seriously.

Coming now to the evening that her mother died, Frances related how Atherton had appeared at the doorway with his gun, and her mother had rushed forward to challenge him. Frances, too, had run towards Atherton but the neighbour, Mrs Marley, had held her back. From where she was, Frances did not have a clear view of what actually happened so was unable to say if her mother had grabbed the gun barrel or not. However, when giving evidence at the inquest, Frances had said that Elizabeth had grabbed the barrel.

Fourteen-year-old Joseph Patrick was also in the kitchen on that fateful day and he gave evidence that his mother had indeed grabbed the barrel of the gun. After hearing the first shot, Joseph ran from the house to get help and only heard the second shot some seconds later. Cross-examined by the defence, Joseph agreed that when he first came into the kitchen, Atherton had his right hand in his pocket and carried the gun under his left arm, pointing down at the floor. It was only during the struggle that the weapon was raised up.

A neighbour, Mary Truden, told the court that she had seen Atherton approach the Patrick house, carrying his gun. He went inside and a couple of minutes later she heard the sound of shooting. Looking at her neighbour's house, Mary saw Elizabeth fall into the street. Seconds later the gun was thrown out and landed close to Elizabeth's body.

Another neighbour, Mary Ann Keogan, also heard the first shot and went outside to see what was going on. After the second shot, she, too, saw Elizabeth fall out of her house and then saw Atherton standing framed in the doorway. The gun was thrown out and then Atherton knelt down and appeared to kiss Elizabeth.

Inspector Dryden of the Gateshead police told the court of a statement Atherton had made on August 12th. On the way to the station, the prisoner had stated, "There is one thing that consoles me — I didn't shoot, she shot herself. I called at the house to frighten them, but she took the gun from me and shot herself. I would have stopped her but the daughter and Mrs Marley stopped me."

Victor Pape was a firearms expert and he testified that he had examined the gun, and the clothing worn by the dead woman at the time she was shot. By conducting experiments with the gun and trying to reproduce the marks found on the clothes, he was able to determine that the gun must have been fired from a distance of about 27ins, possibly more. It was, of course, still possible that Elizabeth had grabbed the gun and that in trying to pull it from her, Atherton had accidentally pulled the trigger but his statement that Elizabeth had shot herself was certainly untenable.

The time came for Atherton to give his own version of events. He explained that after leaving the Patricks' household, he found himself short of money and had planned to sell his gun in order to raise some cash. That was why he had taken the weapon from his lodgings and on the way to sell it, he passed the Patricks' house and decided to call in. Upon seeing the gun, Elizabeth had jumped to the wrong conclusion, rushed across the room and grabbed the gun barrel. He had never pointed the weapon at her, or consciously pulled the trigger, and was as surprised as everyone else when the gun went off. It was only when he saw Elizabeth lying on the ground that he realised what had happened. And as for his attempted suicide, that was because he felt guilty, not for the shooting itself but because he had not had the sense to take the cartridges out of the gun.

For the defence, Mr Griffith Jones in his summing up stated that the dead woman had been like a second mother to Atherton and it was surely unlikely that anyone would want to murder someone who had been so kind to them. It was obvious that the gun had been fired accidentally during the course of a struggle and as such, Atherton was guilty of manslaughter, not murder.

The jury were out for 45 minutes before returning their guilty verdict. Asked if he had anything to say before sentence was passed, Atherton asked, "Can I get a fresh trial?" After telling him that he could not, Mr Justice Walton passed the sentence of death whereupon Atherton announced, "I am innocent." In due course, an appeal was also lost and the death sentence confirmed.

Atherton's conduct in the condemned cell was said to be exemplary. He continued to maintain his innocence and managed to convince himself that he would be reprieved. On December 5th, he received notice that there would be no reprieve and after initially being upset, finally resigned himself to his fate.

The same day, Atherton wrote a final letter to his parents, "Dear father and mother. I write these few lines to you, hoping to find you all well, as you will very likely know the sad news before you get this letter, that there is no more hope for me in this world. But I will have to put my trust in the Lord. He is the One who we will all have to answer to sooner or later. There is one thing that I will not have to answer for, and that is what I am sentenced to death for, of which I am innocent, and my life is on the hands of those I told you about. You can believe me what I told you; it is the God's truth. It won't do me any good to tell lies. I would not have said anything if I had hold of the gun when she was shot, but I never was in the struggle.

"...You can tell all my friends that I send them my best respects. So I will expect you and Katie, Lizzie and Levi coming on Monday, if you can possibly get. That is all at present. From your innocent son, Abel Atherton."

Atherton rose at 6.00am on the morning of Wednesday, December 8th, 1909. Dressing in his own clothes for the first time since his trial, he was then seen by the prison chaplain, the Reverend D. Jacob. Later still, Atherton ate sparingly of a breakfast of bread and butter, washed down with tea.

There had been a sharp frost the previous night and probably as a result of that, no one waited outside the prison at 8.00am when Atherton was placed upon the trapdoor by Henry Pierrepoint and his assistant, William Willis. As the pinioning process was completed, Atherton cried out in a loud voice, "You are hanging an innocent man." They were the last words he ever uttered. Seconds later the lever was pulled and Abel Atherton hurtled down to his death.

CHAPTER EIGHT

A MOST
DETERMINED MAN

I T WAS around 3.30pm on the afternoon of Saturday, March 26th, 1910, when Mary Jane Henderson of 11 Oakwellgate, Gateshead, heard a knock on her front door.

Going to see who it was, Mary was greeted by a handsome looking man who asked, "Does Henderson live here?" Mary replied in the affirmative and, presuming that the gentleman was looking for her husband, asked if he was a friend. It was only when the visitor went on to say, "Yes, I'm her cousin," that Mary realised that the man was looking for her daughter-in-law.

Mary's son, Thomas William Henderson, lived further up the same street in rooms on the second floor of Carter's Yard, which was at 60 Oakwellgate. Only seven weeks before, on February 5th, Thomas had married Annie Finn, a native of Barnard Castle. Mary explained to the man that the woman he was looking for lived elsewhere, and offered to escort him to her son's home.

That home was a small, rather gloomy flat which consisted of two rooms and a small scullery. When Mary and her caller arrived, Annie and her husband were in the front room. Annie instantly recognised her visitor and said, "You're Tommy

Craig, aren't you?" The visitor said that he was and added, "And you're Annie Finn." As they shook hands, Annie replied, "No, I'm Mrs Henderson now." Annie's husband, Thomas, also held out his hand to greet his guest but Craig refused to grasp it. Instead he turned to Annie and asked, "Why did you throw me over?" Annie made a fairly obvious reply, "Because I loved my husband better than you."

The story of Thomas Craig and Annie Finn had begun in the year 1903, as it was then that Thomas, a native of Spenny-moor, had first become acquainted with Annie when he had gone to Barnard Castle in order to do his military training. They started walking out together and even from the beginning, Craig had made it plain that he was a very jealous man and if Annie ever went off with anyone else, she would face the consequences. This relationship had continued for two years until Craig was arrested for an offence he had committed, tried at Durham before Mr Justice Darling, and sentenced to seven years' imprisonment.

For a while, things remained the same between Annie and Craig. They corresponded regularly until around September 1909, when the letters from Annie had dried up. Through writing to other friends and acquaintances, including Annie's sister, Winifred, Craig found out that there was now another man in Annie's life. He still wrote to her but the tone of his letters had changed. Now they were filled with threats and abuse. In one of his last letters, he had said that he still considered her to be his sweetheart and that no matter where she went, he would find her. Craig went on to say that he would fight for her with the last drop of his blood and would repay her for what she had done, adding that she would soon be with her mother. Annie's mother had died five years earlier. The letter ended, "I'll come like death it sealf" (*sic*) However, this same missive was signed with three kisses!

Annie's new husband knew all about her previous association with Craig, and she had shown him the letters and the threats they contained. Thomas Henderson said that he did not think Craig would do anything, but for Annie's peace of mind, he told her to make sure that the front door was locked whenever he was out and she was left at home alone.

Now, though, Annie was not alone and since his mother was also there, and Craig seemed to be reasonably quiet, Thomas Henderson saw no reason to be wary of his uninvited guest. Indeed, as Annie continued to talk to Craig, Thomas carried on with what he had been doing previously. He stood on a chair and began to take a picture down from the wall. While he was doing this, Thomas' mother went into the bedroom and gazed down into Oakwellgate. It was then that this peaceful domestic scene was shattered.

A loud report rang out and immediately Thomas Henderson half jumped and half fell off his chair with a cry of, "Oh! Annie." Annie turned to face Craig now and saw that he had a gun in his hand and was coming for her. Mary Jane Henderson was by now back in the room and she saw Craig pointing something at her daughter-in-law. She could still not actually see that it was a gun but the fact that the room was filled with smoke, and an overpowering stench of what turned out to be gunpowder, left her in little doubt as to what was going on.

Thomas Henderson managed to dash into the scullery as two more shots were fired. Annie was the target now and she tried to run around a table to escape but a total of five more shots rang out. Annie felt a terrible pain in her left breast and knew that she had been hit. Almost immediately, a second bullet tore into her back and she fell upon the settee. Craig now pointed the gun directly at Mary Jane who screamed, "Oh God! Spare me..." This seemed to bring Craig to his senses and he dashed out of the house and into the surrounding maze of streets.

Although badly wounded, Thomas Henderson bravely ran after the man who had shot him and his wife. Thomas, though, took a wrong turning and lost his man, ending up in Gateshead's High Street where he staggered and collapsed. Passers-by rushed to his aid and the police were called. They brought a stretcher and took the wounded man to the police station which was very close by. It was there, within 30 minutes, that Thomas Henderson died, making this a case of murder. Annie Henderson, meanwhile, was rushed to hospital where she eventually made a complete recovery. A massive police search was now launched for Thomas Craig, also known as Crake, but he was nowhere to be found.

The inquest on the dead man opened on March 30th at the Town Hall, before the coroner, Mr John Graham. This was immediately adjourned to April 13th, in the hope that by then, the police would have their man in custody. Three days later, on April 2nd, Thomas Henderson's body was laid to rest at Gateshead cemetery.

The police redoubled their efforts to find Craig. On April 8th, 34 policemen, assisted by civilians, searched Gibside Woods where a man fitting Craig's description had been seen. All they found was a note, signed 'Thomas Craig', saying that they would find his body 'somewhere in the woods' but after a painstaking search, no sign of Craig was found and the entire matter was put down as a hoax.

The search even spread as far as Westmorland, for late on the evening of April 12th, it was reported that Craig had been arrested at Tebay, by Police Constable Woods. This turned out not to be the case, the man in custody merely bearing a strong resemblance to the wanted man.

The next day, April 13th, the inquest was reopened and after hearing the evidence, a verdict of wilful murder against Craig was returned. Immediately Gateshead Corporation Watch Committee announced that they were offering a £50 reward for information which led to the arrest of Thomas Craig.

In fact, Craig was to remain free for three more days. During this period there had been two attempts to break into the house of a gentleman named Price, close to Corbridge, and a man fitting Craig's description had been seen in the area. So it was that an extensive search of Healey Woods was organised and as part of that search, officers eventually came to Dilston House, a farm near the village of the same name. It was there, in one of the outbuildings, that Constable Reuben Reed saw a man's boot half hidden in the hay. Investigating further, Reed found Craig, fast asleep, with a loaded revolver a few feet away. He offered no resistance when Reed woke him and from there was taken to Corbridge railway station where he was escorted back to Newcastle, arriving there at 12.25pm on April 16th. During the journey, Craig was very talkative and admitted that he had intended to kill Annie, not her husband, who he had only wanted to wound. He mentioned, too, that he would have liked to have killed Justice Darling, the man who had sent him to prison, but had not been able to find out where he lived.

Craig's first appearance at the Gateshead Borough police court was on April 18th, when he was remanded for two days. On April 20th, the first of the evidence was heard and Craig's movements since the shooting were outlined. Apparently, after the crime he had set off for Jarrow but when he was almost there, he retraced his steps and ended up at Chester-le-Street instead. After spending some time there, he returned to Gateshead, then passed through Dunston, where he spoke to some young lads before finding himself in Ravensworth Woods.

After hiding in the woods for a couple of days, Craig had returned to Chester-le-Street. He had intended going from there to Scotland but, as he was unfamiliar with the area and dare not ask for directions, he went to Consett instead where he was actually spoken to by a policeman who did not realise who he was and let him go on his way. Eventually he ended up at Corbridge, where one night he had broken into a house and helped himself to a meal of cold meat while the house owner was asleep on the settee in the next room.

On April 20th, the case was held over until April 22nd. From then, the evidence went on until April 23rd, when Craig was finally sent for trial by the magistrate, Mr Michael Corbett. That trial took place at Durham, before Mr Justice Grantham, on June 25th. Craig was defended by Mr Morgan Griffith Jones, while the case for the Crown was put by Mr Bruce Williamson and Mr Willoughby Jardine.

There was certainly evidence that Craig had planned his progress to Gateshead most deliberately. He had been released from Portland prison on March 24th. By the following day he had reached Darlington, for it was there, at 3.00am on March 25th, that he walked into the police station and asked Sergeant Whalen, the officer on duty, where he might find a bed for the night. Whalen suggested a place and after taking a few hours rest, Craig set off again for the north-east.

By 3.30pm on that same day, March 25th, Craig was knocking on the door of Annie's sister, Winifred Finn, who lived at Peel's Yard, Bridgate, Barnard Castle. Winifred, at Annie's request, had written to Craig in prison to tell him that Annie was about to be married and it had been this letter which prompted Craig to write the long, threatening letter to Annie.

Craig demanded that Winifred tell him where Annie was but Winifred said that he would not find out from her. At that, Craig said that he knew she was somewhere in Newcastle and, if need be, he would search the streets until he found her. Craig ended, "If I meet her husband first, she will have no husband to go home to."

By 11.30am on March 26th, Craig was at Stanley Hill Top where he spoke to Thomas Priestman, who was married to another of Annie's sisters. Once again he asked where Annie lived. Priestman claimed that he did not know but eventually Craig spoke to one of Priestman's workmates, a man named Harrison, who finally gave him the information for which he was so desperate. Thomas Henderson worked at Sowerby's

Ellison Glass Works in East Street, Gateshead, and from that Craig knew he would be able to trace his former lover's address. Craig wrote down the details on the back of an envelope.

Now that he had a general location for his target, Craig needed the means to carry out his plans. At 2.00pm he walked into Messrs W.R. Pape & Sons, gunmakers, of Collingwood Street, Newcastle, where Thomas Simpson sold him a revolver which Craig said he needed to protect his property. At the time, Craig gave the name John Wilson, and said he lived at 1 North Road, Durham, but Simpson had subsequently identified Craig as the customer.

Eighteen-year-old William Tate also worked at the glassworks and at 3.30pm Craig stopped him near Chandless Street and asked him if he knew where the Hendersons lived. Tate asked him which Hendersons he meant and once Craig had replied that he was looking for Tommy, Tate showed him where Mrs Mary Jane Henderson lived. For this, Craig thanked him and handed over twopence for his trouble.

Tate was suspicious of the man who had asked him these questions, especially since on the way, they had seen a couple of policemen and Craig had asked Tate to shield him until they had passed. Craig had then darted into a nearby brewery yard until the police officers were out of sight. He later explained that he had been arrested that morning for gambling and did not want any further trouble. Nevertheless, Tate waited around until he saw Craig emerge from Mary Jane's house. As they passed him, Craig muttered, "It's all right." This finally reassured Tate, who carried on with his own business.

The details of the shooting itself were then told, by Annie Henderson and her mother-in-law, Mary Jane. Evidence was also given of the immediate aftermath of the crime. Margaret McShane, who lived at 50 Oakwellgate, had seen Thomas Henderson running down the street after Craig. As he approached Margaret, Henderson gasped, "Oh Mrs McShane, that man's killed me." She then saw him run into the High Street where he fell down on to the tram lines. He managed to pick himself up, staggered another 30 yards or so and then fell against a shop. Margaret ran to offer him assistance and tore open his shirt front. Someone brought him a glass of water but he muttered that he was unable to drink. As the police arrived on the scene, Margaret noticed that blood was beginning to run from Henderson's mouth.

Constable Sanderson testified that he had been the first police officer on the scene and since the shot man was still conscious, he had asked him who had attacked him. Henderson managed to gasp, "Tommy Craig of Spennymoor." Sanderson was present at the police station when Henderson died at 4.25pm.

Dr Charles Edward Harold West had seen the victim at the police station after arriving at 4.00pm while Thomas Henderson was still alive. Two days later, he performed a post-mortem. The only external mark was a single bullet wound in the back, below the right shoulder blade. This bullet had entered between the eighth and ninth ribs and had splintered both of them. It had then travelled in an upward direction, penetrated the lung and finally come to rest in the chest cavity. The cause of death was given as haemorrhage of the lung, due to lacerations caused by the bullet.

Craig's defence was that the killing had been unintentional. He had only meant to 'wing' Henderson and he had, after all, suffered severe provocation from the only woman he had ever loved. As such, he asked that a verdict of manslaughter be returned. In the event, the jury felt that he was guilty as charged, although they did add a recommendation to mercy. Asked if he wished to say anything before sentence was passed, Craig replied, "I have nothing to say sir. I am quite willing to face death."

Despite a petition of 5,000 signatures from his home town of Spennymoor, Craig did indeed face death. Having spent a quiet night in Durham prison prior to his execution, he rose before 7.00am on the morning of Tuesday, July 12th, 1910. After receiving the ministrations of the Roman Catholic chaplain, Canon Brown, Thomas Craig was hanged at 8.00am by Henry Pierrepoint, who was assisted by William Willis. Craig was given a drop of exactly 7ft. Outside the prison gates, nearly 100 people waited for the appointed hour and the death of a man who had been so determined on revenge.

CHAPTER NINE

THE NEWCASTLE
TRAIN MURDER

THOMAS William Charlton enjoyed his work as a foreman porter at Alnmouth Station in Northumberland. Part of his duties involved checking trains once they had pulled into his station and ensuring that they were clean enough for their return journey. It was just such a task that he was performing on Friday, March 18th, 1910.

The 10.27am train from Newcastle Central Station had arrived at Alnmouth at 12.06pm and comprised an engine and four carriages. The first carriage, the one nearest to the engine, consisted largely of luggage accommodation but also included three third-class compartments. The second carriage had a third-class compartment at each end with a first-class section sandwiched between. The third carriage was all third-class, while the fourth and last was similar to the first carriage, consisting of luggage and third-class accommodation.

Charlton checked inside the various carriages until he came upon the first of the three compartments in the car closest to the engine. The compartment was the furthest of the three from the engine and as Charlton opened the door, he could see that something was terribly wrong. Three streams of blood crossed the floor and all seemed to emanate from underneath the seat facing the engine, at the far side of the carriage. Gingerly, Charlton entered the compartment and looked under the seat. There he saw the body of a man lying face down. Close by the man's head lay a hard felt hat and a pair of spectacles, which were broken in two. Also on the floor lay a return ticket from Newcastle to Widdrington. Charlton wasted no time in contacting his superiors who immediately called in the police.

It was a relatively simple matter to identify the dead man. A name band in the hat revealed that he was 44-year-old John Innes Nisbet, a colliery book-keeper, who lived at 180 Heaton Road, Heaton, and who was married with two young daughters, Cecily and Lilian. Nisbet worked for Messrs Rayne & Burn, of Beaconsfield Chambers, Sandhill, and one of his duties was to take the fortnightly pay to the men of Stobswood Colliery some half a mile from Widdrington station.

The motive for the crime was also easy to determine. Although Nisbet's personal property had not been touched — he still wore his silver watch and gold albert and had money in his pockets — a good deal of cash had been taken, for this was one of the days when Nisbet acted as cashier and courier for Stobswood. Thomas Anderson was the manager and cashier for Rayne & Burn and that morning he had handed Nisbet a cheque for £370 9s 6d, drawn on the Collingwood Street branch of Lloyds Bank. When the police checked at the bank, John Bradshaw Wilson, one of the cashiers, confirmed that Nisbet had cashed that cheque and had been given 231 sovereigns, 206 half sovereigns, £35 9s 0d in silver and the balance of £1 0s 6d in copper. The gold had been in three canvas bags, the silver in paper bags and the copper in paper parcels. Wilson also confirmed that before he left the bank, Nisbet had placed all the money into a leather bag, about a foot long, which he then locked. That bag, and, of course, all the cash, was now missing.

One of the first witnesses to provide the police with any

useful information was the dead man's wife, Cicely Nisbet. On the days that her husband had made the trip to Widdrington, it was Cicely's habit to walk down to Heaton station and wait for his train to pull in. They would exchange pleasantries and sometimes, when he had received his own pay, John Nisbet would hand some cash over to Cicely before the train continued on its way. The morning of March 18th, had been no different.

Cicely had waited at the end of the platform where the back of the train would be, since that was where her husband usually sat, but on this day he was not in his usual carriage. Looking down the train, she saw him leaning out of the carriage nearest to the engine and ran along the platform to greet him. They only had time to speak for a minute or two, John Nisbet standing inside the carriage and leaning out of the middle window, and it was during that conversation that Cicely noticed that there was another man in the carriage. This man was at the far end, facing the engine with his hat pulled down and his coat collar turned up. In addition to this, the shadow from the tunnel entrance was thrown across his body but one thing that Cicely was certain about was that there was only one other person in the compartment with her husband.

Once details of the crime were published, two more important witnesses came forward. Percival Harding Hall and John William Spink were also working together as cashiers and were engaged on a similar errand to Nisbet, who they both knew quite well. They had travelled on the same train as Nisbet on a regular basis for some four and a half years and had often passed the time of day with each other. Spink had not seen Nisbet at Newcastle station, but Hall certainly had. The two friends were in the middle of the third-class compartments of the first carriage and Hall was looking out of the window towards the back of the train when he saw Nisbet walking towards him.

Nisbet was apparently with another man, as they were

walking along together and Hall saw them both get into the compartment immediately behind the one he shared with Spink.

Hall and Spink alighted from the train at Stannington. It was now that Spink saw Nisbet for the first time. As they waited for the train to pull away, Spink noticed that in the compartment behind the one he had occupied, Nisbet was sitting, facing the engine. Indeed, Nisbet now acknowledged the two friends by nodding to them. Spink noticed that there was one other man in the compartment with Nisbet, a man with a moustache who wore a black felt hat and sat in the far corner.

It was the evidence of these three people; Mrs Nisbet, John Spink and Percival Hall, which enabled the police to piece together a very basic description of the man in the same compartment as the dead man. This description was published on March 19th and stated that the man was around 5ft 6ins tall, not very old and with a sallow complexion.

By March 21st, the police had come to accept that they were either looking for two assailants, or a single killer who had used two weapons. A medical examination of Nisbet had revealed that he had been shot no less than five times. Four of the bullets used in the crime had been recovered and these proved to be of two different calibres. Two of the bullets were nickel-coated and of .250 calibre. The other two were lead and .320 revolver cartridges. It was, however, on this same day, March 21st, that a new witness came forward; one who was to break the case wide open and lead to the arrest of a suspect.

Wilson Hepple was an artist by trade and he, too, had travelled on the 10.27am, train from Newcastle on March 18th. It was while he was buying his ticket that he noticed someone he had known for more than 20 years. After selecting his carriage, Hepple stood about on the platform for a few minutes and saw his friend walking towards him with another man. The two passed him, but because the platform was quite broad, they were still perhaps 20ft away. Hepple saw them enter a carriage near the engine together; indeed, the stranger appeared to hold open the carriage door for the man known to Hepple. After seeing the reports of the crime in the newspapers, Hepple was sure that one of the men he had seen was John Nisbet but the man with Nisbet, the man he had known for 20 years, was one John Alexander Dickman.

It was late on the evening of March 21st that Detective Inspector Andrew Tait called on Dickman at his home, 1 Lily Avenue, Jesmond. The inspector identified himself and told Dickman that a witness had come forward who reported that he had seen Dickman in the company of John Nisbet on the morning he was killed. Having listened to this, Dickman replied, "I knew Nisbet for many years. I saw him on that morning. I booked at the ticket window after him and went by the same train, but I did not see him after the train left. I would have told the police if I thought it would have done any good."

Inspector Tait asked Dickman if he was willing to accompany him to the police station and make a statement to Superintendent Weddell who was in charge of the case. "Certainly," replied Dickman, and he and Tait then travelled together to the station, arriving there not long before midnight.

At the police station that Dickman made a long statement which read in part, "On Friday morning last I went to the Central Station and took a return ticket for Stannington. Nisbet, the deceased man, whom I knew, was at the ticket-office before me, and so far as I know, had left the hall by the time I got mine. I went to the bookstall and got a paper, the *Manchester Sporting Chronicle*. I then went to the refreshment room and had a pie and a glass of ale. I then went on to the platform and took my seat in a third-class carriage nearer the hinder end than the front end.

"My recollection is, although I am not quite clear on the point, that people entered and left the train at different stations on the journey. The train passed Stannington Station without my noticing it and I got out at Morpeth and handed my ticket, with the excess fare of twopence halfpenny, to the collector.

"I left Morpeth to walk to Stannington by the main road. I took ill of diarrhoea on the way, and I had to return to Morpeth to get the 1.12pm train but missed it. I had to get the 1.40pm. While at Morpeth, after missing the 1.12pm train, I came out of the station on the east side, and turned down towards the town. I met a man named Elliott, and spoke to him. I did not get into the town, but turned and went back to the station, and got the 1.40pm to Newcastle. I got a single ticket for Stannington, but I did not give it up. I gave up the return portion at the Manors. I have been very unwell since I went on this journey to see Mr Hogg of Dovecote in connection with new sinking operations there."

By Dickman's own admission, he had travelled on the same train as Nisbet, and yet had not come forward to say so. He fitted the general description of the man seen with Nisbet and had been identified by someone who had known him for 20 years. He was now cautioned and searched, whereupon the police found that he was carrying £17 9s 5d. Five pence of this was in copper, and 9s 0d in silver. More significant perhaps was the fact that the £17 was in gold and wrapped inside a bag from the Lambton branch of Lloyds Bank. Dickman was now told that he would be charged with murder to which he replied, "I don't understand the proceedings. It is absurd for me to deny the charge, because it is absurd to make it. I only say I absolutely deny it."

The following day, March 22nd, the funeral of John Innes Nisbet took place at the Jesmond Old Cemetery. Dickman made his first appearance at the Moot Hall police court that same day and was remanded until March 30th when a second remand was granted.

On Sunday, April 3rd, the train on which the murder had taken place, together with the same carriages, was driven to platform five at Newcastle, the same platform it had departed from on March 18th. There a number of photographs were taken by the police so that witnesses in the case could describe exactly where they were on the day in question. Pictures were also taken of the gates to platforms four and five, the refreshment room and a cigar booth, all of which were to feature in the evidence.

Dickman was back in court on April 6th, by which time he was being represented by Mr Edward Clarke. Once again he was remanded, this time until April 14th. It was on that date that the first of the main witnesses were heard, and the case concluded the following day, at the end of which Dickman was sent for trial at the next assizes.

The trial of John Alexander Dickman opened at the Moot Hall, Newcastle, on July 4th, 1910, before Lord Coleridge, and the proceedings lasted for three days. Dickman was defended by Mr Mitchell Innes and Lord William Percy, while the case for the Crown was led by Mr E. Tindal Atkinson, assisted by Mr C.F. Lowenthal.

In the early stages of the trial, evidence was given of the timetable of the 10.27am from Newcastle. The first stop was Heaton, where it arrived at 10.34am. From there it travelled through Forest Hall, Killingworth, Annitsford, Cramlington, Plessy and Stannington, where it arrived at 11.06am. The next stop was Morpeth, where the train arrived at 11.12am and departed four minutes later at 11.16am. From Morpeth, it stopped at Pegswood and Longhirst before arriving at Widdrington where Nisbet should have departed. It then travelled on to Alnmouth, calling at other small stations on the way before finally reaching its destination, where it arrived just after noon.

For the prosecution, the important stations were Stannington and Morpeth. Spink and Hall had both seen Nisbet alive and well at the former station and at Morpeth, a gentleman named John Grant got on to the train. He had actually walked past the last compartment of the carriage closest to the engine, the one in which Nisbet's body lay, and had seen that it was empty. Grant got into the first compartment of that carriage but his testimony meant that not only was Nisbet already dead, but that his killer or killers had also made good their getaway. By his own statement, Dickman had alighted at Morpeth and the ticket collector there, John Athey, confirmed that a man had paid him an excess fare and handed in a ticket to Stannington. The man had the money ready in his hand. He was wearing a greatcoat but Athey could not see if he carried a bag or parcel of any kind.

John Grant, who said that the murder compartment appeared to be empty at Morpeth, also stated that when he got on to the train, there was another man already in his compartment. That man was Andrew Bruce who was a carriage inspector for the railway. He did not leave the train until it had reached its destination, Alnmouth, but he told the court that he had seen the two clerks get out at Stannington and nod to someone on the train. Those two clerks were, of course, Hall and Spink, but Mr Bruce had to admit under cross-examination that he had not seen anyone get off the train at Morpeth.

Evidence was now called to show that Dickman had been the man sharing the compartment with Nisbet. John Spink repeated his earlier evidence and said that although the man did look like Dickman he would not swear that it was him. He had attended an identification parade at the police station, and had failed to pick Dickman out from the line-up.

Percival Hall also attended that identification parade which took place on March 24th. There were nine men in a row and after walking down the line once, he approached a police officer and asked him what he should do. The officer advised him to, "…point him out", whereupon he returned to the line and picked out Dickman. However, Hall had also said, "I won't swear that the man I pointed out was the man I saw get in with Mr Nisbet, but if I could be assured that the murderer was there, I would have no hesitation in pointing the prisoner out." This somewhat ambiguous identification would prove to be rather significant later.

More significant was the testimony of Cicely Nisbet. She had told the police of a man in the carriage with her husband and had admitted that he had his hat down, his collar up and was in shadow. Despite all this, there had been an astounding development when she gave her evidence at the magistrate's hearing. Stepping down from the witness box, Mrs Nisbet had suddenly fainted. Upon being revived she had explained that the reason for her collapse was that she had caught a glimpse of Dickman's profile and it had been identical to the man she saw with her husband. She now had no hesitation in saying that John Dickman was the man who sat in that compartment.

Charles Raven was a commercial traveller from Heaton and both men involved in this case were well-known to him. Nisbet he had known for five or six years and Dickman he had known by sight for perhaps nine years. He, too, had been at Central Station on the morning of March 18th, and he now swore that Nisbet had been walking with a companion who he identified as Dickman. He saw them just a few minutes before the 10.27am left but could not say that they were in conversation with each other. They had walked together through the gate which led to platform four and turned right, towards platform five, behind the cigar shop. Raven did not see either man get on the train and could therefore not say whether they travelled together or not. It could be, of course, that the two men had simply been walking to the same train at the same time and happened to walk side by side.

Dickman had said that he was going to a colliery at Stannington to see Mr Hogg about the sinking of a new shaft. He had previously worked in the industry and had a keen interest in new developments. The police had, of course, spoken to William Hogg who now testified that he had known

Dickman since the turn of the century when he had been the secretary to a colliery company based at Morpeth. His company was indeed sinking a new mineshaft at Dovecot but on March 18th, he had no appointment with Dickman and, in fact, spent that entire day in Newcastle. The defence, though, under cross-examination, caused Hogg to confirm that Dickman had already visited him four or five times, each time without an appointment, the last time being two weeks before the murder, on March 4th. Therefore there was nothing unusual in Dickman making yet another visit on the 18th.

Attempts were now made to link Dickman to the robbery itself. Peter Spooner was the colliery manager at the Barmoor East Colliery and on June 9th, he had been making an inspection of a seam at the Isabella Pit, at Hepscott, some three quarters of a mile from Morpeth railway station, when he saw something at the bottom of a ventilation shaft which led to the surface. This turned out to be a leather bag, the one Nisbet had put the money into. The bag had been slit open by means of a sharp knife and most of the contents removed. A few coppers remained inside and others were scattered around the shaft. Eventually a total of 19s 5d was found. The bag also contained the pay slips for the colliery to which Nisbet was travelling. Spooner admitted that he and Dickman had once worked together but had to confirm that this was at a different establishment and he was unable to say whether Dickman knew of the location of the Isabella ventilation shaft or not.

John Bradshaw Wilson, who had cashed the cheque for Nisbet at Lloyds Bank, was called to identify the canvas bag found in Dickman's possession when he was arrested. Wilson was able to confirm that the gold he had paid out to Nisbet was placed inside canvas bags but he was unable to say exactly what sort had been used. The bank used various types, including the one Dickman had had in his pocket. That bag, though, was an old type which had not been produced since 1901.

Samuel Cohen was the manager of the Cash Accommodation & Investment Company of Northumberland Street, Newcastle, and his business was the lending of money. Some time around October 15th, 1909, Dickman had come to his office and enquired about the possibility of raising a £20 loan, stating that he wanted it for about three months. Cohen told Dickman that the interest on such a sum would be £1 a month, with the principle repayable at the end of the three months. Dickman said he would consider the terms and left.

A few days later, on October 18th, Dickman returned to the office and accepted the loan, handing over a promissory note for the £20. The interest had since been paid every month but in January, Dickman had come back yet again and asked for a further three months in which to repay the principle. The last payment of interest had been made on March 17th. Before that date, Dickman had introduced another client, a Mr Christie, who had raised a loan of £200. Dickman had been paid no commission for this introduction however.

This was, of course, an attempt by the prosecution to show that Dickman had financial worries. He had borrowed money and apparently been unable to pay it back. He had even introduced another customer, possibly in the hope of getting some commission, which never materialised. Under cross-examination, however, Mr Cohen admitted that since Dickman's arrest, his wife had paid off the loan in full, this taking place on May 9th. The Crown never suggested that Dickman's wife received any proceeds from the robbery and yet her finances were such that she could pay back £20 long after her husband was in jail.

Frank Christie had known the accused for some six years and he agreed that Dickman had introduced him to Mr Cohen as a possible customer. He had then raised a loan of £200, and had signed the cheque over to Dickman. Eventually, Christie had had the benefit of about half of the money but the rest he left with Dickman so that he could put bets on for him. He had backed horses many times through Dickman and there was nothing unusual in this particular transaction.

John Ketterer was the manager of Kuss & Company, a jewellers, and he testified that on February 14th, Dickman had called into his shop and shown him some items of jewellery on which he said he wished to raise some money. Ketterer gave Dickman £5 and still had the articles in his possession.

Witnesses were called to give details of the various bank accounts that the Dickmans maintained. John Dennis Badcock was a cashier at the National Provincial Bank in Mosley Street and he testified that John Dickman had been a customer since around 1893. On June 30th, 1909, the account had a credit balance of just 7d. Since then there had been only three deposits; one of £4 10s 0d, one of £20 being the cheque from Mr Cohen and another of £200 which was also a cheque from Cohen but payable to Mr F. Christie who had endorsed it on the back. The account was now overdrawn to the tune of 3s 0d.

Robert Plews Sedcole was also a cashier but he worked at the Lambton's branch of Lloyds Bank. He produced details of Dickman's account there from December 10th, 1907, to the time it was closed on December 14th, 1909. The last credit had been received on May 13th, 1909. On August 11th, 1909, there had been a withdrawal of £7 which left a credit balance of 13s 0d. This had been withdrawn and the account closed on December 14th, the bank taking 2s 0d as its charges and the remaining 11s 0d being paid to Mr Dickman.

William Albert Christie, who was no relation to Frank, the man who had taken out the loan from Mr Cohen, was a clerk in the Savings Bank Department of the Post Office. He gave the court details of an account in Mrs Annie Dickman's name. Between 1907 and 1910, the total deposits received amounted to £15 0s 9d. No withdrawals had been made and so that amount was the credit balance on January 1st, 1910. Since that time, only withdrawals had taken place. On January 5th, £12 was drawn out. Two amounts of £1 each were drawn on February 1st and February 16th and a final amount of 10s 0d on March 14th. The balance now remained at 10s 9d.

Thomas Paisley was the treasurer of the Newcastle Co-operative Society and he too produced details of an account in the name of Annie Dickman. The account had been opened in May 1904 and on October 30th, 1907, held a credit balance of £73 17s 2d. Three further deposits had been made after that date but in 1909, withdrawals had become much more frequent. By March 17th, 1910, the balance was just £4.

When Dickman's house had been searched, no gun had been found, but the prosecution now tried to link him with the possession of weapons. Henrietta Hyman ran a stationer's and newsagent's from 35 Groat Street, Newcastle, and Dickman used to buy his newspapers from her. She knew Dickman as Fred Black and it was in that name that he had letters delivered to her establishment, which he would pick up at his convenience. Most if not all of these letters were connected with betting but one day in October 1909 a parcel arrived and from its shape, Henrietta believed that it was a gun. Dickman made no attempt to pick up this weapon for some considerable time and before he did so, a postcard arrived from the company who had supplied the gun, saying that they had sent it in error and would he kindly return it. A second parcel arrived with this postcard but since it was in a box, she could not tell what this one contained.

It was not until January that Dickman came back into the shop. He now told her his correct name, told her, too, that he lived in Lily Avenue, and asked her for a label so that he could send the first parcel back to Glasgow from where it had been sent to him. Other letters had arrived for Dickman since but he had never been to pick them up and she had since passed them all on to the police.

Andrew Craig Kirkwood worked for Messrs W.R. Pape & Co, gunsmiths of Newcastle. His company kept a register of all the firearms it sold and he now produced a register which held an entry under 1907. The entry read, "John A. Dickman, Lily Avenue, Jesmond — bought automatic magazine pistol." Another employee of Pape's gave scientific evidence on the bullets found at the crime scene. Thomas Simpson testified that two of the bullets were .250 nickel-plated and had been fired from an automatic pistol. The others were .320 and lead. The first two bullets could have been fired by the gun referred to by Andrew Kirkwood and apparently purchased by Dickman, but the others could not have been fired from such a weapon. In his opinion, there must have been two guns used. The two nickel-plated bullets would have been held in a magazine and there would be seven bullets when the gun was fully loaded.

Two doctors gave medical evidence. Dr C. Clark Burman was the police surgeon at Alnwick and he had examined the body of John Innes Nisbet both at the scene of the crime and later at the mortuary where he had performed a post-mortem. The back of Innes' right hand was covered in blood and there was a good deal of blood about the face and head. There were five bullet wounds in all. The first was under the left eye and burning around the wound showed that the gun had been only about two inches away when it was fired. This bullet had been recovered and was leaden.

The second wound was over the left forehead and the bullet had travelled downwards into the head. Again there were slight signs of burning on the flesh and this bullet was one of the nickel-plated ones. The third wound, which was not serious, was behind the right ear. The fourth was behind the left ear and had only grazed the skull while the fifth was two inches below this and was again caused by a leaden bullet.

Dr Robert A. Bolam, a professor of medical jurisprudence at the College of Medicine in Newcastle, had received from the police various items taken from Dickman and his home. These included a pair of gloves, a pair of trousers and a Burberry coat. On the palm surface of the left glove, just under the thumb, Dr

Bolam found a small smear of blood although he was unable to say that it was human, or even mammalian. Nine small pinpricks of blood were found inside the left front pocket of the trousers and there was a large area of staining on the left front of the overcoat. The surface of this stain was frayed as if it had been rubbed and it smelt strongly of paraffin. There was no evidence of blood on the coat although the application of the paraffin would have negated many of the tests usually performed.

The time came for the defence to put its case. William Strafford Sanderson was a spirits merchant from Morpeth. On the morning of March 18th, he had left his office to go on his rounds. At around 1.30pm, he was close to the station when he was overtaken by a friend, Edwin Elliott, who was riding his cycle. They walked on together and after a few steps, met up with another man who spoke to Elliott. This man was Dickman and at the time he appeared to be perfectly normal in his behaviour and had no obvious bloodstains upon his clothing.

Edwin Elliott backed up this testimony and confirmed that he and Dickman had spoken about the forthcoming big race. Dickman asked Elliott what he fancied and at that point, William Sanderson had said that he had dreamt that the favourite won. Dickman had scoffed at the suggestion of dreaming winners and then had gone on his way, back towards the railway station.

Dickman himself went into the witness box. He said he had left home at about 10.00am on March 18th, and had been wearing his suit, a black hat, brown overcoat and brown gloves. He caught the tram to Northumberland Street and from there walked to the station. As he queued for his ticket he saw Nisbet in front of him and Nisbet wished him good morning. After enjoying a pie and a glass of ale in the refreshment room, Dickman took his seat on the train towards the rear and as far as he recalled, other people got in and out at various stations.

Once Dickman realised that he had gone past his station, he had thought about crossing over the line and catching a train back, but thought that the walk would do him good. On the way to Stannington, though, he fell ill and had to lie down for about an hour. He then walked back to Morpeth, intending to catch the 1.12pm train back to Newcastle but just missed it so took a walk into Morpeth town intending to go to the Newcastle Arms for a drink. On the way he met Elliott and Sanderson and after talking to them, returned to the station and caught the 1.40pm train. Dickman then tried to demolish some of the individual pieces of evidence that had been given in court.

According to Dickman, Hall had been very reluctant to make an identification at the parade at the police station. It appeared to him as if he was pushed back towards the line by a police officer and was almost forced to make some sort of selection. The gun sent to him at the newsagent's had been returned by him to Bell Brothers, Waterloo Street, Glasgow. The bank bag found on him he had owned for perhaps ten years and he had used it in place of a wallet for some time. Hepple, the man who claimed to have linked him with Nisbet, was rather old and very deaf now. They were close friends and surely if Hepple had seen him he would have spoken and they would have travelled in the same carriage. The stain on his Burberry coat was bicycle oil and he had not even worn that coat on the day of the murder. As for the apparent trouble with his finances, he had raised the loan with Mr Cohen just to see what rates could be obtained so that he could recommend a company to Mr Christie. The jewellery was pledged because he wanted it to be in a safe place as there had been a number of burglaries in the area of late. As for the gold found on his person and his method of earning a living, he took bets and made bets, sometimes of large amounts, and this was just the cash he held for that purpose.

The jury retired at 12.55pm on July 6th, and returned at

3.30pm, with a verdict of guilty. Asked if he had anything to say, Dickman replied, "I can only repeat that I am entirely innocent of this cruel deed. I have no complicity in this case. I have spoken the truth in my evidence, and in everything I have said." The sentence of death was then passed, at which Dickman half-turned and cried aloud, "I declare to all men that I am innocent."

Soon after the verdict, Annie Dickman wrote to her local newspaper to defend her husband and attempt to show that he was not the killer of John Nisbet. She said that when he had returned home to her on the evening of the crime, he was perfectly normal and spotless. She also suggested that the identification evidence in the case was unsatisfactory and this matter was mentioned again, in detail, at the subsequent appeal.

Annie Dickman was not the only woman to have troubles at this time. After Dickman's trial, another court in Newcastle decided that Nisbet's death could be described as an accident and since this had arisen out of his employment, his widow was entitled to compensation. Mrs Nisbet was awarded £300 but Rayne & Burn, her dead husband's employers, appealed against this decision saying that his death had not been accidental. They were trying their best to avoid making any payment.

A petition was organised on Dickman's behalf and sent to the Home Secretary, Mr Winston Churchill. This document asked for a review of the sentence because; Dickman was married with two children; he had only one previous conviction and that for a very minor offence and there was nothing else against his character; the evidence in the case was purely circumstantial and there was no proof that he had possessed the necessary weapons or that he had ever handled the money taken from Nisbet.

Dickman's appeal was heard on July 22nd before the Lord Chief Justice, and Justices Lawrance and Phillimore. The

Home Secretary himself had referred the matter to the appeal court, the first time these powers had ever been used. It was at this appeal that some absolutely scandalous behaviour on the part of the police investigating the case was revealed. A letter from the chief constable was read out in court. In this document the police admitted that while Hall and Spink had been waiting in a hallway at the police station, prior to attending the identification parade, they had been told to look into the room where Dickman was being held. Both men did as they were instructed but could see only the tops of people's hats. When this strategy failed, the police arranged for the door of the room in question to be opened slightly and the two witnesses were again invited to take a look.

Hall only saw the back of Dickman and remarked at the time that he thought him more thick-set than the man he had seen with Nisbet.

Hall was called as a witness at the appeal and agreed that this subterfuge had taken place. He claimed, though, that what he had seen had not affected his identification and as a result of that, and the fact that the judges felt that there was sufficient other evidence to build a substantial case against Dickman, the appeal was dismissed.

No weapon had been traced to Dickman. No money from the robbery was traced to him. Two of the witnesses were largely discredited and even Mrs Nisbet, who made her dramatic identification in the magistrates' court, had known Dickman by sight for 18 years. As for the marks on his coat, Annie Dickman said she had used paraffin to remove an oil stain. She was not called to give that evidence in court. Of course, Dickman himself had claimed that it was a different coat that he had been wearing on that day.

In his last letter to his wife, Dickman wrote, "There is something that still keeps telling me that everything will be made clear some day, when it is too late to benefit me. I can only repeat that I am innocent." Late on the night of Monday,

August 8th, he again repeated that he was innocent of the crime.

Dickman rose early on the morning of Tuesday, August 9th, 1910, and ate a breakfast of porridge, bread and butter, and tea. He was ministered to by the prison chaplain, the Reverend W.F. Lumley, who urged him to speak the truth with regard to the crime. Dickman made no reply. By 8.00am a crowd of 1,500 people had gathered around the prison. A high canvas screen had been erected from the condemned cell to the execution shed so that no one in adjoining buildings should see the condemned man on his way to the gallows.

At 8.00am John Ellis and his assistant, William Willis, entered the cell and began the pinioning process. Dickman walked bravely to the scaffold and at 8.01am those outside the prison heard the loud thud as the doors of the pit swung against the walls of the cell, causing John Alexander Dickman to drop to his death. At the inquest afterwards it was reported that Dickman, who was just under 5ft 6ins and weighed 155lbs, had been given a drop of exactly 7ft. Death had been instantaneous.

It has since been suggested that Dickman had also been involved in the unsolved murder of Mrs Luard in 1908. There is absolutely no evidence to link him to that crime and it may well be that this was just an attempt by the authorities to attach some other degree of guilt to a man unable to defend himself any longer. The fact remains that Dickman went to his unmarked prison grave maintaining to the very end that he was an innocent man.

CHAPTER TEN

DEATH AT THE INN

JAMES WOOD IRONS, who lived at 38 Devonshire Place, Newcastle, had a feeling that this was not going to be a pleasant day. The owner of a number of public houses, he was off to see one of his managers at the Sun Inn at Bedlington — and the news he carried was not good.

The morning of Tuesday, April 15th, 1913, dawned clear and bright and by the time Irons reached Bedlington it was around 10.45am. The events of the next few minutes would never be fully established. What is certain is that Irons told his manager, 35-year-old John Vickers Amos, that he would have to leave the pub, his agreement was at an end and a new manager would be brought in.

Amos, who had worked as a miner in America for four separate periods, had first become manager of the Sun Inn, a public house which held a commanding position in the main street of Bedlington, on January 27th, less than three months earlier. A contract was drawn up and Amos was to receive 30s a week pay, his coal and gas were free and, as a bonus, he was to get five per cent of all money taken over the bar. As was customary, Amos handed over the sum of £30 in cash, as a bond against the stock of beers and spirits held on the premises, but he was to receive four per cent interest on that money as well.

Amos was more than happy in his new position but after almost exactly a month in the job, he found things weren't going exactly as planned. On February 28th, Irons returned to the Sun Inn and did a detailed stocktake of the liquor, after which he told Amos that after comparing cash paid in with the remaining stock, there was a shortfall of £7 5s 0d. Amos said that he simply couldn't understand it. He told Irons that business had been good if not spectacular and he had put every single penny he had taken through the till. James Irons, however, did not seem unduly concerned about the discrepancy, and told Amos not to worry.

Irons made a second visit on March 16th. Once more the stock was checked and now Amos was £21 11s 3d short. This time the owner apparently had real cause for concern. John Amos had always been regarded as an honest man but it looked very much as if either he or his wife, Isobella, had been dipping into the till and helping themselves to James Irons' money. The implications so worried Mrs Amos that she suggested that perhaps they could appoint a professional stocktaker of their own. This, they said, was no reflection on the honesty of the man Irons had been using, but under the circumstances surely Amos was entitled to have a 'second opinion' as it were. Irons said that he was more than happy for Amos to have anyone of his choosing, providing of course that the man was properly qualified.

John Amos did indeed appoint his own stocktaker but on the third occasion that Irons visited, April 1st, the man could not be there so it was once again Irons' appointee who checked the public house stock. The deficiency had grown again and by the time Irons did a fourth check, just a few days later on April 6th, the discrepancy had grown to the grand total of £45 19s 5d. John Amos was at his wit's end.

On April 12th, Mr Irons wrote a rather unflattering letter to John Amos. It read, "The writer will be over to take stock on Tuesday. Your last stock is £17 2s 9d short, which makes the total up to £45 19s 5d. Evidently you are running the Sun Inn for yourself. Will you please ask your wife to see that the place is clean, as I was thoroughly ashamed of the filthy state it was in when I called last week." So it was that when Irons turned up at the Sun Inn at 11.00am on the morning of April 15th, John Vickers Amos had very good reasons to believe that this was the day he would be given notice to quit.

James Irons began by having Mr Jack Sylvester, a professional stocktaker who he had used on previous visits to the inn, check the stock of claret. As this was being done, Mrs Amos appeared with a shot gun. John Amos asked her where she was going and she replied that one of the customers, a man named Richardson, had asked to borrow it to do some practice shooting. Amos, who had more important things to worry about than such trifles, took the gun off his wife, telling her, "That gun is not going out of this house." Soon after this, Amos raised the question of his bond of £30. Irons replied, "We will see about the bond when the stock is adjusted." This apparently did not satisfy Amos because he bolted the back door of the inn. With a shout of, "We will see who is boss here," he went upstairs. James Irons, however, immediately unbolted the door and realising that there might be trouble in removing his manager, left the inn and called at the police station where he spoke to Inspector John Culley. After Irons had explained the situation, the inspector said that he would send along a constable to ensure that things went smoothly.

As Mr Sylvester continued in his work, James Irons now walked to the railway station where he met the man who was to take over from Amos, Richard Grice, who had arrived with the wife of the man who had recommended him to Irons, Mr Craggs. The three returned to the inn, to be joined later by Mr Grice's wife, Sarah Ellen Grice, and Mrs Craggs' husband, both of whom had caught a later train.

At 2.00pm James Irons again went out briefly. Tension was building at the inn and he felt that now might be time he would need help from the police. Irons again visited the police station, asked for the assistance that had been promised and then he and 30-year-old Constable George Bertram Mussell returned to the inn and waited for Mr Sylvester to finish his work. Amos, meanwhile, was asked to fill out a report sheet showing the recent takings and to bring out all the cash he had in the till. The money came to £7 5s 6d. James Wood Irons now counted out 30s of that money and handed it to Amos, telling him that this was his week's wages. Amos was then given a further 2s 6d as his commission for the current week and another 30s for the following week in lieu of notice. As if all this were not enough for Amos to take in, he was now told that he must leave that same day but could store his furniture in the clubhouse until he found a new home for himself and his family. Amos was shocked and unable to grasp what was happening to him. Sitting down he gasped, "Give me five minutes breath."

He was then told that the stocktake was finished and he was a grand total of £68 10s 7d short. Meanwhile, as Amos' mind was still racing, Mr Craggs, Mrs Grice and another friend who had just arrived, Mr Learmouth, were enjoying refreshments in the smoke room where they were speaking with Constable Mussell.

Everything seemed to happen so very quickly after that. Returning to his bedroom, Amos collected the shot gun he had earlier taken from his wife, and walked down a passageway in the pub. Here he was confronted by Constable Mussell and fired both barrels into him. The shots struck Mussell in the neck and killed him instantly.

Mrs Craggs shouted down to the men who were still in the cellar, pleading with them to come up immediately as there was murder going on in the pub. Irons made good his escape through a hatchway, but the others remained where they were for the time being. Thirty-three-year-old Sarah Ellen Grice was at the top of the cellar steps, still waiting for the men to come up, when another shot rang out and she fell down the steps, the back of her head a mass of blood and brain tissue.

Just down the road from the inn, Police Sergeant Andrew Barton was talking to a couple of local men when he heard shots apparently coming from the direction of the pub. Barton was a brave man, a holder of the Board of Trade Medal for Gallantry for his services at the shipwreck of the *Ena McTavish* near Warkworth, on October 17th, 1907, when he courageously swam through raging seas to rescue a sailor. He now ran up the steep pathway that led from Front Street to the inn and immediately made for the back door, followed by a number of other men including William Young and George McQueen. Within a few minutes of Barton entering the inn, another shot rang out and the sergeant fell, a large wound in his chest. All the others who had followed Barton into the inn now ran back outside, fearful that they might well be next.

For some time, John Vickers Amos held the growing crowd at bay. Appearing at his front door at regular intervals he brandished the gun and threatened to shoot anyone who came near. Shortly afterwards he put the gun down while he lit a cigarette but soon picked the weapon up again, telling onlookers that there were two cartridges in it, one for Irons and the last for himself.

Back at the police station, Inspector Culley was asking for help from all the surrounding forces. By car and train, police from Blyth and Morpeth made their way to Bedlington. Superintendent Tough, who was in charge of the Bedlington district, arrived on a motorcycle and immediately arranged a cordon of police and volunteers around a wide area. Captain Fullarton James, the chief constable, arrived by car with six or seven other senior officers. Even when facing all this manpower, John Amos managed to stand his ground for a full hour before finally dashing back inside the inn, then darting out of the back door and making his way across the fields. No one followed him immediately but eventually the police organised a detailed search of the surrounding farms and fields for any sign of the man who had turned from a simple public house manager into an armed and highly dangerous man.

It was some time later when a group of men were searching the neighbourhood of Church Lane and one of them, Joseph Potter, noticed footprints in the flattened grass leading to a culvert underneath the roadway. Gingerly looking down into the blackness of the culvert, Potter thought he could make out the huddled shape of a man. Inspector David Hutchinson was with the group and Potter told him of what he had seen. Hutchinson ordered Potter, who was armed with a shotgun, to fire one barrel into the culvert. Potter did as he was asked and then Hutchinson called on the man inside to come out. Almost immediately a voice from within shouted, "I'll surrender." For two minutes, nothing happened so Hutchinson told Potter to fire the second barrel. At this there was a cry of pain and then, seconds later, Amos emerged from the culvert. There were a few relatively minor pellet wounds in his head and he was marched to the police station, followed through the streets of Bedlington by a large crowd of curious locals.

The inquest on the three bodies opened before the coroner, Mr H.T. Rutherford, on April 17th. Mr Rutherford met the jurors at the Sun Inn, where Sarah Grice's body still lay, before taking them on to the residential quarters of the police station where the bodies of Mussell and Barton had been taken. Formal identification was made by Richard Grice and Superintendent Tough. Matters were then adjourned until April 24th. On April 18th, all three victims were buried and four days after this, on April 22nd, Amos made his first appearance at the Blyth police court.

As he stood in the dock, Amos' head was heavily swathed in bandages. Superintendent Tough again gave evidence, this time about Amos' arrest and went on to say that the prisoner was suffering from two small pellet wounds, one on either side of his forehead. Mr Swinburne G. Wilson appeared for Amos and no objection was made when the prosecution asked for a remand until April 29th.

The inquest convened again on April 24th, and finally on April 28th, when the medical evidence was heard. The following day, Amos was back at Blyth police court, the case for the Director of Public Prosecutions now being put by Mr Lays. Amos, who had by this time grown a short stubbly beard, was then sent for trial on three charges of murder.

That trial opened at Newcastle on July 2nd, 1913, before Mr Commissioner Harrison. Although he faced three charges of murder, the proceedings would hear evidence on only one, the killing of Sergeant Andrew Barton. Amos was defended by Mr W.J. Waugh and Mr Leon Freedman while the prosecution case was led by Mr Bruce Williamson assisted by Mr Willoughby Jardine. The case lasted for two days.

Evidence was heard of the events that had taken place inside the inn on that terrible day. Just before Mussell had been shot, Mrs Grice and Mrs Craggs had joined the men who were down in the cellar. Mrs Craggs had been at the very top of the cellar steps when the first shot rang out and she shouted to the men to tell them what was going on. Irons immediately escaped through a trapdoor which led to the bar and made off for the police station. Meanwhile, Mrs Craggs had gone down into the cellar to grab the children who were in the house and Mrs Grice helped them down the steps. No sooner were the children safe, that the shot that killed Sarah Grice hit her in the back of the head.

Other people, including Mrs Amos and a servant girl, Hannah Stewart, were upstairs and they locked themselves inside a bedroom. Then things went quiet for a time and Mrs Craggs, taking the children with her, thought that this might be a good time to make good her escape. They crept up the cellar steps and as they opened the door that led into the yard, Amos appeared and levelled the gun at Mrs Craggs. She had cried, "Spare me on account of the children." Amos had paused for a few seconds before lowering his gun and Mrs Craggs had run for safety with the children, leaving her husband and Richard Grice in the cellar where they were to remain until the siege was over.

Richard Grice, the husband of the dead woman, said that he had been engaged as the new manager, by Irons, on April 12th. On the day in question, he was introduced to Amos by Irons who then turned to him and said, "You can take charge now." This was obviously the first official notice that Amos had received, because he commented, "Is it the case that I am finished?" to which Irons had replied, "Yes, you have guessed right." Grice told the court that he had heard Amos not only asking for his £30 bond back but had then gone on to tell Irons that he did not intend leaving the house until he got it. Finally, Richard Grice confirmed that he, too, was to place a cash bond with Irons, although in his case it was only for £20.

Witnesses were now called to give more detail of the specific charge of murdering Sergeant Andrew Barton. As the sergeant walked in to the Sun Inn, George McQueen was only feet behind him. Barton had asked Amos to put the gun down but Amos refused. Determined to do his duty, Barton took a couple of steps forward whereupon Amos had shouted, "If you come another step, I'll shoot." Barton moved ever closer and when he was just a few yards from Amos, a shot rang out. Barton staggered backwards but Amos then fired a second time, hitting Barton once again. McQueen himself then asked Amos to put the gun down but Amos told him to back off, adding, "It's not you I want, Geordie." He went on to say that he intended to shoot Irons and then himself.

Hannah Stewart, the servant girl, testified that just before the shooting had started, she had been upstairs with Mrs Amos. John Amos came upstairs, having just been told that he had lost his job and that he could not have his £30 cash bond returned. There were tears streaming down his face and he had said, "Look here Hannah, do you think I would go to the

States and work hard for Mr Irons to take my money off me?" According to Hannah, Amos was not simply upset. His eyes looked strange and he seemed to be out of control.

The time came for John Wood Irons to give his evidence. He agreed that he had written to Amos on February 4th, expressing satisfaction with his management and that on March 16th, when the stock had been shown to be short, he had said, "Well Amos, I am not saying you took the money, or that Mrs Amos took the money, but I hold you, as manager, to be responsible to me for the money." He denied that he had sworn at Amos on April 15th, or that he had told him that he was not to have one minute's notice. It appeared that Irons was simply a businessman who had apparently had his property taken, in one way or another, and had merely sought to remove the cause of that loss, John Vickers Amos. The truth was, though, that Irons was not as blameless as he seemed.

Under cross examination, he confirmed that Amos was held responsible for £3 10s for every barrel of beer in the premises. In order that he should be able to realise this figure, Amos had to sell every single drop from each barrel. Any wastage whatsoever and he would fall short of the £3 10s. Most public house owners allowed their managers to reckon two gallons from each barrel as wastage. There was also the fact that the Sun did a large outdoor trade, when the beer was sold a little more cheaply. None of this had been taken into account in the contract Irons had drawn up and in effect, it meant that the more barrels of beer Amos sold, the more wastage he lost and the more he fell into debt. As if further proof were needed, Jack Sylvester, the professional stocktaker, later confirmed that since Amos had left, the stock at the Sun Inn had still fallen short, by an average of £1 per day. No one was stealing from John Irons. Because of the way he had structured the contracts, his tenants, whoever they were, had no chance to escape ever-rising debts.

There was also another matter which remained unresolved.

Although no one had actually seen the transaction take place, James Irons had claimed that on April 17th, he had given Amos a total of £3 2s 6d as wages and commission. When Amos was picked up, only half a sovereign was found on him. He claimed that he had received no money at all from Irons and said that the receipt Irons produced was a forgery.

Dr James K.J. Haworth gave evidence of the injuries he had found when he went to the Sun Inn at 3.45pm on April 15th. Mussell had a large wound extending from the right side of his jaw to the clavicle. His jugular vein had been divided and death was due to haemorrhage. The staircase near where his body had been found was splattered with blood and even part of his tunic had been blown away.

Mrs Grice had large compound fractures of the right vault of her skull, and her brain matter had been protruding from the gaping wound in the back of her head. As for Barton, his body had been found in the kitchen. He had still been alive when the doctor examined him, but died soon afterwards without regaining consciousness. He had a large wound which penetrated the apex of his left lung and the base of his heart. His pocket book, which was found inside his tunic pocket, had been riddled with pellets.

Inspector John Culley testified that after Amos had been arrested, at 6.50pm he had recovered a loaded gun from the inside of the culvert which was close to Tower Cottage on Church Lane and some 400 yards from the Sun Inn. The gun was an American Winchester with a magazine capable of holding eight shots. There were five cartridges in the gun when he found it; four in the magazine and one in the barrel.

George Oliver ran a cycle shop in the village of Bedlington, but also sold bullets and cartridges. He gave evidence that on the afternoon of April 17th, he had sold a box of 12-gauge cartridges to Amos' 11-year-old son, George. When George himself confirmed this story, Amos held his head in his hands, crying bitterly.

The time finally came for Amos to tell his own story. He had married his wife, Isobella, in 1899 and they had three children ranging in age from three to 12, George having celebrated a birthday since the crime took place. From the age of 12, until October 1912, Amos had worked as a miner and had spent a good deal of time in the United States. In fact he had been there four times, finally being promoted to foreman.

In June 1912, Amos was working in a mine when there was an explosion of coal gas. Two men were killed and 14 were seriously injured. Amos was badly burned while rescuing two men. On July 20th of that same year, Amos was in another explosion. This time eight men were killed and he was blown backwards a total of 15 yards. As a result of these two tragedies, he slept very badly, suffered from severe pains in his head and became very excitable. His memory was affected. So much so that one night he slept in a field although he did not realise what he had done until the following morning.

Amos claimed that while he had been manager of the Sun Inn, Irons had treated him 'like a dog'. On April 15th, Irons had said he was to have one minute's notice and would not get back a halfpenny of his bond. Though he was unable to prove it at the time, Amos knew that he had been scrupulous in his accounting and had not stolen any money from his employer. Amos thought the stocktaking was grossly unfair. Finally, he claimed that after being told that he and his family were to be thrown out that day, he had no recollection of any of the events inside the inn until he was arrested at the mouth of the culvert.

The jury were out for only eight minutes. Asked if he had anything to say, Amos replied, "I don't remember anything about it. They were good friends of mine." Soon afterwards, from the condemned cell, Amos wrote to his father, "I am pleased to tell you that I was baptised on Monday, so I will put myself in the Lord's hands, and leave it with Him, and whichever way has to be, with His help I will try to meet it with a good heart."

Many people felt that Amos had been unfairly treated and a petition was organised for a reprieve. That collected over 60,000 signatures but did nothing to move the Home Secretary who announced that the sentence must be carried out.

On the morning of Tuesday, July 22nd, 1913, John Vickers Amos rose early in the death cell of Newcastle prison. He was attended by the prison chaplain, Mr W.F. Lumley and then ate a light breakfast. As a crowd of more than 1,000 gathered outside the prison at 8.00am Amos walked firmly to the gallows where he was dispatched by Thomas Pierrepoint and William Willis. At the inquest afterwards, it was stated that Amos was 5ft 5ins tall, weighed 164lbs and had been given a drop of 5ft 5ins. He had been buried within the prison precincts, in a plain white wooden box.

On that same day, the *Evening Chronicle* of Newcastle carried a letter from Amos' wife, Isobella. It read, "The last words of my dear husband today were; 'Thanks to all although human aid is of no avail. I am prepared to meet my God.' Will you please convey to the public my thanks for their sympathy. May God reward them for their kindness to me in my trouble. Yours etc., Isobella Amos. 2 South Row, Bedlington."

CHAPTER ELEVEN

A JARROW TRAGEDY

SOME time around early December, 1913, a 50-year-old widower whose name was Robert Upton and his 14-year-old son, Joseph, moved from their room at 29 Back Albion Street, Jarrow, to 42 Stanley Street where they were to share a room with one of Robert's closest friends, Charles Gribben. Gribben lived in a front room at Stanley Street, with the back room of that same house being occupied by James Evans and his family. There was, however, one other person who knew 42 Stanley Street, Robert Upton and Charles Gribben, very well indeed.

Elizabeth Burden was somewhere around 40 years old and, although married, had been separated from her husband, a worker on Tyneside docks, for some 20 years. She had worked as a housekeeper for Robert Upton at Back Albion Street since March 20th, 1912. Shortly after this, in about June of the same year, Gribben, too, had taken advantage of Elizabeth's services and she had also started acting as housekeeper for him at Stanley Street. Along with her cleaning duties, Elizabeth, however, was apparently performing other services of a more physical nature and in due course she began splitting her time between the two homes. At the weekends she slept with Upton and during the rest of the week shared Gribben's bed.

Although the two men were friends, this arrangement, not surprisingly, led to friction between them. On more than one occasion Upton tried to get Elizabeth to leave Gribben and live with him full time but she refused, claiming that she couldn't trust him when he was drunk. There were also quarrels between Gribben and Upton, although it was a testament to their friendship that in more than a year, they had quarrelled only three times, and it was always about Elizabeth and her sleeping arrangements.

Once Robert Upton and his son moved in with Charles Gribben, Elizabeth Burden decided that it would be too difficult for them all to continue under the same roof. She solved the dilemma rather neatly, not by choosing between them but by instead moving out to live with a third man, Jack Bloy, at Queen's Road, Jarrow. This affected Gribben and Upton in different ways. Whilst Gribben seemed to be content to let Elizabeth do what she wished, Upton was furious.

In fact, Upton had already issued threats, not only against Elizabeth but also against both Bloy and Gribben. One night in November he had burst in upon Elizabeth while she was alone in Gribben's room. It was around 9.00pm and Upton, in a most excitable mood, had shouted, "Charlie Gribben will not get you, or Jack Bloy either, for I will have you myself tonight. I will kill the pair of you." He seemed so determined that it was only with great difficulty, and the help of James Evans, that Upton was put out into the street. Even then he waited outside for a time and kicked in one of the panels on the front door.

On December 10th, Elizabeth told Gribben and Upton that she was moving in with Bloy and added that she intended to marry him. Gribben was annoyed, but Upton actually cried. Gribben, though, did not wish to stand in her way, saying that they should not try to prevent her going to a good home and adding that he thought that if the truth be told, neither he nor Upton really wanted her. Upton, however, was not to be placated. He turned to Elizabeth and shouted, "You will never get Charlie or Bloy. I will swing for you first." Knowing that if she stayed there would be further trouble, Elizabeth walked out that same night.

For a few more days, the anger festered inside Robert Upton before, in late December, it exploded into violence. Joseph Upton was alone in the room on the night of Saturday, December 20th, 1913. There was only one bed and that belonged to Charles Gribben. Joseph and his father shared a 'shake-down' on the floor but it was still reasonably early when Gribben came in, much the worse for drink, and within minutes had fallen asleep on the floor in front of the fire. At some time between 11.00pm and 11.30pm Robert Upton returned to number 42 and he, too, was drunk.

Upton had not been back long before he sent his son out to buy some meat. The boy did as he was asked but as he was leaving, he noticed his father lifting Charles Gribben on to his bed. Joseph was away for only a short time but when he returned his father had gone in to James Evans' room and was talking to him and his wife. Young Joseph handed over the meat to Robert Upton and shortly afterwards went to bed. Not long after this, he felt his father get down beside him and the house settled down for the night.

It was 3.30am on December 21st when Joseph Upton was woken by the sounds of quarrelling. Looking around the room he saw his father over by Gribben's bed with his knee upon the man's chest. Robert Upton had one hand over Gribben's mouth but eventually he managed to move his head enough to shout, "Joe, he is cutting my throat."

Joseph Upton rushed forward and pulled his father's hand away from Gribben's mouth, pushing Robert over in the process. Only now did he see the open razor in his father's hand. Gribben tried to rise from his bed but within seconds, Robert Upton threw himself forward again and managed to draw the razor across Gribben's throat, crying, "You will not get up."

Robert Upton had accomplished his aim and now got up

from the bed and ran out of the room. Joseph, seeing the gaping wound in Charles Gribben's throat, ran to the next room and pounded on James Evans' door, shouting, "My father has cut Charlie's throat." Evans pulled on his boots and, without getting dressed, went to verify the boy's story before running to the police station nearby. Mrs Evans waited with Joseph Upton for her husband to return with assistance. Minutes later Robert Upton reappeared in the open doorway, took out the razor and drew it across his own throat.

Sergeant Dixon was the first officer to arrive on the scene, soon to be followed by Inspector Robson and Superintendent Yeandle. It took the combined strength of all three officers to overpower the powerfully-built Upton, even though he was wounded. During the struggle Upton was shouting, "I have done it. Let me die."

Soon afterwards the police surgeon, Dr J.J. Weir, arrived and examined both men. Charles Gribben was already dead but Upton, although in a state of collapse, was still alive. At Dr Weir's instructions, Upton was taken by ambulance to the Harton Workhouse Hospital where he was guarded by a police officer while his wounds were dressed.

The inquest on Charles Gribben opened at Jarrow police court on December 22nd, before Mr Shepherd. Since the coroner felt it important that Upton, who would in due course be charged with a serious offence, should be in court if he so wished, proceedings were adjourned until January 19th. When that date came and the hearing was reconvened, it was announced that Upton, who was still in hospital and had now been charged with murder, did not wish to appear or to have legal representation at the inquest. Evidence was then heard, although Elizabeth Burden was the only witness to testify, and at the end of the day a verdict of wilful murder by Robert Upton was returned.

The trial of Robert Upton opened at Durham on March 5th, 1914, before Mr Justice Ridley. Upton was defended by Mr

Hugh O'Neill while the case for the Crown was led by Mr Bruce Williamson, assisted by Mr Armitage.

Evidence was given that Charles Gribben had been a well-liked man who had once lived in Salem Street. He was regarded as quiet and inoffensive and worked as a caller-up, getting other people out of bed in time to go to their work. Since the death of his wife, Gribben had sunk lower and lower on the social scale until he ended up in the one room in Stanley Street, an area known for poverty and violence. All his family were now dead, except for a married daughter who lived in London. She had recently written to her father, asking him to go to the capital to live with her, but, tragically as it turned out, he had refused.

In addition to his earlier statement, Joseph Upton told the court that when he had returned with the meat, his father had asked him to fetch his knife for him so that he could cut himself some tobacco. Joseph went to look in his father's coat pocket where his knife was normally kept and there he found, much to his surprise, a razor, wrapped in paper. This was normally kept in a cupboard and although Joseph thought it unusual for it to be in the jacket, he made no comment at the time.

Mrs Evans testified that after her husband had gone to fetch the police, Robert Upton had suddenly appeared in her doorway and asked where James had gone. Told that he was out, Upton had continued, "I have done it now; I have done it to old Charlie now." He then drew out his razor again and began to hack at his own throat. At this awful sight, Mrs Evans had screamed and tried to push past Robert Upton in order to escape. He would not let her pass so she and Joseph ran out of the back door together and then waited outside for the police and James Evans to arrive.

James Evans testified that Joseph's screams for help had woken him. After being told what had happened, Evans went into the Uptons' room and saw Charles Gribben sitting up on

the bed, holding his throat. When Evans asked him what had
taken place, Gribben could only mutter, "Bob...Bob..." Evans
then bound Gribben's throat with a cloth in order to staunch
the bleeding, before running to the police station. Evans also
reported that earlier that evening, he had heard Robert Upton
talking to Gribben. The two men appeared to be friendly and
Upton had invited him to go out with him for some beer.

Elizabeth Burden, who had now taken to using the name
Bloy although there is no proof that she had gone through any
formal wedding ceremony with Jack Bloy, also gave evidence.
She told the court that she had moved out of Stanley Street
simply because Upton had moved in. She thought that he was
a dangerous man when he had been drinking, because those
were the only times he ever issued threats. Elizabeth added that
Gribben was the 'quietest man in the world' and although she
had heard Upton threaten him, she never heard Gribben issue
threats to Upton. She went on to give details of the last time
she had seen Gribben alive. It was at 10.10pm on the night of
Saturday, December 20th. Gribben had been a visitor at her
father's house at Leanside Cottages. She had caught a tram
home believing that Gribben, who was intoxicated at the time,
would be spending the night with her father. Before leaving,
she had agreed to visit him at Stanley Street the next morning
but by the time she arrived, at 11.15am on the Sunday,
Gribben was already dead and Upton in the hospital.

Inspector Robson gave details of statements Upton had
made while in hospital.

The first of these read, "I have made a bad job of it
Inspector. On Saturday, Charlie called me a —- Englishman."
He had gone on to say that he was full of drink and had
jumped up in a passion, adding that he didn't know where he
had cut Gribben, or even where he had cut himself. At other
times, Upton had asked what had become of Elizabeth and if
she was still with Bloy. Upton also admitted that he was jealous
because Elizabeth had been with him at first and he thought

that Charlie had, 'come sneaking round' and taken her away from him. On another occasion, Upton had asked if Elizabeth had carried out her intention to marry Bloy because he (Upton) knew her husband was still alive and was working in the area. Finally, when Upton had been coming round, he had apparently mistaken the police officer by his bed for his son and had muttered, "Is that you son? I have killed Charlie. Give us a kiss, son. I've cut my own throat and I'll soon die."

Dr Weir told the court that when he had arrived at the scene, he had found the bed saturated with blood. There was also a large pool of blood on the floor. Gribben had bled to death when the main artery in his neck had been severed. As for Upton, his wounds, although serious, had not been too deep. The doctor also testified that he had examined Upton in jail and had found no evidence of insanity.

The defence, though, tried to show that there was evidence of insanity in Upton's family. Upton's father had committed suicide 20 years earlier and an aunt had died in an asylum. There was ample evidence that the two men had been close friends and that Upton was very drunk at the time he attacked Gribben. Added to this, Mr Hugh O'Neill pointed out, had Upton succeeded in taking his own life, an inquest jury would almost certainly have returned a verdict that he had killed himself while the balance of his mind was disturbed. Taking all those circumstances into account, Mr O'Neill asked the jury to return a verdict of manslaughter instead of murder.

In his summing up, the judge said, "It is difficult in this case to find a sufficient reason for the suggestion that it was not a case of murder." That must have removed any doubts that might have remained in the minds of the jury, for they took only a few minutes to decide that Upton was guilty as charged. Asked if he had anything to say before the death sentence was passed, Upton replied, "I didn't know what I was doing at the time; not one bit."

There was no appeal and no reprieve. On March 23rd,

Upton saw his son Joseph and his other children for the last time. That was to be his last night on earth and, perhaps not surprisingly, it was a restless and disturbed night for the condemned man. On the following morning, Tuesday, March 24th, 1914, Robert Upton was hanged at Durham by John Ellis and William Willis, who gave him a drop of 5ft 5ins. This was the first execution for many years where there were no representatives of the press present.

At the inquest held afterwards, the coroner, Mr R.A. Shepherd, the same man who had presided over the inquest on Charles Gribben, heard the evidence. The jury, having viewed Upton's body, reported that he looked peaceful, although his face was rather discoloured. The cause of death was given as being due to a fracture and dislocation of the neck and in due course, the jury returned the usual verdict that death was due to judicial hanging. It was the 35th such execution in Durham prison since the dark days of public executions.

CHAPTER TWELVE

THE MAN WHO
LIKED TO CONFESS

TWENTY-eight-year-old Frank Steele was very fond of a drink and was known to frequently imbibe to excess. It was perhaps for that very reason that when he confessed to having committed a murder, people thought it was the drink talking and did not take him seriously.

It was around 4.45pm on Sunday, May 16th 1915, when Steele met William Johnson at the Bottle Bank near Armitage's Works. Steele had obviously been drinking and greeted Johnson, with whom he had once worked, by telling him that he had 'done Nana in'. Johnson took little heed, although he did notice that Steele had a mark on his neck and claimed that someone had stabbed him.

'Nana' was 21-year-old Nana Barrett, also known as Nana Spoors, the woman with whom he lived at 31 Nelson Street, Gateshead. The couple had been living together since the beginning of 1915. When they had first met, Nana had had her baby. The child was not Steele's and had died a couple of weeks later. Ever since then, the couple had lived alone.

The day after his encounter with Johnson, Monday, May 17th, Steele visited his mother, Elizabeth Margaret Frost, who lived at 4 Rye Hill, Newcastle. Again he was drunk and she would later describe her son as being 'quite wild with drink'. He mumbled something about having committed a murder and although his mother thought he was talking nonsense she was nevertheless fearful for her own safety, and went upstairs out of his way. In due course, Frank Steele left the house, much to Elizabeth's Frost's relief.

Meanwhile, back in Nelson Street, Steele's neighbours were beginning to grow concerned about Nana Barrett. Although Steele was for ever coming and going, Nana had not been seen since Sunday afternoon. In addition, the blinds at number 31 were drawn and there was no reply to the repeated knocking of people such as Elizabeth Gray who lived next door at number 33.

On Tuesday, May 18th, Steele was back at his mother's house and again he said that he had killed Nana Barrett. There was a strangeness about her son and even though he was drunk again, Elizabeth Frost took him more seriously this time and when Steele asked her to send for a policeman, she did so. It was Police Constable Samuel Weir who arrived at Rye Hill and spoke to Steele about his repeated confessions to having committed murder.

After hearing yet another admission, Constable Weir took Steele to the Westgate police station. Here Steele was searched and in his pocket officers found a bloodstained razor in a case. Steele told them, "I cut her throat with that razor on Sunday afternoon. She came in drunk. I done it. I then cut my own and also my arm." At this point, Steele pulled up his shirt sleeve to show a small, superficial cut on his left arm. He continued, "I went to bed in the house and slept all night. I went to Sunderland and Shields, and have knocked about the country since. I intended to finish myself tonight."

Steele was medically examined and there was indeed a wound in his throat, although that, too, was superficial and certainly not life threatening. Meanwhile, Sergeant James Forsyth, together with Constable Robert Cairns, went to 31 Nelson

Street, to check for themselves what had happened to Nana Barrett. The door was locked and after receiving no answer to their calling, the two officers forced an entry. Nana Barrett was indeed dead. She lay on the bed, wearing only a nightdress and stockings. Her face was covered with a bolster and two pillows and when these were removed, the officers saw that her throat had been cut from one side to the other. The wound was some five and a half inches long and very deep. There was a large pool of blood at the head of the bed and two patches on the carpet nearby. At the foot of the bed lay a man's shirt, heavily bloodstained around the neck band, and on a table in the room lay three empty beer bottles and a flask which, although empty, had once contained rum.

Back at the police station, Steele was told what the officers had found and that he would be charged with the murder of a woman named Barrett. His only reply was, "Spoors, that is what I thought they called her." Later he made a full statement explaining why he had killed the woman with whom he had lived.

Steele made his first appearance at the Newcastle police court on May 19th. Only evidence of arrest was given and he was remanded in custody until May 26th. The inquest on the dead woman opened a couple of days later on May 21st, at Gateshead police station, before the deputy coroner, Mr Shepherd. Most of the witnesses were called but nevertheless, these proceedings were also adjourned, this time until May 28th. There was, however, an incident in the court when William Johnson gave his evidence about Steele confessing to murder at the Bottle Bank. Steele shouted that this was a lie and added, "I defy anyone to say they saw me out of the house from the Sunday dinner time until Monday morning."

There were a number of other court appearances. On May 26th, the police court hearing was again adjourned, until June 2nd. The inquest was concluded on May 28th when a verdict of murder against Steele was returned. On June 2nd, Steele again appeared before the magistrates. Most of the evidence was heard, although the proceedings were adjourned for one last time. On Wednesday, June 9th, he made his last police court appearance when he was sent for trial at the assizes.

The trial of Frank Steele took place at Durham on July 6th, 1915, before Mr Justice Ridley. The case for the Crown was put by Mr J. Scott-Fox, assisted by Mr C.F. Lowenthal and Mr H. Youll, while Steele was defended by Mr S.O. Rowan Hamilton. Steele appeared in the dock wearing a rather shabby navy blue suit, together with a green muffler.

Elizabeth Gray, the neighbour from 33 Nelson Street, stated that at the end of 1914, Nana Barrett, who was then using the name Spoors, had come to live with her. Nana had told Elizabeth she was a single woman even though she did have a new-born baby with her. Although she could not prove it conclusively, Elizabeth Gray believed that Nana was earning her living on the streets. Whatever the truth of that, she did grow close to Steele, who lived next door, and some three or four months before her death had moved in with him. They seemed to get on well with each other and Elizabeth had never heard them argue. Nana had been well cared for by Steele and if she had been a prostitute before, she had certainly stopped that way of life now.

On Sunday, May 16th, Elizabeth saw Nana at noon. That was the last sighting of her alive, although Elizabeth did hear her talking to Steele in their basement room at around 3.00pm. The next morning, Elizabeth saw Steele standing at his front door and pointed out to him that the landlord was just up the road and would no doubt be calling for the rent soon. Steele acknowledged that and went back inside. However, although Elizabeth knew that Steele, and presumably Nana, too, were inside the house, she noted with interest that the landlord got no reply when he eventually knocked on the door of number 31.

The landlord left and some time later, at around 11.00am Elizabeth saw Steele come out of his rooms, lock the door and walk up the street. The blinds remained drawn all that day and the next and she did not see either Steele or Nana again.

Although Elizabeth thought it curious that the blinds were down and knocked on Nana's door a couple of times to see if she was in, the conclusion she came to was that perhaps her neighbour had gone to stay with her mother for a day or two.

Dr Samuel Vernon Robinson had been called to the scene and had examined the body of Nana Barrett. In addition to describing the wounds, Dr Robinson stated that he could find no signs of a struggle or of any defence wounds, implying that there had been no argument before the attack had taken place.

The first suggestions of what might be behind this terrible crime, came from the testimony of another neighbour, Mary Murphy, who lived at 29 Nelson Street. She reported that three or four weeks before her death, Nana had been crying in the street. Mary had asked her what the matter was and Nana confessed that the father of her dead child was a man named Joseph Bell. Recently, Nana had sent a letter to Bell but he had not been at the address on the envelope and as a result, the letter had been returned to her. Unfortunately, Steele had seen the letter and read it. The contents had upset him terribly and ever since, there had been a bad atmosphere between them. Indeed, later still, Mary Murphy had seen Steele reading the letter to Bell and she agreed that he seemed highly disturbed by the contents.

It was now time to discuss this letter in detail. Nana had confessed to Mary Murphy that the father of her child was Joseph Bell. Whilst Steele might not have minded a past relationship, the letter Nana had written seemed to indicate that there was a chance this relationship might well be rekindled. The letter had been sent to the Union Hospital at Gateshead but Bell was not there and the letter had been returned to Nana. Steele now read this letter and for him, the significant part was that Nana informed Bell that she had 'fallen wrong' to him and had a baby which had since died. She then went on to tell Bell that the man she was living with was on the nightshift and it would be safe for Bell to come over to see her.

That letter had since been destroyed by Nana but Steele had tried to obtain a copy. He had gone to the main Post Office and had asked what they did with returned letters. He was told that copies of the names and addresses were kept but the actual letter itself was not copied. All this, of course, was proof that the matter had preyed heavily on Steele's mind.

The defence, though, were not relying on the letter as an excuse for murder. They claimed that Steele had been so sodden with drink, that he had been incapable of forming the intention to kill and had not known what he was doing at the time of the attack. As a result, this was not a case of murder, but one of manslaughter. After hearing the summing up from Mr Justice Ridley, the jury retired to consider their verdict.

After 90 minutes, they returned and asked for clarification with regard to the question of drink. The judge informed them that of itself, drink was no excuse for a crime but if they decided that Steele was so drunk that he couldn't possibly conceive the result of his actions, then he might be guilty of manslaughter instead of murder. The jury retired for a second time but were out for a only few minutes before deciding that no matter how drunk he had been, Steele had known what he was doing and so was guilty as charged.

Asked if he had anything to say before sentence was passed, Steele replied, "Yes, I haven't had a fair trial." The judge said that this was simply not the case. Steele had been defended very ably and the jury had come to the only possible verdict on the evidence. Steele was then sentenced to death.

His appeal was dismissed at the end of July. Soon afterwards it was announced that there would be no reprieve. At 8.00am on Wednesday, August 11th, 1915, Frank Steele was hanged at Durham by John Ellis. The inquest took place two hours later before Mr John Graham and here it was reported that Steele's face was very much discoloured, his neck was swollen and there was a considerable lump beneath his right ear. Nevertheless, the usual verdict was returned.

CHAPTER THIRTEEN

THE DEATH
OF A SAILOR

ON WEDNESDAY, June 20th, 1917, while World War One was still raging across the battered continent of Europe and men were dying in their tens of thousands, four petty officers serving in the Royal Navy took some well earned shore leave in Newcastle upon Tyne.

Arriving in the city at around 6.00pm, Alfred Gough, along with officers Birling, Grant and McDonald eventually found themselves in the Mechanic's Arms in Temple Street some time before 8.30pm and it was there that they met up with two women; Sarah Shearer and Isabella Caroline Smith, a married woman whose husband was a soldier serving in France. Later that same night, another woman, 26-year-old Ruby Wright, came into the public house, along with Margaret Brown, who preferred to be known by the name of Muriel. These two ladies joined the four petty officers and just a few minutes later, another sailor on leave; 27-year-old Henry Arthur Hollyer, arrived at the Mechanic's Arms and joined the happy group.

Closing time duly arrived and Ruby Wright, who lived nearby, suggested that they all return to her house where they could have more to drink and maybe enjoy a sing-song. By

10.30pm the five sailors and the four women were at Ruby's home; 1 West Street, Newcastle.

The party had been in full swing for about an hour when another two men arrived, both of whom were civilians. One of these men, a 29-year-old who called himself William James Thompson, but whose real name was William Cavanagh, was introduced as Ruby's husband while the other, James Innes, was said to be a close friend of his. Ruby produced a bottle of whisky and as the night wore on, songs were sung, jokes were told and everyone seemed to be having a good time. It was then, at around midnight, that one of the ladies made a remark aimed at Cavanagh and Innes.

No one could be sure exactly what was said, but the indication was that they should be wearing khaki and fighting for their country in the trenches in France, just as these brave sailors were doing on the high seas. This argument was now taken up by a couple of the sailors and one of them, McDonald, said something to Innes which he found most objectionable. A full-scale argument began with Hollyer taking the part of his shipmate and Cavanagh joining forces with Innes.

Tempers were raised even higher and it appeared to be only a matter of time before fists began to fly. Sure enough, Cavanagh lashed out and struck Hollyer in the face, knocking him to the ground. After that, everything seemed to happen so quickly. Blows were exchanged between Innes and McDonald. Cavanagh drew out a knife when Gough tried to intervene and stabbed him in the face. Gough and some of the others then left the house and stood outside in the street but not before Cavanagh had turned around and stabbed Hollyer in the back.

The police were called and in due course, Acting Sergeant Daley arrived on the scene, to be followed soon afterwards by Inspector Wood. They found Henry Hollyer lying in the yard at the back of the house, apparently suffering from a number of stab wounds and bleeding badly. He was rushed to hospital, as were James Innes, Petty Officer McDonald and Alfred

Gough. Later that same day, charges were preferred against William Cavanagh and Ruby Wright.

It was also June 21st when the first appearance at the Newcastle police court took place, before the Lord Mayor and Mr W.B. Ellis. Cavanagh, alias Thompson, was charged with wounding Leading Seaman Hollyer by stabbing him in the breast and back and with having unlawfully wounded Petty Officer Alfred Gough by stabbing him in the left cheek. Ruby Wright was charged with having assaulted Petty Officer Alfred Birling and Petty Officer Gough, by throwing bottles and glasses at them.

After the court heard evidence of what had taken place at West Street, the two defendants were remanded in custody for eight days. However, before those eight days had passed, on Monday, June 25th, Hollyer died from his wounds and Cavanagh was now charged with his murder. The inquest on Hollyer opened on June 26th, and was immediately adjourned until July 11th.

On June 27th, Cavanagh made his second appearance at the police court where evidence was given that he had been charged with murder at 10.20am on June 26th, after Hollyer had died at the Northern General Hospital. He was remanded to July 5th. At the hearing which opened on that date, it was revealed that James Innes, a 28-year-old native of Edinburgh, had now also been charged. Innes initially faced a charge of assaulting Gough by kicking him in the right elbow, but the prosecutor, Edward Clarke, made it plain that both Ruby Wright and James Innes would probably later be charged with being accessories, both before and after the murder, and might face even more serious charges once the case was prepared. A further remand was granted, this time to July 13th.

On July 11th, the inquest reopened at the Newcastle Infirmary, before the city coroner, Alfred Appleby. By now, both Cavanagh and Ruby Wright had obtained legal representation. Cavanagh was defended by Mr T.A.B. Forster, while

Newcastle Prison, now demolished, where some of the early cases in this book came to their conclusion. *Newcastle Evening Chronicle.*

Cullercoats at the turn of the century, when the Millers murdered Joseph Ferguson (see chapter 1). *Newcastle Evening Chronicle.*

Mr Justice Darling, who was involved in four cases in this book. He sentenced Perkins to death (chapter 4), put Craig in jail (chapter 8), and was involved in two unsuccessful appeals, those of Cavanagh and Mohamed. *Hulton Getty.*

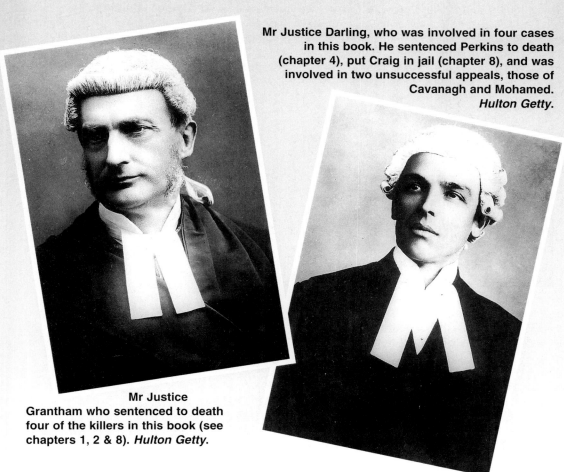

Mr Justice Grantham who sentenced to death four of the killers in this book (see chapters 1, 2 & 8). *Hulton Getty.*

The Royal Victoria Hospital in Newcastle, where some of the victims received treatment before succumbing to their injuries, whereupon their assailants faced charges of murder.

Newgate Street around the time that Henry Perkins murdered his fellow lodger, Patrick Durkin (see chapter 4). *Newcastle Evening Chronicle.*

The street where Thomas Henderson collapsed after being shot in his home and chasing his assailant (see chapter 8). *Newcastle Evening Chronicle.*

John Innes Nisbet, the victim in the Dickman case (see chapter 9). *British Library, Colindale.*

Mrs Nisbet, the wife of the murdered John Innes Nisbet, whose evidence was critical in the conviction of Dickman (see chapter 9). *British Library, Colindale.*

Newcastle Central Railway Station as it was at the time of John Innes Nisbet's death (see chapter 9). *Newcastle Evening Chronicle.*

Sergeant Barton, one of the victims of the Amos case (see chapter 10). *British Library, Colindale.*

John Vickers Amos being taken to Newcastle Prison after his police court hearing (see chapter 10). *British Library, Colindale.*

The body of PC Mussell is removed from the Sun Inn (see chapter 10). *British Library, Colindale.*

Mr Justice Avory, one of the judges involved in the appeals of Cavanagh (see chapter 13) and Johnson (chapter 19). *Hulton Getty.*

Front page of the *Newcastle Illustrated Chronicle*, reporting the murder of Rebecca Quinn by her husband, Corporal Ambrose Quinn (see chapter 15). *British Library, Colindale.*

Hassen Mohamed at the police court (see chapter 16). *British Library, Colindale.*

The café where Hassen Mohamed shot his lover (see chapter 16). *British Library, Colindale.*

Ruth Surtees Rodgers, the woman murdered by Thomas Shelton (see chapter 17). *Public Record Office.*

The letter which Ruth Rodgers sent to Shelton and which caused him to determine on the course of action which cost both their lives (see chapter 17). *Public Record Office.*

Pilgrim Street in 1926, the year when it featured strongly in the murder of Catherine Smith (see chapter 18). *Newcastle Evening Chronicle.*

It was behind these pipes that the body of Margaret Rice was discovered (see chapter 22). *Public Record Office.*

The house (closest to the lamp-post, far right) where George Brown strangled his former girlfriend in full view of her young daughter (see chapter 24). *Public Record Office.*

Margaret Mary Rice, the newly-married WAAF who was battered to death by William Ambrose Collins (see chapter 22). *Newcastle Evening Chronicle.*

The house in Marlborough Avenue where Frank Stokes battered Mrs Violet Ash to death (see chapter 26). *Newcastle Evening Chronicle.*

Lord Goddard, who was for many years the Lord Chief Justice of England. He was one of the judges in the unsuccessful appeals of both Charles (see chapter 23) and Ali (chapter 25). *Popperfoto.*

Ruby was represented by Mr T.H. Smirk. Most of the witnesses to the crime gave their evidence, but the hearing continued the following evening, when the jury returned a verdict of wilful murder against Cavanagh who was then committed for trial. Meanwhile, the very next day, July 13th, Cavanagh, Innes and Wright, now all charged with murder, made their final appearance at the police court. Here it was decided that James Innes and Ruby Wright, would also stand in the dock with Cavanagh at the forthcoming assizes.

The trial took place at Newcastle before Mr Justice Salter, on November 12th, 1917. The case for the prosecution was put by Mr Edward Shortt, MP, and Mr E. Meynell. Cavanagh and Innes were both defended by Mr Charles Mellor while Ruby Wright was represented by Mr G.F. Mortimer.

At the very outset, Edward Shortt announced that the prosecution had examined the depositions very carefully and as a result had come to the conclusion that this was not a case where they had enough evidence against Ruby Wright and had decided therefore to offer no evidence against her. The judge now directed the jury to formally return a not guilty verdict against Ruby and she was then discharged, leaving Innes and Cavanagh to face the charge of wilful murder.

The four petty officers gave evidence of their meeting with the dead man, the four women and the events at West Street once Cavanagh and Innes had made their appearance. They stated that they had first visited the Express Hotel, opposite the Union Club in Westgate Road, before moving on to the Mechanic's Arms. Also, before they had arrived at West Street, they had called at a fish and chip shop in Blenheim Street. All four sailors denied that they were drunk, or that they had taken any drink back to West Street. They claimed that the only alcohol consumed there was a bottle of whisky which Ruby herself had produced and which must have been on the premises already.

Petty Officer Birling testified that he had seen Cavanagh

deliberately stab Hollyer and that Ruby had thrown two glasses at him. McDonald described how Innes had struck him so hard that he had knocked some of his teeth out. Alfred Gough, though, went into much greater detail. He described how after the original remark about Cavanagh and Innes not being in uniform, McDonald had left the house. Innes had followed him into the street, where he assaulted him before returning to the group inside the house. Gough then saw Cavanagh strike Hollyer in the face and knock him down. Seeing that things were getting out of hand, Gough tried to cool things down, but when he tried to break up the fight, Cavanagh took out a penknife from his waistcoat pocket, pulled out the blade and stabbed him in the cheek. Hollyer was still lying on the floor and Gough saw Cavanagh deliberately stab him in the back with the same penknife. Innes then kicked Gough while Ruby was busy throwing glasses around the room at anyone within range. It was Gough, once he had staggered outside, who went to the police station and reported the matter to the officer on duty.

Inspector Wood reported how he had found a bloodstained penknife on a dressing table in the house. Blood was also found on the clothing worn by Cavanagh and Ruby Wright, although there was none found on those belonging to Innes. Next, medical evidence was given. Captain Armstrong of the RAMC, had had Hollyer under his care in the hospital. He reported that there were five wounds. Two were over the heart and one of these had actually penetrated that organ. A third wound was discovered in the left side of the neck while a fourth was some three inches above the liver. The final wound was in the back, just over the right kidney, and from the evidence which had been given by Gough, this was in all probability the first injury Cavanagh had inflicted, while Hollyer was lying face down on the floor.

Major Pybus had operated on Hollyer on June 21st, when he had stitched the wound in the heart. Unfortunately, this had not saved his life and the cause of death was given as inflammation of the heart and lungs as a direct result of the various wounds which had been inflicted.

The time came for Ruby Wright, a barmaid, to give evidence. After the original fracas was over she had told Innes and Cavanagh to take Hollyer out into the yard. She had seen them pick the man up, at which point Innes struck him in the face. Once in the yard, Ruby saw Cavanagh striking repeatedly at Hollyer, although she could not see if he had anything in his hand at the time.

If this evidence was damning, Ruby made things somewhat better for both Innes and Cavanagh by explaining that they were not the only people there who had taken strong drink. Even in the Mechanic's Arms, the sailors were rather jolly and despite what they had said to the contrary, they had in fact brought four bottles of whisky with them to West Street, and all of this had been consumed at her house. By the time the fight started, everyone was intoxicated and it had been Hollyer who struck the first blow when he hit out at Cavanagh.

Neither Cavanagh nor Innes testified on their own behalf, preferring to rely on a plea that the killing had been accidental, during an affray. Having heard all the evidence, the jury came to the conclusion that James Innes was not guilty and he was discharged. Cavanagh, though, was not so fortunate and having been adjudged to be guilty as charged, was then sentenced to death, although the jury had recommended him to mercy. His appeal was heard on December 3rd, before Justices Darling, Avory and Sankey. The grounds were rather unique.

Cavanagh, it seems, had a police record and something of a reputation on the streets of Newcastle. He had, of course, been tried before a city of Newcastle jury and it was probable that some or indeed all of the men on that jury would have known of Cavanagh's character. The defence also contended that the court could not accept the sailor's evidence as correct. They had suggested that they had used no bad language, were sober and had offered no violence but the defence found this impossible to accept. Further, the defence suggested that the civilians in this case had been enraged by insults against them and had merely defended their honour. As for the stabbing, Cavanagh had not even been aware that he had a knife in his hand as he had been drunk when he struck the blows. The knife itself was very small and, if anything, it was extraordinary that fatal wounds should have been inflicted.

In his reply, Mr Justice Avory stated that the trial judge had left the question of scrimmage in the most favourable light possible for the appellant. It was felt that there was no evidence to show that the jury would have been justified in reducing the charge to one of manslaughter because of provocation and the request of the defence to call Innes to give evidence must be refused. There was no reason why the appeal should hear the testimony of a witness who could have given evidence at the trial itself, but chose not to do so. As a result, Cavanagh's appeal was dismissed.

On December 15th, Messrs Bennett and Maddison, the solicitors who had acted for Cavanagh, received a letter from the Home Office, stating that the Home Secretary had failed to discover any grounds in the petition praying for a reprieve. The sentence would be carried out.

At 8.00am on the morning of Tuesday, December 18th, 1917, William Cavanagh was hanged at Newcastle by Thomas Pierrepoint who was assisted by Robert Baxter. He walked firmly to the scaffold while a crowd of 50 or 60 people waited outside the prison in Carliol Square, waiting for the notice of execution to be posted on the gates. At the inquest later, Dr Hardcastle, the prison doctor, stated that Cavanagh was 5ft 3ins tall, weighed 146 pounds and had been given a drop of 7ft 3ins inches. Death apparently had been instantaneous, which was more than could be said for his victim.

CHAPTER FOURTEEN

AN OPEN AND SHUT CASE

REBECCA Jane Quinn worked as a housekeeper for two miners, Elijah Smith and his brother, at 15 West Row, Bebside, a village between one a half miles and two miles from New Delavel. By the middle of August, 1919, Rebecca had worked at Bebside for five weeks and, by all accounts, was very happy in her work.

Rebecca Quinn had been born on December 22nd, 1893, and now, at the age of 25, had a young child who lived at her parents' house, 94 New Row, New Delavel. Rebecca returned home as often as she could in order to see her child and cared deeply for its welfare, so when a visitor arrived at her place of work on the morning of Monday, August 11th, and told her that the child had been in an accident, the concerned mother made immediate arrangements to go to New Delavel.

The man who had brought the message was well known to Rebecca. Twenty eight-year-old Ernest Bernard Scott had been walking out with Rebecca Quinn for three weeks but of late they had fallen out, and she had told him that the relationship was over. It was 9.45am when he called at 69 West Row, Bebside, and asked Mrs Margaret Davison, a close friend of Rebecca's, to take her a message that her child and another had been 'sore scalded'.

During the period that Rebecca had worked for the Smith brothers at Bebside, she had become friendly with Mrs Davison, who was surprised when Scott arrived with his terrible message and asked him why one of Rebecca's relatives had not brought the news themselves. Scott replied that he had come out of kindness and consideration for Rebecca. As a good friend, Margaret Davison rushed to deliver the message and the child's mother was obviously distressed. Shortly after Margaret Davison had returned home, Rebecca arrived at her house in tears and asked her to accompany her to New Delavel. Margaret arranged for someone to look after her own children before the two women set out to walk across the fields and trackways.

They had gone perhaps a quarter of a mile when Rebecca said, "Look, there's Ernie." Margaret Davison watched with interest as Ernest Scott approached them, close by the railway line and asked why it had taken them so long to get there. Rebecca explained that a childminder had to be found for Mrs Davison and the three then walked together. When they reached the Forster pit-heap, close to New Delavel, Margaret asked if that was where Scott was going. After all, he too was a miner and while he might have taken time off to bring the message to Rebecca, he would surely want to get back to his work. Scott replied, "No, I am going straight on; they know I am on this message." With that he put his arm around Rebecca's neck. Margaret Davison assumed that Scott was about to kiss Rebecca so averted her eyes. Seconds later, though, she looked back to see Rebecca stagger and fall over, her clothing covered in blood.

William J. Wilkinson was walking towards the railway station at the time. He saw two women and a man coming towards him along the footpath and then heard one of the women shout as the other fell. The man who had been with them was now running away across the railway line towards Bebside. Wilkinson ran forward to offer what assistance he could.

Rebecca Quinn was lying face down on the ground. Gently, Wilkinson turned her over to see that she was barely breathing. There was a large gash on one side of her throat and a deep hole in the other. Wilkinson stayed with her until she died some two minutes later.

A full scale search was launched for Ernest Scott. Not long after the attack had taken place, Constable Armstrong of Cowpen overtook Scott at Kitty Brewster. When stopped, Scott said, "I've not slept all night. I've been working out a scheme, and it has come off. Rebecca has given me up and was with another man last night. That is more than I can stand. If you had not caught me, I intended to finish myself in the river. I am glad you caught me. Don't keep me in misery. Finish me off at once. I have had two tries to cut her throat. You will find her near the pit-heap at New Delavel." Scott was then taken to Blyth where he was charged with murder. To this he replied, "That is quite correct. I'm happy now."

The inquest on Rebecca Quinn opened on August 13th, before the coroner, Mr H.T. Rutherford, at the Mechanics' Institute, Newsham. Scott was not present as Mr Patrick Quinn, the dead girl's father, gave evidence of identification, adding that his daughter had served for four years in the WAAC. He also told the court that Rebecca had told him that Scott had wanted to marry her but she had objected to his attentions. After this, the matter was adjourned until August 20th when proceedings would continue at the court house at Blyth.

On August 14th, the funeral of Rebecca Quinn took place at Cowpen cemetery. The cortège left her parents' house at New Delavel, passed through Newsham, Blyth and Cowpen. All along the route blinds had been drawn and a large crowd at the cemetery heard the service conducted by the Reverend Father Curran.

Scott made a number of appearances before the magistrates at Blyth until, on August 26th, when all the witnesses had been heard, Scott was asked if he had anything to say. He replied, "I am guilty of killing the woman I love. That is all." He was then sent for trial. That trial took place on November 5th, 1919, at Newcastle, before Mr Justice Lawrence. The case for the prosecution was put by Mr J.A. Compston and Mr W. Valentine Ball. Scott refused to take any advice as to his defence and was therefore not represented in court. In reply to the charge, Scott answered, "Not guilty sir, of murder."

Evidence was given that when Scott had first arrived at the Davison household to give the false message for Rebecca about her child being injured, he had also left a letter addressed to Elijah Smith. This letter was now produced and read in court; "Just a few lines to let you know I cannot part with my love so easily. I am doing this for the love of her. There is nothing wrong with the child, but I cannot part from Becky. In death we will be happy, the same as the nights we passed together. God forgive this rash act, but it is for the best. Here is my goodbye and Becky's. Love to all we left." The letter was signed in the names of both Ernest Scott and Rebecca Quinn and ended with the words, "Only forgive me Mr Smith."

This letter had earlier been read out at the inquest on Rebecca Quinn. At the time, Scott had claimed that there was a page missing and insisted that it be found. What had been read out clearly showed that Scott had planned the act and deliberately carried it out. Mentioning this, the coroner had said, "It does not affect me." To this Scott had replied, "But it affects me sir." At the trial, though, Scott made no objection to the letter and made no reference to the page he alleged was missing.

Mrs Davison was an important witness for the prosecution. She explained that the last time she had seen Scott before the day of Rebecca's death had been on Saturday, August 9th, when they had been standing by her back door, talking, at around 4.00pm. She next saw Scott on August 11th when he brought the message about Rebecca's child being scalded and he had given her the letter to pass on to Elijah Smith. This she had done that same afternoon, by which time, of course, Rebecca was already dead.

Referring to the attack itself, Mrs Davison admitted that when Scott had put his arm around Rebecca, she had not seen any weapon in his hand. As soon as Rebecca had fallen, Scott ran off over the railway line and she had shouted to a gentleman who had been walking towards them. This had been Mr Wilkinson and Margaret had cried out, "Be sharp. Be sharp. He has murdered Becky." Whilst Wilkinson tried to administer assistance, she had run into New Delavel and knocked on the door of a house to raise the alarm.

Police Constable Michael Callaghan of New Delavel told the court that he had arrived at the scene at 12.05pm. Rebecca was dead by then, so Callaghan concentrated his efforts on finding her killer. He followed a trail of blood which led from the body towards Bebside. The trail led over the railway line and on the opposite side, Callaghan found a broken razor in a field. This was about nine yards from where Rebecca lay. Later that same day, Constable Callaghan took possession of the letter which had been addressed to Mr Smith.

The razor Constable Callaghan had found was identified by Frederick Thomas Robson, a barman from New Delavel. He testified that Scott had asked him if he could borrow a razor and this particular one had been handed over at 9.00am on the morning of August 11th, the same day Rebecca had been attacked.

Elijah Smith said that Rebecca had worked for him and his brother since July 6th. He had been at work when Rebecca received the message so was unable to shed any light on that, but he had received the letter from Mrs Davison later that same day and had then handed it over to the police.

Dr T. Gallagher, who had examined Rebecca at the scene of

the crime within 20 minutes of her death, gave evidence as to her wounds. He said that great force had been used to inflict the injuries. The instrument used had passed over the windpipe and cut down to the bones of the neck. In his opinion, two savage blows had been required.

Scott was asked if he wanted to give evidence. He replied, "No sir, I am guilty of taking her life right enough, but not guilty of murder. Anything but murder. But I took her life right enough. That is all I want to say sir."

The jury returned their guilty verdict without even leaving the box. Asked if he had anything to say as to why the sentence of death should not be passed, Scott said, "Not in the least. I will get the happiness I want then. I have long looked for it. I was deprived of it. I will not be deprived of it in the next world." The entire proceedings had lasted just over an hour. Scott had remained cool and composed throughout the hearing and had remained motionless as the sentence was passed. A woman in the public gallery was not so calm, however. Upon hearing the sentence of death she cried aloud, "Oh Ernie...," and had to be led out of court.

Scott made no attempt to appeal against the sentence, but he did write several letters from the condemned cell. In one, to a friend, he joked, "This is a good Government we have now; do you not see my new suit? See how low it is round the neck! You know what that fashion is for."

One of his last letters was to Mrs Davison who had proved so valuable a witness at his trial. To her Scott wrote, "I take the pleasure of writing these few lines, hoping it finds you well, as it leaves me quite happy and content. I am going to meet with friends I love dearly, and with whom I have never to part again through Christ, Who will carry me to them...I earnestly hope my parting from this earth will be a lesson to some; as you know, it is a big price I am paying for their learning."

On the eve of his execution, Scott spend a quiet night and slept soundly. He enjoyed a good breakfast and after being ministered to by the chaplain offered no resistance to the pinioning process in his cell. He walked firmly to the scaffold as a good sized crowd gathered outside the prison, despite the gloomy weather.

At 8.00am on Wednesday, November 26th, 1919, Ernest Bernard Scott was hanged at Newcastle by John Ellis, who was assisted by Edward Taylor. No bell was tolled in deference to the subject of the next chapter, Ambrose Quinn, who was waiting to keep his appointment with the hangman.

At the inquest, held by the city coroner Mr Alfred Appleby, it was stated that Scott was 5ft 5½ins tall, weighed 151lbs and had been given a drop of 7ft 3ins. Death had been instantaneous and Ernest Scott had at last escaped the unhappiness of his life.

CHAPTER FIFTEEN

THE MAN WHO DIDN'T LIKE DANCING

IN THE year 1917, Ambrose Quinn, who was then 26 years old, joined the Royal Air Force as a mechanic, leaving behind his wife of three years, Elizabeth Ann, and their two children, the youngest being just a baby.

It was not until June 16th, 1919, that Ambrose began a three-month leave period but on returning home he found that his wife wanted more of a social life than he was prepared to accept. Elizabeth loved to go to the cinema and Ambrose thought she spent far too much time and money there.

Things, though, did not come to a head until July 19th when the country united to enjoy a day of peace celebrations. Although the war had ended in November 1918, it had taken some months to ship the large number of British soldiers home from the killing fields of France and Belgium. Now there were street parties and dances and Elizabeth, perhaps not unnaturally, wanted to go to a dance to be held in the street that night. Ambrose objected strongly to this and a heated argument followed. Threats were issued, and there were even some blows struck, but eventually Ambrose demurred and Elizabeth was allowed to go to her dance.

It was later that same night that Ambrose Quinn began to hear rumours of his wife's conduct while he had been away serving his country. Apparently, on Whit Monday, June 9th, she had gone to a friend's wedding. After the reception, she had been seen home by two men, one of whom was named Joseph Shepherd. It transpired, though, that Shepherd had left Elizabeth's company in Scotswood Road and it had been the other man who had seen Elizabeth home to her father's house at 63 Hawes Street, where she had been staying during her husband's absence. According to gossip Elizabeth had given herself to this other man — whose name Quinn did not know — in a nearby passageway.

Inevitably, Ambrose Quinn faced his wife with these reports but, equally inevitably perhaps, she denied everything. The matter simmered for another couple of weeks until, on Friday, August 1st, a meeting was arranged between Ambrose and Elizabeth Quinn and Joseph Shepherd. Here Ambrose was told by Shepherd that he and another man had indeed started to escort Elizabeth home and that Shepherd had left her with this other man, but he steadfastly refused to name him. Ambrose insisted and at one point, Shepherd asked Elizabeth if she wanted him to give out the name. Elizabeth, adamant that nothing improper had taken place, told Shepherd to go ahead, saying, "Yes, I don't know him. I want to take him to the man in order to prove there was nothing wrong between us." Despite this, Joseph Shepherd still refused to name the other man.

Two days after this incident, Ambrose Quinn again met Shepherd and now at last he got the name of the man he believed had made love to his wife. From that moment he appeared to become obsessed with the idea that his wife was an unfit mother and any hopes of a reconciliation between them seemed to disappear. The next morning, August 4th, Ambrose again accused his wife of adultery and on August 5th, he walked out of her father's house and went to live with his mother. That same night, he returned to Hawes Street to inform Elizabeth that it was his intention to take the children from her. A day or two later, Ambrose moved in with his sister, Mrs Little, and her husband Robert, who lived in Herbert Street.

On the morning of August 6th, Ambrose Quinn was back at Hawes Street where he informed Elizabeth that he was prepared to, '...give that bloke £10 to go to court and swear that he had misconducted himself with you'. Once again Elizabeth denied that she had been unfaithful saying, "I've told you the truth, and I've got my brains hammered out." It was at that point that Ambrose Quinn snatched up a knife that was lying on the table and hurled it at Elizabeth. Fortunately it missed her but embedded in a door and had been thrown with such force that it buckled.

On the night of Saturday, August 9th, 1919, Ambrose Quinn was out drinking with a group of his friends, although he only had a total of three gills. Last orders were called at 10.00pm and by 10.15pm Ambrose was in Scotswood Road, talking to his friends. From there, he walked into Hawes Street where he happened to see his wife walking back to her house at number 63.

Ambrose walked over to his her and was seen to put his left hand on her right shoulder. They walked on a few steps and Ambrose then put his right arm around her neck. A sudden upward movement followed whereupon Elizabeth began to stagger. She fell to the floor, managed to pull herself to her feet again but fell for a second time just a few paces from her front door. As neighbours rushed to her aid, it was seen that there was a gaping wound in her throat. Ambrose Quinn, meanwhile, had run off towards Scotswood Road.

It was 10.35pm when Quinn rushed into the police station on Scotswood Road and announced to Superintendent Potts, "Hurry up. A woman has cut her throat in Hawes Street." Quinn was almost out of breath and as Superintendent Potts detailed two officers to go to Hawes Road, a man named McKenzie, who had apparently seen the entire affair, entered and told the police what he had witnessed. Ambrose Quinn was then informed that he would be detained.

Sergeant Rogerson was told to search the prisoner and he noticed that there were extensive bloodstains on the inside and outside of his left sleeve. The thumb and fingers of his right hand were also heavily bloodstained. Meanwhile Superintendent Potts had travelled to the crime scene and there he found the dead body of Elizabeth Quinn lying on the road opposite her front door. Back at the police station he charged Ambrose Quinn with murder. Sergeant Rogerson took the prisoner down to the cells and Quinn, apparently in a daze, asked, "Did he say I killed her?" Superintendent Potts asked Quinn if he wanted the charge read over to him again and once it had been, Ambrose muttered, "I did not intend to kill her, sir."

Ambrose Quinn made his first appearance at the Newcastle police court on August 11th. Here he was defended by Mr T.H. Smirk and after hearing evidence of arrest, Quinn was remanded for one week. A further week's remand followed on August 18th and, meanwhile, the inquest returned a verdict of wilful murder against Quinn, who was sent for trial on that charge.

The trial of 28-year-old Ambrose Quinn took place at Newcastle on November 6th, 1919, before Mr Justice Lawrence. The case for the Crown was put by Mr W.J. Waugh and Mr H.S. Mundahl, while Quinn's defence lay in the hands of Mr Walter Hedley.

Robert Little was Quinn's brother-in-law and he had been drinking with Quinn on the night in question. Mr Little testified that after they had come out of the public house, they had met his wife and then all three stood for a while on the corner of Tulloch Street. After a minute or two, Quinn had walked away, saying he would be back directly. In fact he did not return and becoming rather suspicious, Mrs Little rushed home to Herbert Street where she found that a razor was missing. She dashed back to her husband and the couple went to Hawes Street, just in time to see Quinn attack his wife.

There had been many people in Hawes Street at the time of the attack and all now related what they had seen. Mary Robson who lived at number 57, just a few doors down from Elizabeth's house, said she had seen Ambrose draw a razor across his wife's throat. Ralph Calvert also saw this but after Quinn had run off, Calvert gave chase. Seeing that he was being followed, Quinn stopped, turned to face Calvert and brandished the razor as if to attack him. Fortunately, though, Calvert was faster on his feet and he managed to dodge the blow and hit Quinn with his fists. Quinn fell to the ground and lost the razor but then managed to get up and run off again.

Thomas Ridley, Elizabeth's father, reported how ever since Quinn had found out that his wife had been escorted home after the wedding party, he had been insanely jealous. On more than one occasion since he had threatened to murder Elizabeth and Ridley had also witnessed the accused striking out at his daughter. Even before these incidents, though, Quinn had tried to restrict his wife's social life, complaining that she went out too much and complaining that she used too much powder on her face.

Police Constable George Parkin had been on duty in Scotswood Road when Quinn had come up to him in a state of near-collapse, asking to be taken into custody. Parkin walked with him to the police station and at one stage had to support Quinn when he did collapse.

Superintendent Potts told of the events inside the station but also stated that on August 5th, Quinn had come in and complained that his wife had committed adultery and as such, he wanted to have her separation allowance stopped. Superintendent Potts had advised Quinn that the best course of action was to speak to his regimental paymaster. However, he also took Quinn's complaint of child neglect seriously and

Inspector Dale had been sent to Hawes Street to check that the children were well. That officer had found no sign of neglect and reporting back to Quinn had suggested that it might be best if he returned to his family and tried to sort things out.

Medical evidence was given by the police surgeon, Dr George Edward Stephenson, who described a six-inch long wound which had completely severed the jugular vein and had also damaged the windpipe. In his opinion, death would have been almost instantaneous.

Ambrose Quinn went into the box to give evidence on his own behalf. He described how his wife had admitted she had been to the wedding and had been escorted home by two men. After Shepherd had left them, it had started to rain but she and the other man had still spent some time in a passageway near her home. This had caused Quinn to wonder what they might have been up to and these suspicions were reinforced when Elizabeth started to bring this man up in conversation over and over again.

Turning to the night of Elizabeth's death, Quinn claimed that he recalled standing talking to his brother-in-law when it suddenly came in to his head to give his wife a fright. He remembered going back to his lodgings in Herbert Street and then going to Hawes Street. He knocked on the door of number 63, but there was no reply. He turned to go away and at that very moment, Elizabeth appeared. The next thing he knew, the razor was in his hand and after that, everything was a blank until a police officer gave him a cigarette in the station.

The jury took only ten minutes to decide that Ambrose Quinn was guilty of murder, although they did add a strong recommendation to mercy. Asked if he had anything to say Quinn replied, "No sir. But I did not intend to kill my wife. I never intended to do that." As the death sentence was handed down, Quinn was crying bitterly and wiping tears from his eyes with his sleeve. In the public gallery, his sister, Mrs Little, was also crying and as the last words of the sentence fell from the judge's lips, she fainted and had to be assisted from the court.

There was no appeal and no reprieve. At 8.00am on Wednesday, November 26th, 1919, the subject of the last chapter, Ernest Scott, had been hanged on the scaffold at Durham. Seventy-five minutes later, Ambrose Quinn followed him to the same fate. At the inquest afterwards, it was stated that Quinn had been 5ft 5½ins tall, had weighed 137lbs, and had been given a drop of 7ft 10ins by the same executioner, John Ellis who on this occasion was assisted by Robert Baxter.

CHAPTER SIXTEEN

JARROW JENNY

THE BUILDING at 107 East Holborn, South Shields, was well known to the Arab community of the area. The front room of that establishment was used as a shop, but the kitchen at the back served as a meeting place where coffee was served. On the evening of Monday, 12th March, 1923, there were three Arabs in that kitchen, and one young English woman.

The men were Salem Ali, the gentleman who owned the premises, and two friends of his; one named Sam Ali, who was no relation to Salem, and a man named Nagi. Coincidentally, the English woman was also named Nagi. Originally her name had been Jane Brown but she had married one Mohamed Nagi who had died about a year before. Some people knew Jane as Brown, some knew her as Nagi and her friends in the Arab community also often referred to her as Jarrow Jenny, since that was where her home was.

Jane Brown, who was 25 years old, was in fact engaged to be married to another Arab, Hassen Mohamed, who was a native of Aden and lived quite close to the café at 79 East Holborn. So, it was no surprise when, a few minutes after Jane had gone into the kitchen on this late winter's day, Hassen also appeared at the doorway. The couple, though, had obviously argued for when Hassen asked Jane to go out with him, she told him, "No, I have finished with you." Hassen did not speak again but walked out of the house, only to return three or four minutes later. Once again he stood framed in the kitchen doorway, although now he was smoking a cigarette. Then, much to the surprise of everyone in the room, Hassen drew out a revolver, pointed it at Jane and fired a bullet into her chest.

Jane managed to stagger to her feet and made her way into the yard at the back of the building. Hassen tried to make good his escape through the front door but Sam Ali and Salem barred his way. Jane, meanwhile, had fallen to the ground and by the time Salem and one of the servants, Elizabeth Marshall, could reach her she was dead. They carried her body back into the kitchen and placed her on a couch where she was found by the first police officer to arrive on the scene, Police Constable Walsh. Soon Sergeant Ernest Gray joined his colleague and Hassen was taken into custody.

The following morning, March 13th, Hassen Mohamed made his first appearance before the South Shields magistrates. Although Hassen spoke rather broken English, he did understand the language and said that he did not require the services of an interpreter. One was, however, provided as some of the witnesses said that they would prefer to give their evidence in Arabic.

At this first hearing, it was revealed that Hassen was a sea-going fireman who had only just completed a voyage, having been discharged from his ship in the Bristol Channel on Wednesday, March 7th. Letters from the dead woman found in his possession when he was arrested showed that Jane Brown had suggested meeting Hassen in Cardiff once he was paid off. He agreed and after meeting Hassen from his ship, the couple had travelled back up to South Shields together on the Thursday.

Hassen and Jane had spent those first two nights together, but by Friday, she was back at her father's house at 17 Curry

Street, Jarrow. She stayed there from Friday, March 9th, until Sunday, March 11th, although from time to time during that period, she returned to South Shields to see Hassen.

Little could be ascertained about the movements of either the dead woman, or the man accused of her murder, from Sunday morning until the afternoon of Monday, March 12th. The couple were seen together at 4.00pm on that day when a furious argument took place between them. That meeting had also taken place at the café run by Salem Ali and it was witnessed by Irene Alice Rab who lived at 32 Woodbine Street, South Shields, and who had known Jane Brown for some years.

According to Irene, Jane was much the worse for drink and efforts were made to persuade her to go home and sleep it off. Not only did Jane refuse but she said that she was 'looking for trouble' and having decided that this should be directed at her fiancé, Hassen, she went out to find him. She visited a number of shops and caused a disturbance in one by breaking some eggs. The shop owner called the police but by the time they had arrived, Jane had left the shop and finally found Hassen.

Irene was still with her and she told the court that Hassen had also tried to get Jane to go home, but she had refused to move and when Hassen took hold of her coat, she leapt at him and attempted to scratch his face with her fingernails. Eventually Hassen managed to calm her down a little and he, Jane and Irene then went to 1 West Holborn, an establishment known as the White House. Here, though, the quarrel resumed and Jane leapt on the slightly built Hassen, tried to strangle him and screamed that she would 'swing for him'. Finally, Hassen lost his temper and moved to retaliate but was restrained by several other men while Jane Brown was escorted from the premises.

It was 7.30pm by the time the couple met up again for the last time, at 107 East Holborn. After the shooting had taken place, Hassen told the police officers who took him into custody, "Me fire one shot. Me sorry." He was taken to Laygate police station where he was formally charged with murder. In reply to the charge, Hassen said, "She come from Jarrow and get in trouble in another house. Another man tell me about her being drunk in street. I go down Holborn and see her in street. I brought her to the car and gave her two shillings. I have kept her for eight months." At that point, the proceedings were adjourned and Hassen was remanded in custody for eight days.

It was also on March 13th that the inquest on Jane Brown opened before the deputy coroner, Mr A.E.E. Boulton. Only evidence of identification was given, by Jane's father, Mr Michael Brown. Those proceedings were then also adjourned, until March 16th.

It was when the inquest finally re-opened on the 16th, that the deputy coroner, Mr Boulton, engaged in some gratuitous racism. Commenting on the relationship that had existed between Hassen and Jane, Mr Boulton announced, "I am sorry to say that in my experience of inquests at South Shields, I have come into contact with a number of cases in which white women have married coloured men. I feel very strongly on the point, not that it has any bearing on this case, but it seems a great pity that white women should marry men of a different nationality altogether and that trouble more or less arrives from such unions.

"I don't consider it is fair to the children who may be born to any such marriages, and it seems to me that steps should be taken to prevent these unions if possible. I am sure we should not have been here today had such a wedding as was contemplated in this case not been about to be celebrated." Having listened to that lecture, the jury then returned a verdict of murder against Hassen and he was committed for trial on the coroner's warrant.

No doubt the coroner felt that the events of March 19th vindicated his words. It was on that date that a black man was involved in an attack in the same thoroughfare of East Holborn. At 11.35pm that night, Police Constable Sidney Ainslie was patrolling his beat when he discovered a known thief, John Lowgower, inside Mr Levy's outfitters shop. Constable Ainslie called for Lowgower to come outside and give himself up. Lowgower emerged but immediately pulled a knife and lunged at the officer. Constable Ainslie and a passer-by, Walter Callaghan, were both wounded and Lowgower found himself facing two charges of attempted murder.

The following day, March 20th, Hassen was back in the magistrates' court where for the first time his defence made the suggestion that what looked like an open-and-shut case was in fact nothing of the kind.

According to Hassen's testimony, he had tried to get his fiancée out of the café but Salem Ali, Sam Ali and Mr Nagi all resisted his efforts. It had been Sam Ali, during a struggle with Hassen, who had brought out the revolver and Jane had been hit when it went off accidentally. Nevertheless, with the evidence of those three witnesses all agreeing that it had been Hassen who had deliberately pulled the trigger, there could be no other outcome but that Hassen would be sent for trial.

That trial took place at Durham on July 3rd, 1923, before the Lord Chief Justice, Lord Hewart. Hassen was defended by Mr A.P. Peaker while the case for the Crown was put by Mr L.R. Lipsett.

Evidence was given as to the character of Jane Brown. Some months before her death, Police Constable Henry Gardner was escorting two men to the police station when they turned on him and began attacking him. Jane saw this and shouting that she was as good as any man, leapt into the fray and helped Gardner control the men and even blew his whistle for him in order to summon further help.

For her action, she was commended by the chief constable and awarded a gold locket by the officers of the force. Of course, while this showed Jane to be brave, it also underlined that she was the kind of person who would not think twice about offering violence to Hassen or anyone else who offended her.

In addition to the evidence she had already given at the police court and the inquest, Irene Rab confirmed that Hassen and Jane had arranged to marry on March 14th, just two days after she was killed.

Salem Ali and Sam Ali both repeated their earlier story that after leaving the café, Hassen had returned and within a few minutes had deliberately aimed a revolver at Jane Brown and fired one shot. They had then held Hassen until the police arrived and it had been Sam Ali who disarmed the killer. This testimony was backed up by Elizabeth Marshall, although she added that not long after Jane had first come in, at around 7.00pm, two police officers, one of whom was Constable Walsh, had arrived to talk to her about the eggs she had broken in the other shop. They, though, had been left a full five minutes before the brief argument between Hassen and Jane had taken place.

Medical evidence of her injuries was given by Dr Charles Marks who had been called to the scene and later performed the post-mortem.

The single bullet had entered her left breast and had passed through three vital organs, the heart, the stomach and the left kidney. The bullet had finally come to rest just below the kidney and death would have occurred very soon after the wound had been inflicted.

The time came for Hassen to give his version of the events of March 12th. He claimed that when he first went in to the café, he found Jane sitting on the knee of one of the men. Objecting to this, Hassen had demanded that Salem Ali allow him to take Jane out but Ali had refused. In fact, Sam Ali and Salem Ali then tried to forcibly eject him, during which Sam Ali drew the revolver. This went off accidentally and once it was seen that Jane was dead, Hassen had been dragged back into the café and held until the police arrived. He was then identified as the culprit when in fact he was totally innocent of any involvement.

With all the other witnesses agreeing on a wholly different version of events, there could only be one verdict and Hassen was duly sentenced to death. He did enter an appeal and this was heard on July 24th before Justices Darling, Slater and Swift. The defence complained that at the trial, the Lord Chief Justice had summed up in such a way that the jury were told they could not believe the evidence of the accused man. The defence claimed that the transcript of the summing up did not show the inflection in the judge's words and it was this to which they were objecting. The appeal was dismissed, Justice Darling rather contemptuously adding that he was unable to find it laid down anywhere that the court must have a gramophone record of a summing up in order to understand its meaning.

At 8.00am on Wednesday, August 8th, 1923, Hassen Mohamed, still only 33 years old, was hanged at Durham prison by Thomas Pierrepoint, who gave the small man a drop of 8ft 6ins. It was reported that Hassen had been a model prisoner but as he was placed upon the drop, he twice screamed out the name of Allah. Those cries could clearly be heard outside the prison walls.

CHAPTER SEVENTEEN

SUSPICION

JOHN CLEMO TROTTER had served as a detective in the police force at Newcastle upon Tyne and upon retirement he had decided to use the knowledge and experience he had acquired to set up his own private detective agency based at 11 Saville Row. It was not, however, at those offices but at his home, 2 Lovaine Crescent, that Trotter received a visitor on the afternoon of Thursday, January 29th, 1925.

Trotter's visitor identified himself as 25-year-old Thomas Henry Shelton of 51 Southway, Sheriff Hill, and asked the detective if he would perform a service for him. Trotter made notes as Shelton explained that he believed his sweetheart, Ruth Surtees Rodgers, was seeing another man. He went on to give details of her address, said they were formally engaged and had been for four years, but that of late she had taken to not wearing her engagement ring. Shelton believed that Ruth was going out alone at night, and meeting other men. If this was the case, Shelton said that he wanted to know who these men were. In order to make Trotter's task easier, Shelton handed over a photograph of his fiancée and some letters that she had sent him. After listening to this story, Trotter promised to investigate the matter and told Shelton to return the following morning. It was, however, an appointment that Shelton would be unable to keep.

Eleanor Holmes Hindhaugh Vest, the wife of Thomas Edmund Vest, lived at 66 Back Elliott Street, Felling, and was one of Ruth Rodgers' sisters. She had chosen January 29th to visit Ruth at her place of work, the offices of the City Floorcloth & Linoleum Co, Forth House, in Pink Lane, Newcastle, and after a short conversation, Ruth had asked Eleanor to call at their mother's house; 30 Abbey Street, Gateshead, where Ruth still lived, and pass on a message. Eleanor was happy to oblige and told Ruth that she would see her there later that night.

It was at around 7.10pm that Eleanor, by now installed at her mother's house at Abbey Street, heard a heavy knocking at the front door. She went to answer it but halfway down the hall, heard the unmistakable sound of someone moaning outside. Dashing towards the door, she threw it open to discover to her horror that her sister Ruth was lying curled up on the floor with her head close to the doorstep. Eleanor crouched down and cradled Ruth's head whereupon she heard a male voice she recognised.

Thomas Shelton, standing in the roadway, shouted, "I've done her in Mrs Rodgers. I've done her in. I've done her in." Eleanor gently rested Ruth's head on the pavement again, ran over to where Shelton stood and demanded to know what he had done. Shelton made no answer so Eleanor returned to her sister's side and with the help of other members of the family carried the stricken woman inside and upstairs to the bedroom.

In fact, there were two people who had witnessed exactly what had taken place between Thomas Shelton and Ruth Rodgers. Beatrice Ivy Scarth lived at 18 Abbey Street and had known Ruth for some considerable time. She also knew Shelton and had seen the lovers together on a number of occasions. At 7.05pm on this particular day, she was returning home and as she turned into Abbey Street, she saw Ruth and Thomas together, near number 30. Beatrice walked to her own home, unlocked the door and put the parcels she was carrying inside the hallway before going back outside. As she turned to look up the street, Beatrice saw Ruth run into the middle of the road. Immediately Shelton ran after Ruth and grabbed hold of her. A struggle followed, ending when Ruth broke away from Shelton and fell to the ground, moaning as she did so.

Beatrice's first thought was that Ruth was having some kind of fit so she ran over to see if she could help. As Beatrice drew nearer, she saw Shelton fall on top of Ruth. Within seconds, Shelton was up again and now he, too, was groaning. Beatrice, meanwhile, raised Ruth's head and shoulders and tried to get her to her feet but was unable to do so. Then she saw that Ruth had blood on the right side of her face, so she helped her to her doorway and once Eleanor Vest appeared, Beatrice helped her to take Ruth inside. Only later, when Beatrice returned downstairs and saw a bloodstained razor, did she realise that she had just witnessed Thomas Shelton cut Ruth's throat.

The second witness was Percy Makin Sale, a man who was lodging temporarily at number 34 Abbey Street. He was leaving that address just seconds after the initial attack had taken place. Sale saw a man lying down near number 30 and dashed across to help him to his feet. He asked the man if he was all right but the only reply he received was a gurgle. At this point the door to number 28 was also opened and after shouting for assistance, Sale helped take the injured man into that house, before running off to fetch a doctor.

Number 28 was a house occupied by John and Annie Carr. They had been startled by someone knocking violently on their front door, so lighting a candle Annie went to see who it was. As the door opened, Shelton staggered forward, helped in by Percy Sale, and Annie heard Shelton mumble, "I've killed Ruth…done it with a razor." Annie Carr took Shelton into her kitchen where she placed him in a chair and noticed for the first time that he was bleeding from a wound in his throat. She wrapped a cloth around Shelton's throat to staunch the bleeding. For his part, Shelton was silent for a few minutes but then, in a low voice, asked, "Is she dead?" Then Annie sat with the injured Shelton until her husband arrived.

It was 7.50pm by the time Dr Samuel Vernon Robinson, the police surgeon, arrived at Abbey Street, where he was met by Inspector Thomas Moore. At number 28 he saw Shelton lying on the floor, suffering from a superficial wound to his neck. The doctor also visited number 30, where he examined Ruth Rodgers and confirmed that life was extinct. Shelton's wound was dressed before he was taken to hospital, accompanied by Inspector Moore.

Moore had arrived at the scene some time after 7.15pm. He made an examination of the area, finding fresh pools of blood in the street. The door to number 30 was open and nearby Moore found a closed razor, covered in blood. He also saw a lady's handbag and a right-hand glove, both heavily blood-stained. Outside the door to number 28 Moore saw a hat, also badly stained.

It was inside this latter house that Moore saw Shelton. The man was only partly conscious and Moore saw that he had received some basic medical attention and was not in a serious condition. Then he went next door and saw Ruth Rodgers who died a few minutes later. Moore then returned to where Shelton was and waited for the doctor to arrive.

At the hospital, Inspector Moore found that Shelton was carrying a number of letters on his person. One was addressed to his mother, one to Mrs Rodgers, Ruth's mother, and another addressed 'to whom it may concern'. These letters all said much the same thing: that Shelton considered Ruth to be his wife as they had been sleeping together for five years and he couldn't bear to lose her now.

It was not until February 9th, once he had been discharged from hospital, that Shelton was charged with murder at Gateshead police station. The first police court hearing took place the same day, when Shelton, wearing a smart blue suit but with his neck wound covered by a thick silk muffler, made no reply to the charge. He looked pale and had to be supported through the brief hearing by a police officer who later helped him down to the cells after a seven-day remand had been granted. The second hearing, was on February 16th, and this was when Shelton was sent for trial.

The trial of Thomas Henry Shelton took place on March 5th, 1925, at Durham, before Mr Justice Acton. Mr G.F. Mortimer and Mr Ronald Powell appeared for the prosecution, while Mr Archibald Wilson represented Shelton.

One of the first witnesses was Hannah Quigley who worked as a laundry manageress for the Gateshead Industrial Co-operative Society. She had known Shelton for some two and a half years, as a customer of the laundry, and when he came in they often chatted about his family and his sweetheart, Ruth. Hannah now testified that Shelton had come in to the laundry on Saturday, December 27th, 1924. She remembered the occasion particularly because they normally closed at 6.00pm. Shelton was five minutes late and apologised profusely.

Hannah went to fetch Shelton's laundry and after she handed it over, he said that he would walk along Jackson Street with her, she having already mentioned that she needed to go to the Post Office in West Street. Hannah pointed out that this was in the opposite direction to where Shelton lived but he said he would catch the tramcar at the bottom of the road.

It was during that walk along Jackson Street that Shelton mentioned that he had argued with Ruth. He said that she had started going out at night without him and had refused to tell him where she was going. She had joined some kind of club, although he had no idea which one, but this concerned him and as he said, "I'm afraid she might go wrong with somebody else by going to this club." Shelton went on to say that he was convinced Ruth was seeing someone else and added ominously, "If I don't get her, nobody else will."

Shelton had called at the laundry on a few occasions since that date, but he had never spoken about Ruth again. His last visit had taken place on January 29th, the date of Ruth's death. He stood in silence for five full minutes, looking down at the ground and seemed to be preoccupied. Hannah, thinking he might be ill, asked him if he was off work. He replied that he had been off for three days but no one at home knew it. He then muttered, "I will see her at dinner time," although he had not specified to whom he was referring. A minute or so later he produced a razor, placed it in the palm of his hand and said, "Look at that." Hannah, told him not to be silly, and to think of his mother. Shelton put the razor away and Hannah assumed that whatever thoughts had occupied him, were now forgotten.

William Pearson was a book-keeper at the company where Ruth worked as a confidential clerk. He had known her ever since he started work there some three years before. On Wednesday, January 28th, at some time between 1.00pm and 1.15pm, he had noticed Shelton, who he knew by sight, pacing up and down near the County Hotel, opposite Newcastle Central Station. Shelton saw Pearson and came over to talk to him. "Where is Ruth?" Shelton had demanded. Pearson told him that she had left the office already. At this Shelton remarked, "She has dodged me again" He went on to say that he had telephoned the office and arranged to meet her, adding that since she was no longer wearing her ring, he could only assume that the engagement was off. Well into his stride by now, Shelton said that they were meant for each other and no one would have her if he couldn't. He ended, "I will do her in and myself also. I am not afraid of the consequences." Pearson could only advise Shelton to get back to his work, go out and enjoy himself and put the matter out of his mind. After all, there were plenty of other girls.

Shelton, though, ignored the remark and said that things had been all right between him and Ruth until Mr Shiel had come on to the scene. Before that, Shelton had been in the habit of meeting Ruth when she was on her way to the bank on company business. Now she had told him that he must not do this anymore as Mr Shiel had told her that he would report the matter if it continued. Shelton also mentioned a letter he had found when Ruth's handbag fell off a table. This letter was signed 'Walt.' Ruth had claimed this was from an old boyfriend, but Shelton knew that Shiel's first name was Walter and this had made him even more suspicious. Pearson said that it was a pity Shelton had not kept the letter as it would have proved what he had been saying. It was at this moment that Pearson noticed Ruth on the opposite side of the street, and pointed her out to Shelton, who immediately crossed over to join her.

Walter Shiel was the 45-year-old office manager at the linoleum company, having taken up that position on April 22nd, 1924. He testified that he knew Shelton, having seen him waiting for Ruth on a number of occasions. He had spoken to him for the first time around the beginning of January. It was on that day that, coincidentally, he and Ruth had caught the same tram to the Low Fell Terminus. She seemed upset at the time and he had tried to comfort her. When the tram arrived at the terminus, they remained together for perhaps 20 minutes before Shelton appeared. He had then asked Shiel if he was a married man and Shiel said he was, and that he had three children. Shelton appeared to be pleased at hearing that.

It was about a week later when Shiel next saw Shelton. Work had finished for the day, Shiel had been speaking to Ruth and as a matter of courtesy, said he would see her to the tramcar. They walked over the bridge to Gateshead and there bumped into Shelton. Shiel raised his hat and now walked on a few yards ahead. After a few minutes, Shelton had walked off and Shiel then escorted Ruth to the bottom of Abbey Street where he left her at around 7.20pm.

By January 26th, Ruth had told him that the problems she was having with Shelton were so serious, that Shiel advised her to tell someone in authority. The very next day, she showed him a letter which so alarmed him that he telephoned Ruth's sister Georgina and arranged to meet up with her and Ruth's mother to discuss the matter.

Finally, on the day of her death, Ruth had left work at around 6.10pm and that was the last time he had seen her.

Shiel denied emphatically that there had been anything improper between him and Ruth or that he had ever met her in secret, or that he had ever taken her to a club. However, at this point, Mr Wilson for the defence asked Shiel if it were true that since he had given evidence at the Gateshead police court, he had attempted to take his own life. The judge intervened and asked if it were necessary to deal with that matter and the question was not pursued.

Georgina Hindhaugh Rodgers was Ruth's sister and lived with her and their mother at Abbey Street. She testified that she had known Shelton for six years and that he and Ruth had been engaged for the past four. The couple had argued over the festive season and for a time, Shelton was not welcome at their house, but he and Ruth had made things up on New Year's Day and he had since visited Ruth at home again, the last occasion being January 28th.

It was on that same day, January 28th, at 11.00am, that Walter Shiel had telephoned Georgina and arranged a meeting between her and her mother. Some time after that meeting had taken place, she was about to board a tramcar in Durham Road, Gateshead, when she heard Shelton call out to her. The two of them then went for a walk down Durham Road and West Street.

Shelton knew that she had met Shiel earlier and wanted to know what had been said. Georgina replied that she wished to hear both sides of the story before deciding for herself what exactly was going on. By now they had reached the Town Hall and it was here that Shelton issued more threats against Ruth, adding that he thought Shiel had some kind of hold over her.

Shelton then showed her a letter which read, "Dear Tom, It must be plain to you that things have not been what they should for a considerable time, and it has therefore come to this, that in the interests of us both, we should part. As I have repeatedly told you that I should never marry you, will I hope be sufficient reason, so that you may look for someone else to share your companionship. We shall, of course, part friends. Nothing more can be said as I am determined to choose and keep my own friendships. Yours sincerely, Ruth."

At 8.30pm that night, Georgina arrived home to find Ruth and Shelton already there. They seemed friendly enough but about half an hour later, Shelton drew Georgina's attention to a piece of paper in a music book. Georgina withdrew the paper to find that it was a note, in Shelton's handwriting, saying that there was another 'chap' in Ruth's life, asking her to find out for him who it was, and asking her to write on the bottom when they could meet and discuss the matter further. Georgina wrote that she did not think she would be able to find out anything, but would see him at the house on Friday night. Soon afterwards, Shelton left and Ruth saw him out, spending five minutes with him at the door.

John Clemo Trotter, the private investigator Shelton had visited, had read reports of the killing of Ruth Rodgers in his local newspaper and came forward to tell the police what Shelton had told him. He had had no time to make enquiries into Ruth's circumstances and could only add that at the time of their conversation, Shelton seemed to be excited and very jealous.

Albert McAttee was an 18-year-old apprentice carpet salesman at the same company as Ruth. He had seen Shelton waiting for Ruth although he didn't know the man to speak to. On January 29th, Albert left work at the same time as Ruth, around 6.10pm and they walked up Pink Lane together. They had not gone very far when Albert saw Shelton, who came over and joined Ruth. They walked off together and appeared to be quite friendly with each other, although Albert noticed that Shelton seemed to have 'a strange, vacant stare'.

Ruby Winifred Banns also worked with Ruth and had known her for seven years. Indeed, Ruby had even been at Ruth's engagement party four years before and had often seen her and Shelton together. On December 17th, Ruby and Ruth were at a dance at the Heaton Assembly Rooms. It was there Shelton demanded that Ruby tell him which club Ruth was going to. Ruby replied that she knew nothing about any club and for the rest of the night, he and Ruth did not seem to be very friendly with each other.

In early January, Ruby saw Shelton in Pink Lane and he asked her if she knew Ruth's whereabouts. Told that she had already left, Shelton told Ruby that Ruth had changed towards him and that she no longer wanted to marry him. As a result, he was miserable and unable to sleep.

Charles William Taylor was an omnibus driver of 47 Frank Street, Gateshead. He had known Shelton for three months, although not by name. On January 18th, Taylor was on a bus from Gateshead to Newcastle and Shelton was one of his passengers. They fell into conversation and Shelton told him that he had had a row with his girl.

On January 29th, at 6.30am Taylor saw Shelton, wearing work-clothes, on his way down High Street. Once more they chatted and Shelton said that he had argued with Ruth again. Threats were issued and Shelton told Taylor of a letter he had found. It was from a married man and asked Ruth to leave Shelton and go to him.

Later that same day, at some time between 10.00am and 10.30am, Taylor saw Shelton again. He was on the bus going into Newcastle and announced that he was going to try to see Ruth when she was on her way to the bank. By 1.30pm, though, Shelton was on the bus back to Gateshead. Taylor saw him twice more that day and on the last occasion, Shelton, who was now dressed in better clothes, told him that he had been to see a private detective and was going to have Ruth watched at night.

Inspector Moore produced the letters found on Shelton, together with a diary in which Shelton had written, "Things concerning Miss Ruth Rodgers." In the letter to his mother, Shelton had written, "I will see you in Heaven." and to Ruth's mother, he had asked her to bury them together adding, "Ruth is mine forever."

Samuel Robinson, the police surgeon, had also performed the post-mortem on Ruth's body. He described a wound which started two inches below her left ear and ran for four and a half inches towards the right. The sterno mastoid muscle had been cleanly cut, as had the jugular vein and common carotid artery. The surgeon also reported that Ruth appeared to have been a virgin.

A statement was read out from Dr James Stanley Johnson, a house surgeon to Mr Leech at the Royal Victoria Hospital. He had examined Shelton once he had been admitted and said that he had a three inch wound but this was not serious. Shelton was discharged on February 9th and throughout his stay had seemed to be unnaturally cheerful and unconcerned. Finally, Dr Robert Stuart, the medical officer of Durham prison, said that although Shelton had attempted suicide once, some years before, there was no sign of insanity.

No evidence was called by the defence and in his summing up, Mr Wilson suggested that although there could be no doubt that Shelton took the life of Ruth Rodgers, there was enough evidence to suggest that both before and after the crime, Shelton was not responsible for his actions. In the event, it took the jury one and a quarter hours to decide that Shelton was guilty. Asked if he had anything to say, Shelton spoke in feeble tones, "Shiel is the trouble; that is the man."

Shelton's appeal was heard on March 30th. Mr Wilson maintained that the judge's summing up was misleading in that he had failed to direct the jury on vital matters which might have favourably affected the jury in favour of his client. The Lord Chief Justice stated that Shelton had been heard to issue threats by more than one witness and had then carried those threats out. There was nothing in the appeal and the original verdict and sentence must stand.

Whilst Shelton waited in the condemned cell, his widowed mother, who had been in poor health for some time, finally passed away. Neither this, nor a petition for a reprieve, moved the Home Secretary of the day and in due course, Shelton became resigned to his fate.

The execution of Thomas Henry Shelton took place at 8.00am at Durham prison on Wednesday, April 15th, 1925. Shelton walked firmly to the scaffold and was hanged alongside Henry Graham who had killed his wife at Sunderland. Due to this circumstance, the hangman, Thomas Pierrepoint, had three assistants. The principle one was William Willis but also present were Henry Pollard and Lionel Mann, possibly so that they could gain some practical experience.

At the subsequent inquest on both men, the coroner, Mr John Graham, stated that he was opposed to capital punishment, believing that a man who committed murder was by definition abnormal and should be confined behind bars for life. It would be many years before Mr Graham's wishes became law.

CHAPTER EIGHTEEN

FAMILY TIES

THE HOUSE at 6 Silver Street, Newcastle, was home to no fewer than three families in 1926. On the ground floor lived Mrs Bruce and her family. The first floor housed James and Margaret Courtney and on the top floor lived the Scott family who consisted of George and Catherine Scott and their children, 21-year-old John, 15-year-old Ellen and Catherine, the eldest, who was a married woman. Her surname was Smith and her three children, one aged almost eight, another six years old and a baby, just a few months old, also lived at Silver Street.

Although Catherine was only 26, she had already had a fairly colourful and eventful personal life. She was first married in August 1918, to a man named David Weddell. They had never actually lived together, because Weddell had married Catherine at the Gateshead Registry Office but had refused to go through another ceremony in a Roman Catholic Church. Nevertheless, four months after the wedding, Catherine had given birth to her first child.

On June 10th, 1921, Catherine had given birth again but this time the father was a tramcar conductor named Ernest Long. Catherine had been to court and taken out a bastardy order against Long, who was ordered to pay the mother 10s 0d a week. As a result of this liaison, Catherine's legal husband, David Weddell, divorced her.

It was some time in 1924 that Catherine started seeing another man, 23-year-old James Smith. He was already known to the family and indeed Catherine's mother had known him for many years. The couple married, or at least they said they had married, in January 1925, at the Newcastle Registry Office, although there is no official record of this ceremony. What is true is that after this 'wedding' had taken place, Catherine's mother, who rented out seven rooms at 23 Silver Street, allowed James Smith and her daughter to move in there. The Roman Catholic service which Catherine considered so important, took place at St Andrew's Church in April 1925.

Even before this Catholic marriage, however, trouble had broken out between the newly-weds. Catherine Scott visited her daughter in February 1925, after hearing that there had been an argument between them. She found her daughter sporting a black eye and noticed that there were finger marks on her throat. Catherine Scott acted at once, ordering James Smith to get out of her property, which he duly did, and the new Mrs Smith moved back in with her family at 6 Silver Street. In due course, the couple did get back together, living first at New Gateshead and then later moving in with Smith's mother at 40 Dog Bank, Newcastle.

In June 1925, James Smith, who was a ship's fireman by trade, went to sea and Catherine Smith once more moved back in with her family at Silver Street. It was not until February 1926 that he returned to Newcastle and the couple then moved back to New Gateshead but the arguments started again and as a result, it was only two weeks later that Smith returned to his mother, and Catherine returned to hers.

When he visited his wife at Silver Street and argued with her, he found the rough edge of his mother-in-law's tongue. The trouble, it seemed, had arisen because Smith believed Catherine was seeing other men. She denied the allegation, protesting that she had been faithful to him ever since their marriage. In December 1925, she had given birth to her third child. There was no doubt, she said, that James was the father.

For a time, James Smith, who was by now claiming dole money, visited his wife and child at least once a week and handed over 7s 0d towards their upkeep. There were still frequent arguments between man and wife as James Smith would not now accept that the baby was indeed his. Catherine Smith swore that it was, but the rows continued and whenever the two were together, the atmosphere was one of heightened tension.

On April 18th, 1926, Catherine Scott visited her property at 23 Silver Street and found a number of men, one of whom was her son-in-law, James Smith, gambling in the yard. Mrs Scott did not approve and told them to get out. Initially they did as they were told but when they returned and resumed their gambling, Catherine Scott contacted the police who put a stop to the betting and noted down the names of some of those present. James Smith, however, managed to escape the clutches of the law and his name was not taken by the police.

The next afternoon, after the public houses had closed, and shortly after 3.00pm Catherine Scott heard Smith and some other men shouting from Pilgrim Street, a thoroughfare which her house overlooked. Mrs Scott went to the window and upon seeing her, James Smith and some of his gambling friends began shouting abuse at her.

Seeing that her husband was involved, Catherine Smith went downstairs with her mother and her sister, Ellen. James Smith was told to go away as he was only aggravating the situation. He would agree, he said, but only if his wife went back to live with him. Smith raised his hands as if to strike his wife and, seeing that the situation might well get out of control, Mrs Scott now returned to her house to get her shawl, her intention being to go to the police station again. Catherine Smith decided to stay with Margaret Courtney on the first floor but her sister Ellen did accompany her mother.

Mrs Scott had not walked very far when she met Constable Turnbull at the junction of Pilgrim Street and Mosley Street. She told him what had happened but by the time the officer had accompanied her back to Silver Street, the group of men had dispersed. James Smith, though, had entered the property and was now in Mr and Mrs Courtney's home with his wife.

As Mrs Scott and her youngest daughter walked into the Courtneys' home, they heard James and Catherine Smith arguing yet again. The husband appeared to be very drunk and was frothing at the mouth as he screamed at his wife. Once again he was demanding that Catherine come back to him and in an attempt to cool the situation, Margaret Courtney suggested that he find a place for them so that they would have somewhere to go to. At this point, Catherine Smith added that he should come for her when he had some money to his name. Mrs Scott said that it would be better if he left and Margaret tried to emphasise the point by gently pushing him towards the door. His response was immediate and frightening, for he drew out a dagger and shouted, "I'll do the ****ing lot of you in." He did, however, allow James Courtney, Margaret's husband, to escort him to the front door but as he left, Smith turned, looked at his wife and said, "If I get you out here, I'll do you in."

For a time, things quietened down. Mrs Scott did see her son-in-law in the street on April 20th, but he did not cause any problems and just walked past the house. It was not until some time after 2.00pm on Monday, April 26th, that James Smith once more knocked on the Scotts' door at 6 Silver Street. Mrs Scott answered the door and reminded him that he had been told to stay away. Catherine Smith was sitting by the fire, gently rocking her baby back and forth, and her husband asked, "Kitty, can I speak to you?" His wife placed her child into its cradle and said that she would talk to him. He seemed calm enough and she might be able to reason with him. Catherine Smith went outside on to the landing and Mrs Scott closed the living room door behind them so that they might have some privacy. She then sat by the fire and began to read the newspaper. Shortly, Ellen Scott returned home and passed the couple on the landing. She entered the flat and sat reading with her mother, by the fire. It was perhaps five or six minutes later that the noise of something falling reached Mrs Scott's ears. Almost immediately, Catherine Smith's head appeared around the door and she cried out that the 'staircase was falling'.

Mrs Scott took little notice. The plaster on the stairs was always dropping off and she thought that her daughter was referring to this. Silence reigned again for a minute or two then Mrs Scott heard her daughter shout, "Mother!" This time her voice was loud and piercing and Catherine Scott ran to see what was happening. As she reached the landing, she saw Smith dragging his wife down the first flight of stairs by her hair. He was pulling her with his left hand. In his right, he held a dagger and to her horror, Mrs Scott saw that Catherine was bleeding badly from the area around her shoulder blade.

Then James Smith released his wife and ran down the stairs. She tried to get up and cried, "Oh Mother, I'm done. He's stabbed me." With that she collapsed back on to the stairs as Ellen came out of the flat, saw what had happened and ran off to summon a policeman.

James Smith had not run very far. Francis Patrick Simon was a grocer who ran a shop at 223 Pilgrim Street. He was walking down Pilgrim Street at the time of the attack upon Catherine Smith ran towards him in a zig-zag, erratic fashion and appeared to be foaming at the mouth. Seeing Simon, who had known him since his childhood, Smith stopped, threw his arms around Simon's neck, hugged him and asked him to fetch a policeman. Simon pushed Smith away, whereupon James said, "I have done her." He then handed over the blood-stained dagger.

Believing that he might do more good if he attended the injured woman, Francis Simon left Smith where he was and ran to the Scott's house in Silver Street. There Simon saw Catherine Smith lying on her right side on the staircase. She appeared to be unconscious and made no reply when Simon spoke to her. He searched for a pulse and finding one, bunched up Catherine's green silk jumper and pressed the area around the wound in an attempt to stop the bleeding. Simon was still in this position when Smith returned in the company of a police officer, also named Smith. James Smith moved forward, bent down and kissed Catherine but she still did not stir.

Winifred Hardy lived at 3 Silver Street, and was naturally curious when she saw people running into number 6. She saw James Smith standing on the corner as a policeman approached him. The officer asked her to go to the Central police station for assistance. In due course, help arrived in the form of Constable Archibald Scott, who helped Constable Smith to take the prisoner to the police station, and Sergeant Joseph Bird and Constable Watson, who together helped take Catherine to the ambulance. By the time she reached hospital, she was dead and James Smith was facing a charge of murder.

The inquest on Catherine Smith opened before the coroner, Sir Alfred Appleby, on April 27th, when evidence of identification was heard. The proceedings were then adjourned until April 30th, when a verdict of murder against James Smith was returned. Smith made a number of appearances in the Newcastle police court, the evidence being finally heard over two days, May 18th and 19th, when he was sent for trial.

The case against James Smith was heard at Newcastle on July 2nd, 1926, before Mr Justice Wright. Smith was defended by Mr Archibald Wilson while the prosecution case was put by Mr Russell Vick.

In addition to giving details of the relationship between her daughter and James Smith, Catherine Scott told how Francis Simon and James Courtney had helped to carry her daughter up the stairs to the landing so that she could be attended to more easily. As Simon entered the house, he carried with him the bloody dagger that Smith had used and he now handed this over to Margaret Courtney. Margaret had handed the dagger to Mrs Scott and she put it inside her flat for safekeeping. When Constable Smith arrived, Mrs Scott handed the weapon over to him saying, "There's the dagger and there's my bairn's life blood on it." She had then turned to James and said, "You've killed my poor bairn" to which he had replied that he 'couldn't help it'.

Mrs Scott told the court that James Smith had been very jealous of her daughter but there had been no foundation in his suspicions. Catherine Smith rarely went out without her mother. Referring to the incident of April 19th when Smith and his friends had been shouting abuse in the street, Mrs Scott said that the reason her daughter had stayed behind with Mrs Courtney was because she was afraid of James and what he might do.

George Scott, Catherine's father, testified that his daughter had left Smith four times since their marriage, the final split taking place in February, 1926. On the day of Catherine's death, he had gone to work at 7.30am. Later in the day, at 3.20pm, Ellen had arrived at his work with a message telling him to go home as Smith had stabbed Kitty. Arriving at Silver Street he found that his daughter had been rushed to the Royal Victoria Infirmary. By the time he got there, Catherine was dead and he had made the formal identification of her body.

Ellen Scott, the dead woman's sister, told what she had seen on April 26th. At 1.50pm Ellen had gone on an errand, not returning to her home until about 2.20pm or later. She saw the couple talking on the landing and at the time they did not appear to be quarrelling. Ellen went inside the flat and sat down near her mother until they both heard the terrible scream from outside. Ellen saw Catherine on the stairs as Smith dashed out into the street and tried to follow him, but by the time she got outside, he had vanished. A minute or two later, Ellen saw Mr Simon approaching, carrying the dagger.

Looking further in that same direction, she saw James Smith standing on the corner of Silver Street with his hands in his pockets. Ellen walked past him without speaking and went to find a policeman. Returning with Constable Smith, Ellen saw James Smith, who was now standing under the railway bridge, and pointed him out. Constable Smith immediately took him into custody. Ellen then returned to her home with the policeman who was now escorting her brother-in-law.

Ellen continued by saying that ever since their wedding, James and Catherine Smith had argued. He drank far too much and never seemed to give his wife enough money. Referring to the events of April 18th, she explained that she was with her mother when they found Smith and others playing cards in a wash house at 23 Silver Street. She was also with her mother when they went for the police on April 19th after Smith, who was very drunk at the time, began shouting from Pilgrim Street.

Margaret Courtney told the court how she had heard the abuse Smith shouted on April 19th. At the time he appeared to be excited and rather drunk. When Catherine Smith went outside with her mother and sister, Margaret saw him attempt to strike his wife two or three times, but each time he missed her. Later, when Mrs Scott went for the police, Catherine and the baby waited in her flat but Smith opened the door and walked in without knocking. Smith had said to his wife, "Now Kate, I intend to get a room," to which Catherine had replied, "When you get work, I will go with you."

When Mrs Scott and Ellen returned, a new argument began and Smith claimed that Catherine was arranging to meet another man. Catherine said that he was a liar whereupon the knife had been produced and Smith had threatened to kill everyone. Luckily they managed to get him outside and Margaret Courtney did not see James Smith again until the day of Catherine's death.

On that day, Margaret was lying in bed in the kitchen when

she heard a scream coming from the staircase. Rushing outside she saw Catherine Smith lying on the stairs being supported by her mother. Catherine was still conscious and seeing Margaret had said, "Oh Maggie, he has stabbed me." Those were the last words that she heard Catherine utter and soon afterwards she slipped into unconsciousness. Mrs Courtney then told how Mr Simon had returned and handed her a bloodstained dagger. She had later passed this on to Mrs Scott.

James Courtney said he had known Catherine Smith for 11 or 12 years and had never seen her drunk. He had been present when Smith burst into his flat on April 19th, and brandished the dagger. Courtney had bravely taken hold of Smith's sleeve and said, "What is the use of going on like that?" He finally managed to get Smith out of the house and said that as he left, he was still carrying the dagger and had begun frothing at the mouth.

Turning to the events of April 26th, James Courtney had been called out by his wife after they had both heard the scream. He had been shaving in the kitchen and had heard no disturbance prior to this. Later he saw Francis Simon with the dagger and it had been he and Mr Simon who carried Catherine up to the next landing. When Smith reappeared, Courtney had said to him, "What have you done this for man?" and Smith had replied, "I could not help it. She made me do it."

Francis Simon repeated the evidence he had given at the inquest and the police court. He also described how, when he saw him, James Smith was crying and made no effort to get away. He added that he had seen soldiers in France during the Great War behave in much the same way when they were suffering from shell shock.

Police Constable Michael Hedley Smith said that he had been on point duty at the corner of Mosley Street and Pilgrim Street, at around 2.50pm on April 26th, when he was told what had happened and went towards Silver Street. On the way,

James Smith was pointed out to him. Constable Smith approached the man and asked, "Are you Smith?" He had replied, "Yes, I have killed Kate. I am very sorry." He was taken into custody and escorted back to Silver Street. Later still, when Smith was being taken to the Central police station, he kept repeating, "She made me do it." It was at the police station that Smith was searched and the sheath which had contained the dagger was found on his person.

Ann Leonard lived in Silver Street and also worked as a housekeeper for John Larman whose house was opposite an alleyway which led to 6 Silver Street. Before the street arguments of April 19th, Ann had been approached by Smith who asked her if she knew if his wife had given his name to the police over the gambling.

Ann knew the family well and said that Catherine had said nothing. To this Smith had replied that Catherine was, "…not so bad, it's that swine of a mother."

On April 26th, Ann Leonard was looking through her window when she saw Smith staggering down the alleyway that led to number 6. Although he was walking as if he was drunk, she did not think he could be as she had seen him earlier, at around noon, and he was certainly sober then.

Some minutes later she heard a shout and ran to the alleyway to meet Smith coming the other way. He was saying, "Oh, I have done it. I cannot keep it." She did not see anything in his hand at the time but he seemed to be in an emotional state and was almost falling down. He certainly appeared to be very drunk.

Charles Edward Pearson was a friend of Mrs Bruce who also lived at 6 Silver Street. On April 26th, he visited the house but found that Mrs Bruce was not at home. Her door was unlocked, though, so he waited inside her rooms for her to return. He heard a scuffle of some kind on the stairs, followed by a cry of, "Mother!" He knew Catherine Smith well and recognised her voice. After going outside, Pearson saw James

Smith standing on the corner and was still watching as Constable Smith and Ellen approached him.

Alexander Jamieson was a ship's fireman and he testified that James Smith had signed on the SS *Newminster* on April 20th. They had sailed to Hamburg and returned to Gateshead at 9.00am on April 26th. The two carried on working on the ship until 12.30pm when they went to the Henry IV public house in Gateshead where they had three drinks. By 1.00pm they had left this pub and moved on to the Golden Tiger in Pilgrim Street where they had a couple more pints. They parted at 1.20pm when Jamieson boarded a tramcar to go home.

Dr Thomas Henry Blench, the police surgeon, described the wounds that Catherine Smith had suffered. There was one wound two inches below her left collar bone and six wounds in her back towards the base of her ribs. Later he examined Smith at the police station. He seemed to be dazed but could not be described as drunk. His unsteadiness might well have been caused by a mental disturbance or by emotion.

Weldon Patrick Tyrone Watts was the resident medical officer at the Royal Victoria Infirmary. Catherine Smith had been admitted at 3.20pm on April 26th and was dead on arrival. Her clothing was soaked in blood and the cause of death was shock due to haemorrhage. Cross-examined about Smith's possible mental state at the time of the attack, Dr Watts stated that an acute mental disturbance could cause a person to froth at the mouth as Smith had done.

One of the final witnesses was the pathologist who had performed the post-mortem. Dr Ralph Patterson Smith was later asked if malaria could cause incipient madness and said that he had heard that it was possible. At this point, the trial judge, Mr Justice Wright intervened and asked, "Are people subject to great fury when they are not mad?" Dr Smith agreed that this could be the case.

The jury retired to consider their verdict and, not

surprisingly, decided that James Smith was guilty. As he was being sentenced to death, Smith took a photograph from his pocket and gazed at it tenderly.

Smith's appeal was heard on July 26th. The grounds were that at the time of the attack, he had exhibited signs of insanity. Rejecting the appeal, the Lord Chief Justice stated that it would have been astonishing if the trial jury had not rejected that defence and as such, there was nothing in the application and the appeal was lost.

Efforts to obtain a reprieve failed. On the morning of Tuesday, August 10th, 1926, James Smith rose early but ate none of the breakfast which had been provided. At 9.00am he walked unaided to the execution chamber at Durham prison where he was hanged by Thomas Pierrepoint, who was assisted by Thomas Phillips. It was the first time that a man sentenced to death at Newcastle, had been executed at Durham.

CHAPTER NINETEEN

MEDICAL OPINION

POLICE Sergeant William Alexander Grigor and Constable George Thomas Unwin were strolling down Scotswood Road, Newcastle upon Tyne, at 10.10pm on the night of Thursday, May 9th, 1929, when a woman approached them. She identified herself as Mary Annie Johnson and complained that her husband had just assaulted her. A message was sent to the local police station and another officer, Constable Thomas Gray, was sent by motorcycle to the address she had given his colleagues.

Meanwhile, the other two officers accompanied Mary back to her home at 68 Cannon Street, and there found a number of people including her husband, 43-year-old James Johnson, who was sitting in a chair in the kitchen. Soon after they had arrived, Constable Gray joined them and the three policemen now listened to Mary Johnson's complaint. At one stage, she walked over to where her husband kept his overcoat hanging on a hook behind the kitchen door. Drawing out a pearl handled razor, she showed it to Constable Unwin saying, "This is what he keeps for me." Meanwhile, Constable Gray had noticed that Johnson was apparently sporting a fresh head wound. Asked about this, he said that he was not sure exactly what had happened but Mary admitted that she had struck him with a rolling pin during their argument.

Sergeant Grigor took the razor from Mary and handed it over to her married daughter, 20-year-old Agnes Mitchell, for safekeeping before advising the couple that if they could not live peaceably together, then it might be better if they separated. It was at this point that James Johnson stood up and asked the sergeant if he would go into the bedroom with him as there was something he wished to tell him in private.

The two men went into the next room, along with another of Johnson's daughters, Nancy, who was aged 13½. Here Johnson admitted that he had only been out of prison for some six weeks adding, "Since I came home, I have been told that while I was in prison, my wife was carrying on with Billy Ridley." James Johnson turned to Nancy and said, "Tell the policeman." Nancy did not speak but nodded her confirmation that what her father had said was true.

At that point, Agnes Mitchell entered the room and she too, confirmed that while her father had been away, Ridley had stayed there for six weeks but she did not believe that anything had been going on between him and her mother. Ridley had once worked for her father, as a clerk, and had needed lodgings while Johnson had been in prison. He had stayed as a lodger, sleeping alone in the small bedroom. Indeed, since James Johnson's suspicions had been made public, Ridley had sent him a rather abusive letter, denying that there had been any untoward behaviour between him and Mary. Whatever the truth of all this, the entire affair was, of course, just another tiresome domestic dispute. The police officers spoke to both James and Mary Johnson and eventually matters were calmed down and the couple were left to their own devices.

James Johnson had told the police that he had not long been out of prison and, indeed, that was the case. In fact, he had quite a long criminal record. His first court appearance came on November 7th, 1917, when he was fined 10s 0d for gaming. Since Johnson was a bookmaker by trade, such offences were perhaps to be expected and his next two court appearances were also connected with that trade. On October 14th, 1921, he was fined £10 for paying out bets and on July 3rd, 1924, another prosecution for betting cost him a fine of £20.

On March 13th, 1925, he was found guilty of being drunk and disorderly, for which he was fined 20s. Just two months later, on May 19th, he was fined £5 for common assault when he slashed a man with a razor during an argument. His next appearance was on January 26th, 1926, when he was fined 10s 0d for using indecent language and another charge of drunk and disorderly followed on December 2nd, 1927. For that offence he was fined a further 20s. Betting was once more the charge on July 25th, 1928, when for two offences, Johnson was fined a total of £30. Finally, on December 27th of that same year, he received 60 days in prison for stealing purses.

After the incident of May 9th, things quietened down at 68 Cannon Street, until the early hours of Sunday, May 12th. On the previous night, May 11th, Mary and James Johnson and George Mitchell, Agnes' husband, had been in the Gun Tavern together. The Johnsons had gone home alone, arriving there at about 11.15pm, and the house soon fell silent.

At around 1.00am, however, Thomas Edward Held, who lived on the same floor as the Johnsons, heard a thud through the wall, followed by some low moans. Held's father, William, also heard the noises and went to wake George Atkinson Muckle, the next-door neighbour and Mary's brother-in-law. These two men tried to rouse the Johnsons but could get no reply to their knocking. Concerned for the safety of the family, they now forced James Johnson's front door, whereupon they detected a strong smell of gas. After the gas taps had been turned off, the police were called once more and again it was George Thomas Unwin who attended. Meanwhile, the three children, who had been semi-conscious when found, were taken into William Held's home where they made a full recovery.

There was, in fact, another child in the family, three-year-old Irene, but she had been unwell for some time and had been admitted to hospital on May 10th.

Inspector Arthur Purdue was on duty in Westgate Road and in response to a message from Constable Unwin, he went to Cannon Street, arriving at number 68, at around 2.10am. Looking through the premises by the aid of his torch, Purdue found James Johnson in bed in the larger bedroom. He was rather dazed and Purdue noticed that both his hands were bloodstained. In the same bedroom were Nancy Johnson, another daughter, eight-year-old Jenny and five-year-old James. In the smaller bedroom, Inspector Purdue found Mary Johnson lying dead on the bed. Her throat was cut and there was blood everywhere, on the bedclothes, mattress and floor. Purdue also noticed that the dead woman was barefoot and that her feet were clean.

The children and James Johnson were given medical attention. Purdue, meanwhile, continued his investigation and noticed that there was an open bloodstained razor lying on the dressing table in the smaller bedroom where Mary Johnson's body had been found. The chimney in the other bedroom had been blocked by means of a woman's skirt and there were footprints, in blood along the floor, which indicated an adult foot, wearing stockings. James Johnson was seen to be wearing a night-shirt, a pair of black woollen socks and a pair of drawers. The socks were caked in blood on the soles and the night-shirt and drawers were also heavily stained. James Johnson was now taken to the Central police station where, at 8.00pm that same day, he was charged with the murder of his wife. To this, Johnson shouted, "Never! My wife is not dead"

Inspector Purdue had, however, also found a letter at Cannon Street and this seemed to indicate that James Johnson was indeed guilty of murder. Addressed to George Muckle, the letter read, "Dear George, You know I have positive proof of my wife and B. Ridley being in bed together all night on one occasion if not more, but I have further proof that it has been going on for some time before he came to stay at my house with my wife and he stayed six weeks with her and she kept him that time for her own purpose. You know what that was for, improper purposes. My own daughters have told me about them sleeping together in the little room and she told them not to tell their father anything or they would be thrashed. I only hope the scoundrel will be punished for the ruin he has done here. I can't get him as I want to get her as well, so I am taking one out of the road. He has blackmailed her into this intrigue through threats about things that she was an innocent victim of and she has fell for it. Best of Luck, Yours, Jimmy Johnson."

In fact, James Johnson faced a total of five charges. In addition to the murder of his wife, he was charged with the attempted murder of Nancy, Jenny and James junior, and with attempted suicide. His first appearance at the police court was on May 13th and after a number of remands, he was sent for trial on all five charges.

The trial of James Johnson opened at Newcastle on July 2nd, 1929 and lasted two days. The case for the Crown was put by Mr Arthur Morley and Johnson was defended by Mr R.F. Burnand. The jury was all male and the judge was Mr Justice Finlay.

Many of the witnesses were police officers. Constable Unwin described the scene when he first entered the house. He also described the incident of May 9th when Mary had not wanted to stay in the house with her husband but had relented when her daughter, Agnes Mitchell, said she would stay too.

Sergeant George Frederick Black testified that he had examined the premises and had traced footprints, apparently made by stockinged feet which were covered in blood. These prints led from the small bedroom, through the large one and into the kitchen. Here there was a cupboard where the gas meter was kept and outside this cupboard there was a complete and clear footprint showing that they had been made by an adult.

Evidence was also given that there had been trouble between James and Mary Johnson before her death. On Friday, April 26th, Agnes Mitchell had visited her mother who told her that James had put the family cat into the gas oven, turned on the gas and gone out of the house. Fortunately, the cat had been rescued unharmed. On May 9th, Agnes also witnessed her father strike Mary with a soup ladle. More importantly perhaps, Agnes also testified that some years before, Johnson had been in the habit of switching on the gas taps in the bedroom and the children and Mary had switched them off. Surprisingly, such incidents were never referred to the following morning.

Kate Muckle, who was Mary Johnson's sister, also visited on May 9th and she saw Mary hit James with a rolling pin. In retaliation, James chased Mary with the poker and when Kate Muckle tried to intervene, she was struck by a milk bottle for her pains.

The problems arose when the medical evidence was heard. Dr George Edward Stephenson, the police surgeon, stated that wounds on the dead woman's hands showed that she had tried to defend herself. This meant that some sort of struggle had taken place and therefore, in Dr Stephenson's opinion, this was a case of homicide rather than suicide. This, though, conflicted with the findings of Dr Gerald Newton of Newcastle who was called by the defence.

Dr Newton noted that the wound which had caused Mary Johnson's death had only severed the external jugular vein and was, comparatively, a surface wound. In his opinion, although he could not positively rule out homicide, this was much more likely to be a case of suicide. If this had been a case of murder, he would have expected the fatal wound to be much deeper. Finally, Dr G.H. Shanley of Pelaw, again for the defence, stated that he had no doubt whatsoever that the wound had been self-inflicted. The court had therefore heard three doctors; one of whom said it was definitely murder, another who said it was definitely suicide and a third who said it could be either but was more likely to be suicide.

There could then only be two possibilities. Either James Johnson had murdered his wife over her affair with Ridley, and then tried to gas the children and himself, or Mary had taken her own life. The prosecution, of course, also had the letter to Muckle, and the fact that Mary would have had to have cut her throat, placed the razor down on the dressing table and then walked about her home, leaving a trail of bloody footprints as she did so. The jury took 20 minutes to decide that the first scenario was more likely, and James Johnson was adjudged to be guilty of wilful murder.

The judge asked him if he had anything to say before the sentence of death was passed. For a few seconds he did not speak but as the judge began the dread words of the sentence, Johnson choked out, "I wanted to speak." Mr Justice Finlay paused while Johnson said, "I haven't had a chance to explain several things. I've been ill since November and haven't had a chance. I didn't expect the case to finish so soon. I wanted more witnesses called, but they haven't been called." The trial, though, was over and James had been found guilty. The death sentence was then passed and it was noted that throughout this, and the pleadings of Johnson, one of the jurymen had been in tears.

James Johnson's appeal was heard on July 22nd, before the Lord Chief Justice, and Justices Avory and Branson. The grounds were that Johnson had not been physically fit enough to give evidence at his own trial and there had been other witnesses he had wished to call.

The Lord Chief Justice, giving the court's verdict, stated that the medical evidence showed that Johnson was not incapable of giving evidence and the other witnesses had apparently not been called because the defence had chosen not to do so. In the view of the judges, there was nothing in the appeal and it must be dismissed.

Back in the condemned cell, Johnson was visited by his two brothers, John and William, and to both he swore that he knew nothing of the crime and was innocent of the charge. Nevertheless, on August 5th, it was announced that the Home Secretary had found no reason to advise the King to reprieve Johnson, and the sentence would be carried out.

Early on the morning of Wednesday, August 7th, 1929, a crowd of around 100 people gathered outside Durham prison. Two of those people were Johnson's brothers who stood tearfully as the appointed hour approached. At 8.00am James Johnson was hanged by Thomas Pierrepoint. He never admitted that he was responsible for his wife's death.

CHAPTER TWENTY

MURDER OR MANSLAUGHTER

O N DECEMBER 26th, 1936, William Parker married Jane Ann Daley, also known as Jean, and soon afterwards, the couple moved in to 23 Edwin Street, Newcastle upon Tyne. Just three months later, on March 23rd, 1937, the union was blessed with the birth of a daughter, Theresa Shirley and less than a year after that, on February 15th, 1938, Jane Parker gave birth to a healthy son, Cecil Edward.

It was 10.30pm on the night of Monday, April 25th, 1938, when William Parker walked in to the Forest Hall police station and approached Sergeant Albert Reader who was on duty on the desk. Parker, who was wearing a blue suit, a white muffler, but no cap, announced, "I have something to say." Sergeant Reader prepared to make a note of what the gentleman wished to report but was shocked when Parker continued. "I think I have killed the wife. I hit her with a hammer on the head last Friday night." Parker then went on to tell Reader where this had taken place, whereupon he was cautioned and taken into custody.

Formally interviewed by Inspector James Taylor, Parker continued to expand upon his story by adding, "My wife, Jane Parker, strangled the two bairns, then she came to me with the poker and I hit her with a hammer several times. I don't know how many. I lost my senses." At that point, William Parker fainted.

Sergeant Reader and Inspector Taylor went to Parker's house at Edwin Street. Using the key which Parker had handed over, the two policemen entered the building where they found all too terrible confirmation that there were three dead bodies in the house.

Mrs Parker lay in the back bedroom, covered by three coats. She had been battered repeatedly about the head and a piece of string had been tightly knotted around her throat. The two children were in a front bedroom and both had string tied around their necks, although it was a different kind to that around their mother's. Inspector Taylor left Sergeant Reader with the bodies and went to fetch a doctor.

Back at the station, Parker had apparently recovered from his faint and began to talk to the officer who had been left to guard him, Constable Matthew Masterman Moore. Once again Parker claimed that his wife had attacked the children and he had defended himself when she came at him with a poker. Having rendered his wife unconscious, or perhaps having already killed her, he went to check on the children and found that they were both dead. He returned to where his wife lay, picked her up and carried her into the back bedroom.

Parker went on, "I suddenly remembered about the cord she had placed around the babies' necks and I did likewise and placed it around her's. After, I discovered she was dead." Constable Moore noted all that Parker said, although he asked him no questions and made no suggestion that the prisoner should make any further statement.

Inspector Taylor returned to the police station and informed Parker that he had seen the bodies of his wife and two children, after which Parker made a full statement detailing what he claimed had happened since the previous Friday night.

He said that on Friday, April 22nd, he had left the house at

9.00pm to get some cigarettes from Mitchinson's shop. When he left, his wife was sitting on a stool by the fire, nursing Theresa. The youngest child, Cecil, was asleep in his cot in the kitchen. Having made his purchase, Parker stood at the corner near the Ritz Picture Hall for a couple of minutes so that by the time he returned, it was about 9.15pm.

As he entered the house, Parker saw that his wife had Cecil by the throat and she shouted, "You're too late." He asked what she was doing but before she could answer, he saw the string tied around Cecil's throat. At this, Jane Parker threw the child into his cot, seized a poker and ran at her husband, lifting the poker as if to strike him. William Parker ran through the open scullery door and grabbed for the handle to slam the door behind him, thus keeping his wife at bay. Unfortunately he missed the handle so grabbed at the first article to hand, which happened to be a hammer.

By now, Jane was almost upon him but her blow with the poker just missed him. She raised the weapon for a second strike but Parker stepped back into the kitchen and as her next blow also swished harmlessly through the air, he struck out with the hammer. His first blow did not stop her so he continued to hit her, claiming that he lost control of his senses and was unaware of exactly how many times he lashed out.

Once Jane lay still on the kitchen floor, Parker carried the cot containing Cecil up to the front bedroom. Here he discovered that Cecil and Theresa were both dead so he covered them and returned to where Jane lay. She was apparently also dead so he carried her up to the back bedroom and covered her too. Having spent some time cleaning up the blood on the kitchen floor, Parker made no attempt to contact the authorities but spent that night sleeping in the front bedroom where the bodies of his children lay.

On the Saturday morning, Parker left the house at 10.00am and went up to the Northumberland golf course to act as a caddie. He remained there until 7.30pm, then travelled to Forest Hall where he spent some time just walking about. Eventually he entered the Old Picture Hall, just to occupy some time. Before he went in he saw Inspector Taylor and a sergeant at the end of Delavel Road and had intended to report what had happened to them, but seemed unable to pluck up the courage to do so.

After the picture show had finished, Parker walked around again until it was almost midnight. Then he went to his mother's house at 26 Myrtle Crescent, Forest Hall, where he spent that night. He rose at 8.40am on Sunday, washed and dressed and then returned to the golf course to caddie again. This time he stayed until 6.00pm when he called at Joe Crosby's shop at West Moor while on the way home. From there, Parker wandered around the streets until 7.15pm when he again went to the Old Picture House. He bought some apples and pears from Barker's shop which was next to the cinema and spoke to Charles Murphy, a neighbour, who was in the queue. Inside the pictures he sat next to John Langlands and after the pictures finished, he walked towards Forest Hall police station. Parker then went to Jerrard's fish shop, which happened to be near the police station, which he intended to go to, but he once again found that he could not go in and report the deaths of his wife and children.

Leaving the fish shop, Parker now passed through West Moor and for a time stood talking to Pete Halliday at Four Road Ends. By then it was 11.00pm and after Halliday had said goodnight, Parker sat on a seat for a few minutes before wandering through South Gosforth and Benton and on towards Wallsend. It was 2.00am on Monday by the time he returned to his mother's house. Sleeping there again, he rose at 7.00am, walked back through Benton and finally into Newcastle city centre. He looked around the shops before walking back to Gosforth High Street where he stole a bicycle. In fact, he had stood around watching the cycle for perhaps 30 minutes first, to see if anyone came back for it and when no one did, he rode off to Berwick. It was around 5.20pm by the time Parker arrived there. He stayed only a short time, contemplating his situation before going back home and finally walking into the police station.

This long and detailed document was taken down by Inspector Taylor, in the presence of Sergeant Reader. When it was complete, Parker signed it and was told that he would be charged with the murder of his wife. His first appearance at a special sitting of the Moot Hall police court took place the following morning, Tuesday, April 26th, when after hearing evidence of arrest, the magistrates remanded Parker for one week. The hearing had lasted less than 15 minutes.

On May 4th, Parker was back in the police court when a further remand was requested as the Director of Public Prosecutions was not in a position to proceed. On May 11th, Parker appeared again and this time the court was told that he faced two new charges. In addition to the murder of his wife, he was now accused of killing his children too. Another remand was granted and finally, on May 19th, the evidence was heard, the case for the prosecution being put by Mr E.G. Robey and Parker's defence resting in the hands of Mr Swinburne G. Wilson. In due course, William Parker was sent for trail on three charges of murder.

The trial opened on June 16th, at Newcastle, before Mr Justice Atkinson. Although three charges had been preferred, as is customary in English courts, evidence was to be heard on only one charge, that of the murder of Parker's wife, Jane. The case for the prosecution was led by Mr Russell Vick who was assisted by Mr Norman Harper, while Parker was defended by Mr G.H.B. Streatfeild and Mr Clifford Cohen. The charge was read out and Parker tightly gripped the ironwork of the dock as he replied, "Not guilty."

The early speeches outlined some of William Parker's history and circumstances. A miner by trade, Parker worked at the Weetslade Colliery where he earned 7s 9d per shift.

Unfortunately, he only chose to work some 75 per cent of the time and this had caused the family to suffer from financial problems.

Mrs Hildreth King lived in the flat below the Parkers. Over the past year she had become friendly with the family, often visiting them in their flat. Hildreth King said that although the children were well looked after, Jane Parker had often told her that they did not have enough money for food and as a result, the entire family were somewhat undernourished. To her knowledge, Parker had refused to go to work on 12 different days recently.

Mrs King heard the Parkers arguing over money, especially after Cecil had been born. On one occasion, when Cecil was just four days old, Mrs King had been present in the Parker's flat when they had rowed and William had threatened to knock Jane's head off. Two weeks before the tragedy, Mrs King had gone to Parker's flat to give the family a cot blanket. He had opened the door and she noticed that his eyes were very red. He then admitted that there had been another argument over money.

The money problems did not get any better, for on Thursday, April 21st, the day before Jane and the children were killed, Mrs Parker had borrowed a shilling from Mrs King, so that she could buy her husband some cigarettes. Mrs King's evidence now moved on to the day of the tragedy.

At 3.00pm she had knocked at the Parker's flat to see if they wanted any potatoes from the shop. It was William who answered the door and he shouted up to Jane to ask if she did need anything. Jane shouted back downstairs, "Yes, she knows I do."

Mrs King returned from the shops at some time between 4.50pm and 5.00pm. She saw Jane at that time, delivered the shopping and returned to her own flat.

By 7.00pm Mrs King was back at the Parkers' flat. The door was again answered by William Parker and Mrs King asked him for the return of a flat-iron she had lent to his wife. As Parker returned the iron, he carried Theresa in his arms and said that Jane was about to bath her. Between 8.00pm and 8.30pm Mrs King heard shouting from upstairs. The noise appeared to come from the Parkers' kitchen and Jane was accusing William Parker of lying to her. At one stage Mrs King clearly heard the man say, "Put that poker down."

This was followed by a noise which sounded like the poker being thrown to the floor, to be followed immediately by Jane saying, "I won't have any more of your lies. You are a proper liar."

At 9.00pm Mrs King left her home. As she closed the front door, someone inside the Parker's flat looked out of the front bedroom window, although she could not say whether it was William or Jane. Mrs King returned at 9.45pm and soon afterwards she heard strange noises coming from the flat above. It sounded like someone was dragging a tin bath across the floor, and also moving a table around. In due course the noises stopped but it was 2.45am before she finally retired for the night.

The following day, the ever-present Mrs King was again knocking on the door of Parker's flat, but there was no reply. That same night she saw Parker at a fairground in Delavel Road, and asked him where Jane was. He replied that she was ill and staying at her mother's house. At the time Mrs King felt that this was rather curious since whenever Jane had been ill previously, she herself had normally looked after her. As for the suggestion that Jane Parker had confided in her that she had thought of killing herself and the children, Mrs King denied that she had ever said such a thing.

There was confirmation of some of William Parker's movements on the days in question. Robert Wilkes, a neighbour who knew him well, saw him approaching Mitchinson's shop some time around 9.00pm on April 22nd. Wilkes greeted Parker as he passed, but received no reply. He watched Parker go into the shop and emerge a few minutes later when he said "Hello" again. Once more Parker ignored him and walked off in the direction of his home.

Ethel Mitchinson, who ran a general dealership at 12 Forest Hall Road, said that Parker had come into her shop at about 8.50pm. He bought some cigarettes and seemed to be in something of a hurry. At the time she had assumed that he was in a rush to catch the second house at the cinema.

Earlier that same day, at some time before 4.00pm, George Dickinson who worked at the same colliery as Parker, had seen William at the pay window collecting his money. Not long afterwards, George Henry Williams, another workmate, saw Parker playing pitch and toss at Bigges Main with a large group of men. He stayed there until close to 5.00pm and when he left, Parker was still playing.

When Williams next saw Parker, on the Sunday, at the golf course, he asked him how he had fared and Parker replied that he had won a few shillings.

Evidence was given of Parker's poor attendance record at work. His foreman, Thomas Lockney, said that Parker was employed as a haulage hand. He had last been at work between 1.00am and 8.40am on April 22nd, but during the last 12 weeks, had been absent for a quarter of the time. He had produced only four sick notes to explain those absences.

Roland Noke was the assistant caddie master at the Northumberland golf course. He testified that Parker had acted as a caddie for a number of years. Noke had seen Parker on April 23rd, last noticing him there at about 6.00pm. He also saw Parker on the following day, April 24th, when he believed he was there from 9.00am until 6.00pm.

Further confirmation of Parker's movements on April 24th, came from John Langlands, who lived at 48 Delavel Road, Forest Hall. He saw Parker outside the picture house at 7.15pm. They fell into conversation and went into the cinema together. During the course of their conversation, Parker explained his absence from work on the previous day, the Saturday, by saying that he had had diarrhoea. The two men left the pictures at 10.15pm.

Arthur Halliday, who was known to his friends at 'Pete', reported that he had indeed seen Parker at Four Road Ends at some time between 11.00pm and 11.30pm on April 24th. He also saw Parker the following day, Monday the 25th, when he noticed that Parker had a bicycle with him. The cycle had belonged to Ronald Wilmot who worked in a fish shop on Gosforth High Street. He had gone to work at 8.00am on April 25th, leaving his bicycle outside, propped against the kerb. The bicycle was still there at 11.00am when he briefly popped outside, but by 1.00pm it had gone. Ronald was able to identify the bicycle found in Parker's possession as his.

Parker's father, also called William, lived at 26 Myrtle Crescent, Forest Hall. He confirmed that his son had let himself into the parental home some time after midnight on April 24th. He also returned between 2.00am and 2.30am the following night. William Parker senior had wanted to challenge his son and demand to know why he had turned up at such a late hour but the boy's mother had intervened and stopped him from doing so.

Joseph Crosby, a general dealer of Front Street, West Moor, confirmed that Parker had been in his shop on April 23rd, at 6.00pm. He had purchased a bottle of lemonade and a cake, as well as cigarettes and matches. Parker had called in again at the same time the next day, when he bought lemonade and shoe laces.

Dr Henry Anstey Cookson was the pathologist at Sunderland Royal Infirmary and he had performed the post-mortem on the three bodies on April 26th. He stated that Jane Parker had multiple injuries to her skull and brain, these being the result of six or seven blows. One of those blows had fractured her skull and although this wound would have eventually killed her, she had still been alive, although probably unconscious, when the ligature was tied around her throat. The actual cause of death was strangulation, shock and heart failure. Both the children had died from strangulation but it was impossible to say if their deaths had occurred before or after Jane's, but all three had been dead for some time.

Dr W.A. Freedman had examined Parker after his arrest. He testified that he had found two dried clots of blood on the accused, one behind his right ear and the other on the left side of his forehead. These clots were not of the same type as William Parker's blood but their presence was explained by Parker's admission that he had not washed or shaved in the three days since his family had died. Since Parker had no visible injury apart from a small scratch on his little finger, which he said he had done at work, the blood was therefore almost certainly that of his wife.

The trial came to an end on June 17th. In his summation, Mr Streatfeild said that it was for the jury to decide if Parker's killing of his wife was done as a deliberate act with the intention to kill or to cause grievous harm, or whether the crime could be reduced to manslaughter if they came to believe that he had 'seen red' after finding that his wife had murdered his children, and what more provocation could there be than that? The prosecution for their part said that they doubted that Jane Parker had played any part in the death of her children and that all three had died at William Parker's hands.

In due course, the jury announced that they had found Parker guilty of wilful murder. As the sentence of death was passed, Parker fainted in the dock but recovered enough to shout, "Oh Jane, why did you do it?"

The appeal was heard on July 11th before the Lord Chief Justice and Justices Hawke and MacNaghten. The grounds of the appeal were that in his summing up, the trial judge had reversed the order of the defence, putting self-defence first when he should have mentioned the possibility of provocation first. Only in this way could the court have excused the extreme violence that Parker had used. The appeal court judges ruled, though, that the order was unimportant as all the various defences had been fairly put, and the appeal was lost.

Parker wrote a number of letters from the condemned cell, including one to his mother asking her not to visit him and repeating that he was innocent of murder. His last visits came on July 25th when a number of his other relatives called on him. The following day, Tuesday, July 26th, 1938, William Parker, still only 25 years old, was hanged at Durham prison, by Thomas Pierrepoint, at 8.00am. No more than 20 people waited outside the prison for the execution notices to be posted on the gates.

CHAPTER TWENTY-ONE

THE HYPOCRITE

SEVENTEEN-year-old William Elliott had just left his home at 240 South Eldon Street, South Shields. The date was Sunday, January 19th, 1941, and the weather was cold and frosty, with a light dusting of snow covering the ground. It was 6.20pm when William reached the junction with Bertram Street and turned right towards South Frederick Street. At the junction of Bertram Street and Back Eldon Street he encountered a man and a woman who appeared to be arguing.

When Elliott first saw the couple, he was perhaps 6ft away from them. The woman had her back to the wall and the man was facing her, holding her clothing with his left hand and hitting her in the face with his right. Although the man was much older that he was, Elliott immediately forced his way between the couple and said to the man, "Come on Jack. Break it up."

At this intervention, the assailant put his hands into his pockets as the woman, who was by now quite hysterical, begged Elliott;" Will you take me to my grandmother's? It's just up the road." The man who had been attacking her seemed to be calmer now and he spoke before Elliott could decide what to do, saying to the woman, "You have someone else to meet."

The woman was still begging Elliott to escort her away from her attacker but he now turned to Elliott and said, "I don't want to cause any trouble with you but if you just go along it will be all right." Satisfied that there would not be any further trouble, Elliott nodded his agreement and walked on his way, turning as he went to see that things had settled down.

Elliott, though, had not gone more than four paces when he saw the man once more grab hold of the woman and rapidly draw his hand across her throat, twice. Though William Elliott did not see anything in the man's hand, there must have been some kind of weapon there for the woman now broke loose, gasping for breath. She dropped the items she was carrying, including her umbrella and her bag.

William Elliott took the woman's right arm with his left hand and ran with her down Bertram Street towards South Frederick Street. Once they reached number 47, a shop owned by Mr Urwin, Elliott took the woman inside and sat her down in an armchair in the living room behind the customer area. It was while the poor woman was sitting there that her head fell backwards and Elliott and Mr Urwin saw that there was a deep wound in her throat which was bleeding very heavily. Elliott went back outside the shop and saw that the woman's assailant had moved from the place where the attack had occurred, and was now standing across the road at the corner of South Palmerston Street. Without any further delay, Elliott ran to Laygate police station where he reported what he had seen.

It was 6.33pm by the time Detective Constable Henry Littler heard the report of the crime from William Elliott. He summoned an ambulance and then he and other officers accompanied Elliott back to the shop in Bertram Street. By the time they arrived at the shop, the woman's assailant was also there, sitting on a table, and he too was now bleeding from wounds in his throat and wrists. They were both given first aid and when the ambulance arrived, were rushed to the General Hospital.

It was Constable Littler who now examined the shop and found an open bloodstained razor on the floor. Also on the floor were a hat, a right-hand glove, an umbrella and some overshoes which were just inside the door and looked as if they had been thrown in, possibly by the assailant. Constable Littler asked the shopkeeper how the man had been injured.

Ernest Foster Urwin was a shipwright who lived on the shop premises which were run by his wife. He said that he had been quietly sitting by the fire in his living room, the shop door being partly open. At the time he was alone in the building and upon hearing footsteps in the shop area, went to see what the customer wanted. The customer turned out to be William Elliott, assisting a woman who seemed unable to speak. Elliott explained what had happened and the woman was taken to the back of the shop where she collapsed into a chair. Urwin said he would look after her and told the boy to run for the police, which he did.

Soon after Elliott had left, the man came into the shop, his hands in his pockets. He walked through to the back room, looked down at the woman and said, "I told you I would kill you, you bugger. Meeting somebody else and double crossing me." Urwin now turned to the man and seeing that the woman was probably close to death muttered, "She is finished."

The man, still looking at his victim, seemed unmoved. He merely said, "If there is one, there is going to be two." With that he took his right hand from his coat pocket and drew it across his throat, dropping the razor he had used on to the floor. Without another word, he then walked across to where a mirror was positioned on the wall and gazed at the wound he had just inflicted upon himself. Returning to the razor, he now took it up again and slashed his left wrist. The razor was once more thrown to the floor and then the heavily bleeding man sat on the table until the police arrived.

At the hospital, it was determined that the woman, now identified as 34-year-old Emily Wardle, was dead. Her attacker,

39-year-old Henry Lyndo White had his wounds stitched and was then spoken to by Constable James Higginson. That officer had been one of those who went to Bertram Street with Constable Littler and he had travelled to the hospital in the ambulance in order to keep White under observation. It was 7.35pm by the time White was able to make a brief statement but even then his breathing was very laboured and he could only utter two or three words at a time. Constable Higginson took down the words in his notebook.

According to this brief statement, White was an unemployed labourer and he had bumped into Emily as she was walking down Bertram Street, towards Eldon Street. They had known each other for 13 years and he had heard that she was going to meet another man. They had words about this and Emily said that she wished to go home and started to shout at him. White continued, "I had an open razor in my pocket and I took it out. I don't know why I did it, but I slashed her and I don't want to live. I then tried to kill myself." The finished statement was read out to White at 9.10pm and his signature was then witnessed by Eileen Rau, one of the nurses.

The inquest on Emily Wardle opened on January 21st, at the Central police station, South Shields, before Mr W.M. Patterson. Only evidence of identification was given, James Patterson Wardle, the dead girl's father stating that Emily had lived with him and his wife at 113 South Palmerston Street. James was accompanied to court by his wife, Barbara Crooks Wardle, but she did not give evidence. Superintendent J. Scott of the police told the court that a man was being treated in hospital and that if he recovered from his injuries, he would be charged with the capital offence. Under the circumstances, the proceedings were adjourned for 14 days, a copy of the father's evidence being sent to White in hospital since he had been too unwell to attend the hearing.

It was 9.30am on January 24th, when Detective Inspector Thomas Davison went to the hospital and cautioned White.

Told that he would be charged with murder and attempted suicide, White replied, "I have nothing to say." He was then taken to police headquarters where in response to the formal charge, White said, "Not with malice aforethought" However, when the suicide charge was read out, White would only say, "Yes, that's right. I tried to commit suicide."

That same day, White made his first appearance at the South Shields police court. His neck was still heavily bandaged and he spent the time leaning against the dock rails with his head bowed. Only evidence of the arrest was given and the entire proceedings were over in three minutes, matters then being adjourned until January 29th.

The case did indeed open on January 29th, Mr R. Smithson Young handling the prosecution while White was defended by Mr Ernest Gompertz. White was allowed to be seated in the dock while the evidence was given. When Ernest Urwin told the court that White had said, "I told you I would kill you, you bugger." White jumped to his feet and shouted, "It's a lie sir. It's a lie." He was told to sit down and be quiet.

Eventually all the evidence had been given, and White was sent for trial at the next assizes on the charge of murder. The charge of attempted suicide was allowed to remain on file.

The trial of Henry Lyndo White opened at Durham on February 14th, 1941, before Mr Justice Charles. Dr J. Charlesworth led the prosecution with White being defended by Mr J. Harvey Robson. White pleaded not guilty, his voice being no more than a whisper as he spoke.

Fourteen-year-old Lilian Scott had been walking along Bertram Street at 6.30pm on the day of the attack. She was a neighbour of Emily's, living at number 109, and so knew her quite well. Lilian saw Emily with two men at the junction of Bertram Street and Back Eldon Street. Lilian heard Emily shout, "Leave me alone. I want to go to my grandmother's." Lilian carried on walking but stopped close to Urwin's shop. From there, she saw White with his arm around Emily's neck.

There was a shout and then Emily ran away towards the shop. Indeed, as Emily went into the shop, she grabbed Lilian's right hand, but loosened her grip as she continued into the shop. At this, Lilian carried on home but added that she had seen blood on Emily's mouth.

Barbara Wardle, Emily's mother, testified that to her knowledge, her daughter had been seeing White for seven years and for the past three, White had visited her at home three times a week. Only now had Barbara discovered that White was a married man with two children. Had she known that at the time, White would not have been allowed inside her house.

She went on to report that on January 5th, exactly two weeks before Emily died, her daughter had arrived home with a very red nose which appeared to be bruised. That was, as far as she knew, the last meeting that had taken place between Emily and White. Turning to the day of Sunday, January 19th, she said that her daughter had left home between 6.20pm and 6.25pm. The next time she had seen her, it had been at the mortuary at 10.15pm that same night.

George Mankin was White's father-in-law and lived at 32 Martin Street, South Shields. White lived in the flat below, at number 30, and the two men had been on very good terms. Mankin testified that White had always used an open razor to shave, until three years ago. Since then, he had only ever used a safety razor although Mankin had seen his son-in-law stropping a cut throat. This, of course, implied that if White had been carrying an open razor, it must have been a deliberate act since he no longer used such an instrument.

Charles Marks was the South Shields police surgeon. At 8.30pm on January 19th, he had examined the body of Emily Wardle at the mortuary. By then she had been dead somewhere between one and two and a half hours. There were three distinct wounds, two to the face and one right across the throat. Of the two facial wounds, one ran from eye to eye across the bridge of Emily's nose, while the other started at her lips and went as far as her chin. The third and fatal wound was on the left side of the neck and had divided the jugular so much that the edges were inches apart. The right internal jugular was also divided, but only partially. Either of these two injuries could of itself have caused death, which would have taken place within five minutes of the attack. Marks had also examined White and found a wound five inches long, but that no vital tissue had been damaged. The wound to White's left wrist was also superficial.

White did not go into the box to give evidence on his own behalf but his wife, Annie did. She said that her husband suffered from headaches and could not sleep at night. As Annie gave her evidence, White wept. When it came time for the defence barrister, Mr Harvey Robson, to sum up for his client, he asked the jury to consider the state of White's mind at the time of the attack. The judge immediately intervened saying, "There is no evidence of insanity and I shall tell the jury that I cannot allow it to be put to them. No one has suggested either by question or by calling evidence, that this man is not as sane as I am. "

The case was, of course, overwhelming and in his summing up, Mr Justice Charles pointed out that jealousy had been the cause of the crime. White had claimed that Emily had double-crossed him by seeing another man but throughout all this time, White had been married and cheating both Emily and his wife, showing the utmost hypocrisy. The jury did not even bother to retire, conferring briefly in the court and then returning their guilty verdict.

There was to be no appeal. White spent his days in the condemned cell writing letters in an endeavour to obtain a reprieve, but on Thursday, March 6th, 1941, Henry Lyndo White was hanged at Durham by Thomas Pierrepoint. There was no large crowd outside the prison. Only three police officers and two press representatives waited for the appointed hour of 8.00am. The notices of execution were afterwards pinned to the prison gates but no one bothered to read them. Later that morning, the inquest returned the customary verdict that death was due to judicial hanging and Henry White was buried in an unmarked grave

CHAPTER TWENTY-TWO

NO FORETHOUGHT

ON April 21st, 1942, at the height of World War Two, Margaret Mary Liell, a 24-year-old WAAF corporal from Epping, married Patrick Leslie Rice, a lieutenant in the Royal Artillery. Soon after the marriage, Patrick returned to his unit at Woolwich while his new wife, now Margaret Rice, travelled north to her base at The Uplands, Kenton, Newcastle. For some time the young lovers could only speak of their feelings in letters and telephone calls, but then, finally, late on Wednesday June 10th, Patrick Rice was told that he could have a 48-hour leave and travelled north to see his new bride.

The couple spent a wonderful two days together but all too soon the time came for Patrick to go back to Woolwich. It was almost midnight when Patrick and Margaret Rice stood on the platform at Newcastle's Central Station ready to say their tearful farewells. By the time the train pulled out, it was 1.00am on June 13th, and as it was a pleasant night, Margaret set off alone to walk back to her billet.

James Jones was a milk van driver for the Newcastle Cooperative Society and by 8.40am his round was almost complete. It was then, as he was driving his van down Claremont Road, Town Moor, that he caught a glimpse of something unusual on the far side of the road. At the time, workmen had positioned some large pipes along that side of the street, ready to lay them over the next few days, but there, almost directly opposite numbers 22 and 23, there was a pale shape partially concealed behind one of the pipes.

Leaving his two delivery boys to take care of the van, Jones walked across the grass and looked over the pipe. What he saw made him freeze in horror. There lay the body of a young woman, naked from the waist down, her legs wide open in the classic rape position. Some of her garments lay scattered around the wet grass and there was a great deal of blood on her face and head. Jones regained his composure and called the police.

It was 8.42am when Inspector Moses Venner received the telephone call which took him to the scene of what was obviously a brutal and vicious murder. He noted that the woman was still wearing a silk shirt blouse, a blue jumper, a pink brassiere and a maroon coloured cardigan jacket, although all these items had been pushed high up on to the dead woman's chest. The clothing that had once covered her lower half now lay in a number of piles on the left hand side of the body. Other personal items scattered about, including letters found in a handbag, identified the dead woman as Margaret Mary Rice.

By 9.00am Chief Inspector Jacob Smith had reached the scene and taken charge of the investigation. He was present when Dr George Edward Stephenson made an initial examination of the body, at 9.30am. The doctor saw that there was comparatively little bruising to the body itself but that the head had been badly beaten. Dr Stephenson performed a full autopsy that same afternoon and he found evidence of bruising around the neck consistent with the pressure from four fingers and a thumb. Strangulation, though, was not the cause of death. The doctor also found a total of 14 wounds on Margaret's head. Five were on the left side of the forehead, two on the right side and seven on the back of the scalp. Several of these wounds had penetrated down to the bone and the skull had been fractured. The wounds suggested a frenzied assault. Someone had battered Margaret, held her down by the throat, stripped her and raped her and left her for dead.

Although the murder weapon was not found at the scene of the crime, evidence was found which suggested what that weapon might be. Police Constable George Herbert Rodham had been one of the officers searching the immediate area around Claremont Road and at 7.15pm on the day that Margaret's body was discovered, he found a piece of vulcanite on the grass verge, just off the footpath. At 6.20am the following morning, Constable John Brennan found a second piece, 12ft from where the body had been discovered and these seemed to indicate that the weapon used had been a revolver. The two bits of vulcanite had come from the hand grip of a gun and the police knew that if they found such a firearm with a broken butt, it would probably lead them to their killer.

It was 6.45pm on June 13th, when a young man walked up to Sergeant Thomas Hogg, who was on duty in an incident room set up in a garage in Claremont Road, close by the spot where Margaret had been murdered. He identified himself as 21-year-old William Ambrose Collins who lived at 17 Framlington Place. Collins explained that he had just been in a nearby public house, the Royal Oak, and had been talking to some of the other customers, one of whom told him that the police wanted to speak to anyone who had been in the area of Claremont Road, late the previous night, so he had come forward to tell them what he knew.

Collins said that he had been out for a drink with a friend the previous night and it had been 1.30am by the time he was walking down Claremont Road. He did not see any woman but had noticed a man on a bicycle who passed him. The man was wearing a dark-coloured uniform and might even have been a policeman. Sergeant Hogg thanked Collins for coming forward and said he would take a written note of what he had said. Collins then went into greater detail about his movements.

According to his statement, Collins had gone to the Royal Oak at around 7.00pm on the Friday. After having a couple of drinks by himself, Collins then enjoyed a game of darts with a friend named Eddie Morgan. These two then drank in each other's company until around 8.30pm, when they left the Royal Oak together and went on to the Traveller's Rest on the Great North Road, at Gosforth. Here they continued drinking until closing time which was at 10.00pm.

From Gosforth, Collins and Morgan went to a dance at a hall in Seaton Burn, where they stayed until 12.40am on the Saturday morning, after which they both climbed into Morgan's car and drove into the centre of Newcastle where, at some time around 1.00am, they had called at the railway station and had pie and lemonade in the refreshment room. They stayed there for perhaps 30 minutes before Morgan drove Collins home, dropping him at the corner of Park Terrace and Claremont Road. Waving goodbye to his friend, Collins then walked to his home at Framlington Place, and the only person he saw was the man on the bicycle who passed him, peddling towards the Haymarket, at 1.40am.

By the time the police had spoken to Patrick Rice, and reconstructed his wife's movements on the night she died, it was plain that there was some kind of link between Collins and the dead girl. Both had been at the Central Station at around 1.00am and both had been in Claremont Road, close to where Collins lived, at about the same time. Further links were revealed when the police spoke to Collins' friend, Edward Bircham Morgan, of 16 Burdon Terrace.

Morgan said that he had first met Collins some ten days before the murder. He gave much the same details of his night out with Collins but added that he had sold his young friend a revolver on the night Margaret Rice died. They had indeed been in the Royal Oak but later had gone to the Traveller's Rest at Wideopen where the transaction was completed. Later still they had been to a dance and then gone on to the Central

Station which they left at some time around 1.00am to 1.30am. After giving Collins a lift, he watched him put the gun, which had a vulcanite grip, into the right-hand pocket of his raincoat and that was the last he had seen of him. The police decided that it was time to talk to William Collins again.

At 5.45pm on June 15th, Detective Constable John Martin went to Claremont Road and there met Sergeant Hogg who was still on duty in the incident room. Martin told Hogg that he wished to interview Collins and that he intended waiting for him in Framlington Place. Shortly after Martin had arrived, he was joined by Detective Sergeant William Checkley and in due course, when a police patrol car arrived, the two detectives got inside and waited for Collins to come home.

It was 6.20pm when Sergeant Hogg saw William Collins opposite the Royal Oak in Claremont Road. Hogg stopped Collins and asked him where he was going. "Home for tea," replied Collins and Sergeant Hogg said he would walk that way with him. As the two reached Framlington Place, Hogg signalled to the officers inside the police car and Martin and Checkley identified themselves. Constable Martin said that he understood that Collins had been in Claremont Road at around 1.30am on the day of the murder. He asked Collins to come to the police station to make a formal statement, which he agreed to do.

It was in that first written statement that Collins elaborated on his meetings with Eddie Morgan, but gave much the same timings as before. Collins was now cautioned, by Chief Inspector Smith and told that his statement did not agree with the known facts. Charged with murder, Collins was taken down to the cells by Staff Sergeant Rex Hetherington.

As the heavy iron door was swinging shut, Collins said, "Can I have a word with Inspector Smith?" Hetherington asked if the matter was urgent, whereupon Collins replied, "Yes, I would like to make an alteration." Hetherington locked Collins into his cell and immediately reported the conversation to Inspector Smith. Within minutes, Smith, accompanied by Superintendent Weir, was in Collins' cell, asking him what he wanted to say.

Collins had been charged that he "did feloniously, wilfully and of his malice aforethought, did kill and murder one Margaret Mary Rice". Collins now insisted that the charge was wrong as there was "no forethought". He said that he wished to make a new statement. Taken back upstairs, Collins finally told the police what had really happened in Claremont Road. It was well after midnight by the time he had finished. Collins admitted that he had also met Eddie Morgan on June 11th, when Morgan had mentioned that he had a gun for sale. Collins said he was interested but did not have enough money on him. Morgan said he would keep the weapon for him and arrangements were made to complete the transaction the following night.

On Friday, June 12th, Collins had visited his family's solicitor, Mr T.A.B. Forster. This gentleman was the executor for Collins' grandfather who had left the young man some money in his will. Collins withdrew £5 of this money, to pay for his forthcoming night's entertainment and the gun he had been promised.

The timing of the meeting with Morgan in the Royal Oak was now much the same as before. The gun was examined and Collins agreed to pay 30s for it. At the time, Collins was short of change so inside the pub he gave Morgan only 10s 0d, paying the balance as they left together. The gun was a .45 Webley and came without ammunition.

Later that night, as Morgan had dropped off Collins, a young woman walked past. Collins claimed to have no memory of what happened next but said that he must have hit her with the butt of the gun. There followed a brief struggle and he recalled grabbing a wallet that had fallen from the woman's pocket. He then ran off home, but on the way, shoved the wallet down a drain.

Back at home, Collins had looked at some trinkets he had also stolen from the woman he had attacked, including a wrist bangle, a handkerchief and a small purse. After some minutes, he went back outside and pushed these items, too, down various drains in the streets around his home. The next day, the handkerchief was flushed down the toilet in the Dun Cow public house. Meanwhile, having disposed of most of the property he had stolen, Collins took a torch and returned to where he had struck the woman. Finding that she was still in the same place, he noticed to his horror that she was in a very bad way and that she had been stripped to the waist. He couldn't recall doing any of that, but supposed it must have been him. He now snatched further property from the body, including the rings from her fingers.

When it was daylight and news of the murder was spreading through the community, Collins had grown frightened and gone to the coast to think. That night, back in his old haunts, he had disposed of further items, including a powder compact by putting them down other drains. As for the gun, he had wiped it clean and put it underneath his pillow at home.

The next morning, Detective Sergeant William Checkley, together with Detective Sergeant Taylor, returned to 17 Framlington Place, where the door was opened by Kate Isobel Dorling, William Collins' mother, who had remarried after William's father, George Collins, had died. She was told that her son had been charged with murder and that the officers had a warrant to search the premises.

There, underneath his pillow, just as Collins had said, was a Webley revolver, serial number 87526. The vulcanite grip was broken. A suitcase underneath the bed contained another piece of vulcanite and when all this was later assembled it was shown that the pieces found near the murder scene had indeed come from this weapon.

The trial of William Collins opened at Newcastle on August 26th, 1942, before Mr Justice Cassels. Mr Paley Scott appeared for the prosecution, assisted by Dr J. Charlesworth, while Collins was defended by Mr J. Harvey Robson. The trial lasted for two days. Collins pleaded not guilty to murder, claiming that he was not responsible for his actions.

Peter Croucher was a foreman in the city cleansing department and he gave evidence of items he had found in various locations. On June 15th, he had examined a manhole opposite the back of 14 North Terrace. Here he found a comb and a bracelet which had subsequently been identified as items which had belonged to Margaret Rice. In a gully outside 70 Back North Terrace, he had found a handkerchief, again shown to belong to the dead woman. Finally, in another gully at the corner of Framlington Place, he had discovered a powder compact. All these locations matched those given in Collins' second statement to the police.

Lewis Charles Nickolls was the director of the North Eastern Forensic Science Laboratory at Wakefield. The gun found underneath Collins' pillow had been passed on to him by the police. He found that the flat portion of the butt end was heavily bloodstained. This blood proved to be human and was of type 'O' which was the same type as the dead woman. Mr Nickolls had also received various items of male clothing, taken from 17 Framlington Place. He found blood of the same type on the shirt, at the cuffs and also on the front of a pair of trousers. These same trousers bore a stain near the fly which tests showed to be seminal fluid. Collins' raincoat was extensively spotted with blood and there were smears of blood on the underpants he admitted to wearing on the night Margaret died.

In addition to the evidence of Collins' statements, Chief Inspector Smith also testified that when searched at the police station, Collins had been found to be carrying an Irish threepenny bit. Patrick Rice had already testified that he had given his wife just such a coin as a good luck charm.

Although the jury perhaps had no difficulty in deciding that Collins was responsible for the death of Margaret Rice, was he, as he claimed, not responsible for his actions? Dr B.G. Derry was the medical officer at Durham prison where Collins had been held after his arrest. Since his incarceration, Derry had examined Collins a total of eight times in order to determine his mental condition. Dr Derry had spoken to Collins' mother and she had pointed out that a paternal grand-uncle had been diagnosed as an imbecile. Collins himself said that four years before, in 1938, he had been involved in a bad cycle accident in which he received a severe blow on the head. He had suffered from concussion and lost his memory for a time. However, Dr Derry was able to say that he had found no evidence of insanity or epilepsy in the prisoner and indeed described him as being of superior intelligence. As a result, the jury took only 20 minutes to decide that William Collins was guilty as charged. Before Mr Justice Cassels passed the sentence of death, he told Collins, "It was a wicked crime that you committed in taking the life of this young woman because she resisted and struggled with you and would not let you have your desire."

Collins' appeal was heard on October 12th. Once again the defence tried to put forward the suggestion that Collins had not been responsible for his actions but the evidence was such that there was no chance of success. The appeal was lost and in due course it was announced that there would be no reprieve.

On Wednesday, October 28th, 1942, William Ambrose Collins, a Merchant Navy apprentice, who killed a defenceless young woman while he was at home waiting for a ship, was hanged at Durham prison by Thomas Pierrepoint.

CHAPTER TWENTY-THREE

A MOST
SIMPLE TRIANGLE

POLICE Constable Robert Redhead had been enjoying a moderately uneventful evening on Thursday, November 29th, 1945. Just before midnight, however, all that had changed.

At 11.30pm on that night in the first few months of peace after World War Two, a young woman in her early 30s; Hannah Burns, rushed into the police station and explained that a man had been shot at her home. Constable Redhead alerted his superior, Detective Inspector Thomas Davison, and after the woman had given a few more basic details, the inspector ordered Constable Redhead to the scene of the alleged crime, 14 Albermarle Street, South Shields.

Arriving at Albermarle Street, Robert Redhead knocked on the door of number 14 and in due course it was opened by a man wearing only his underwear. Of the truth of Hannah's story there could now be no doubt. The man was bleeding from bullet wounds in his arm, abdomen and thigh. It was remarkable that he could stand, let alone hobble to the door and within minutes he had been placed in an ambulance and rushed to the Ingham Infirmary.

The story Hannah Burns had outlined at the police station

was a simple one and, over the years, depressingly familiar. The man who had been shot was 35-year-old John Duplessis, her current lover, and the man who had fired the bullets into him was Arthur Charles, who was her ex-lover. Both were black. The motive was as old as time itself, pure jealousy.

Until fairly recently, Charles had been living with Hannah in Albermarle Street but now that he had been supplanted in her affections, he had moved to a temperance hotel at 6 Dean Street. It was there that Inspector Davison called at 11.50pm that same night. The man who ran the hotel, Robert Watson, confirmed that Arthur Charles was a resident. Further, Mr Charles had come in that night at some time between 11.00pm and 11.15pm. They had exchanged 'goodnights' and Watson was certain that Mr Charles had not left the building since.

When Inspector Davison knocked on the door to Charles' room, it was opened within a minute. Charles was told at once that he was being arrested for the attempted murder of John Duplessis, but he denied that he was responsible, saying, "I did not do it. I have not been to 14 Albermarle Street tonight. I was in the Railway, had two drinks and then went into a café where I had supper. I came here and went to sleep." Charles' room was searched but no revolver was found. Charles, meanwhile, was taken into custody and formally charged. In reply to that charge he again stated, "I did not do it sir."

It became clear that John Duplessis would probably not survive his injuries. He had by now been moved to the Shotley Bridge Emergency Hospital, where he could receive better treatment, but his condition was deteriorating and it was decided to take a deposition from him. At 3.30pm on December 15th, Mr Cuthbert Barrass, a Justice of the Peace from South Shields, together with the accused man, Arthur Charles, under a police escort, and legal representatives for Charles and Duplessis, attended the hospital and took details of what Duplessis wanted to say.

The statement was a lengthy one, but gave much background to what had taken place on the night of November 29th. It read, "I am a seagoing fireman. I am a native of Cape-town, South Africa. I have been living in England now for a few years. I came to South Shields about nine months ago and when not at sea I lived at 14 Albermarle Street, South Shields, at the home of a woman named Hannah Burns.

"I know the accused. I have known him for one year. I signed on the steamship *Tilsington Court* at Glasgow on the 12th of September, 1945. The accused signed on the same ship on the same day. When I was in South Shields, I lived with the woman Hannah Burns as if she were my wife. I know that before I came to South Shields the accused had been living with Mrs Burns. I had no trouble with the accused when on board the ship. We were paid off the ship at Glasgow on the 28th of November 1945.

"After the crew had been paid off, I came by rail to South Shields. The accused travelled in the same compartment to South Shields. I went straight to Mrs Burns' house. I stayed there that night. The following afternoon I went into the Loco-motive Hotel, Coronation Street, South Shields. I saw the accused there when I went in.

"I went to Mrs Burns' for tea and after tea, I went out again. Mrs Burns had arranged to meet me either at the Locomotive Hotel or the Railway Inn, Coronation Street. Eventually I met her in the Railway Inn. She was in the company of the accused and two other men and two other women.

"The accused went out and Mrs Burns went out afterwards. I left the Railway Inn at closing time and went into a café in Church Way, for my supper. When I got in the accused was there having his supper. I was not sitting at the same table as the accused when Mrs Burns and another woman and two of my countrymen came in. They all came and sat at the table where I was sitting.

"The five of us were laughing and joking among ourselves. We were not laughing at the accused. The accused left and a good few minutes afterwards the five of us left the café. This was shortly before 11 o'clock. The others went their way and I accompanied Hannah Burns to her house. I had a cup of tea and then she got me some warm water to wash my feet. I washed my feet and then went to bed in the kitchen. Mrs Burns unbolted the door to empty the water from the dish in which I had washed my feet.

"She had opened the door and I then saw the accused standing in the doorway. He was holding a revolver in his hand and was pointing it at me. He told me three times to get up. I told him I was not going to get up and said; 'What chance would I have when you have a revolver in your hand?'

"He said nothing but started to fire the revolver. He fired six times. I was hit five times, once in the hip, once in the knee and once in the thigh. Hannah Burns had left the room. She must have left by the front door. The accused went out and returned a few minutes later. He pointed the revolver at me again but it must have been empty because it did not fire. When he pointed it at me he said; 'Do you want some more?' The next thing I remember was that the police were in the room and they took me to the infirmary. When the accused shot me he was not drunk"

Having made this statement, Duplessis was now questioned by Mr Donald Haring the solicitor who was acting for Arthur Charles.

The specific questions he asked were not recorded but the answers were given on the deposition. They were, "I have been living with Hannah Burns for nine months. I knew that the accused was finished then with Mrs Burns. I went to the Locomotive Hotel about seven o'clock and left about ten o'clock, closing time. I had had more than ten pints of beer. The back door of the kitchen opens on to the back yard. The accused was just one step inside the door into the kitchen. The electric light was burning. I am sure it was the accused who stood in the kitchen doorway and shot me and that it was not any other man. He stood in the doorway two minutes before he shot me."

From those answers it is possible to determine that Mr Haring was trying to suggest that Duplessis had himself drunk quite a lot of alcohol and since it was dark, he might well have been mistaken about just who he saw in the kitchen doorway. Now it was the turn of Mr Rothfield, representing the Public Prosecutor, to question the badly injured man. Again his single question was not recorded but the answer was. "I am sure the accused shot me and that it was not any other man." The document was then signed by Cuthbert Barrass who witnessed the mark made by John Duplessis. In fact, Duplessis was to hold on to life for more than two weeks longer but on New Year's Eve, Monday, December 31st, 1945, he died, making the charge against Arthur Charles one of wilful murder.

The trial of Arthur Charles took place at Durham on February 14th, 1946, before Mr Justice Oliver. Dr J. Charles-worth led for the prosecution while Charles was defended by Mr William Temple.

One of the most important prosecution witnesses was Hannah Burns. She testified that although she was a married woman, she had been separated from her husband for some years. She had first met Arthur Charles some 16 months earlier when they had fallen into conversation in the Mill Dam café, South Shields. They hit it off from the start, went home together that same night and began to live as man and wife.

The couple had shared the house at Albermarle Street happily enough for some four months. During that time, Charles had returned to sea on a couple of occasions and when he was away, he made Hannah an allowance of £12 a month from his wages. Unfortunately, towards the end of this time, the relationship began to deteriorate and he became violent towards her. Once he hit her and knocked some of her teeth out and she told him to leave, which he did. A month later they were back together but this second attempt to live together lasted only a week. A third attempt was also made but they had been finally parted for about eight or nine months when John Duplessis had come on the scene and they now started living together.

When Duplessis returned from his last sea trip, on November 28th, 1945, he had returned home to Hannah at Albermarle Street. On the next night, they arranged to meet up in the Locomotive Inn but on the same day, a letter had arrived for Charles and she took it out with her on the evening of November 29th, in case she ran into him. When Hannah went in to the Locomotive, Charles was there and she gave him the letter and got talking to him. Even though they were no longer together, they were still on friendly enough terms and Charles bought drinks for Hannah and her friend.

She and her friend left the pub soon afterwards but returned at 8.00pm. They had one drink before moving on to the Railway where they again saw Charles with some of his friends. Again he bought them drinks and he now mentioned that he was expecting a telegram, asking Hannah if she would make sure he got it as soon as it arrived. She promised she would hand it over and they stayed chatting together until 8.45pm, when John Duplessis came in.

Hannah then bought drinks for herself and one each for Duplessis and Charles although they did not sit together. After finishing his drink, Charles left the Railway and not long afterwards, Duplessis also left, having first arranged to meet Hannah in the Locomotive at closing time. In fact, Hannah and her girlfriend were in the Locomotive soon after 9.00pm. Charles was there once more and again sent a drink over to Hannah. He left the pub, some time before 10.00pm but after Duplessis had arrived.

After the pubs had closed, Hannah, her girlfriend and Duplessis went to the café in Church Way. She knew that this was a place which Charles visited most nights and so was not surprised to see him sitting there, finishing off his supper.

Duplessis met a couple of men from South Africa and they began conversing in Afrikaans. As they joked amongst themselves, Charles beckoned for her to come over and when she went across, Charles asked her if she knew what the men were laughing at. He had become convinced that they were saying something about him but Hannah tried to reassure Charles that they were just telling jokes and his name had not been mentioned.

Back at Albermarle Street, Hannah drew some warm water for Duplessis to wash his feet. By now it was almost 11pm and when Duplessis finished she went to empty the water down the drain in the yard. As she opened the door she was surprised to she Charles standing on the second step. She dashed back into the kitchen and then Charles appeared inside the doorway, a revolver in his hand.

Hannah Burns pleaded with him 'not to be silly', but Charles ignored her, pointed the gun at Duplessis and said, "Come on, get up, you are a fighting man." In the normal run of things, John Duplessis was not afraid of Charles, but he was not about to take on a man carrying a gun. The pair argued and Charles repeatedly asked Duplessis to get up and fight, but the latter simply replied, "Shoot if you are going to shoot." Charles smiled and said, "Alright, I have been waiting for this." The first shot then hit home.

Hannah Burns, horrified to see Duplessis bleeding from a wound in his arm, turned and ran for the front door. Before she had reached the street, she heard three more shots. She had then dashed to the police station and reported the matter to Constable Redhead. Finally, under cross examination, Hannah confirmed that the violence Charles had shown towards her was over his belief that she had been seeing yet another man, one Fasil Mear. She had denied that there was any truth in the rumours Charles had heard while he had been at sea.

Evidence was now given of some previous problems

between Duplessis and Charles. On November 26th, 1944, just over a year before the shooting, Police Constable Charles Welsh had been called to Albermarle Street at 10.39pm. There he saw Hannah Burns, John Duplessis and Arthur Charles. It was Duplessis who was doing all the shouting and at one stage he rushed at Charles as if to attack him and had to be restrained by Welsh. Hannah explained that she had met Duplessis for the first time that very night and had brought him home. Charles had come home and objected to this, whereupon Hannah had asked Duplessis to leave, telling him that she wished to stay with Charles. It all seemed to be simple enough but Duplessis was claiming that he had been living there for some time and now Charles had reappeared and Hannah had changed her mind about him. This seemed to be confirmed later, for when Constable Welsh said that it might be better if Duplessis left, as Hannah Burns wished, he walked around the rooms in the house, collecting items of his clothing. This was hardly indicative of someone who had arrived on the scene for the first time that night.

Constable Welsh could only act on what he had seen. Charles was very quiet at the time, and causing no trouble. Hannah Burns stated clearly that it was Duplessis she wanted to leave and that he was the one issuing threats and shouting. Welsh escorted Duplessis from the premises and advised Charles that if he wished, he could see a magistrate and swear out a complaint against Duplessis. The last time the officer saw Duplessis that night, he had been walking off with his belongings, saying that he was going to stay at lodgings at 19 Dale Street.

Next the police surgeon, Dr Charles Marks, gave evidence of the injuries inflicted on John Duplessis. There were two wounds in the left thigh, and two in the right forearm, although one of these was an exit wound. That particular bullet had passed through completely, fracturing the right radius as it did. There was also a bullet wound in the upper part of the abdomen on the right-hand side, just below the ribs and a minor wound on the ring finger of the right hand. An X-ray showed two bullets in the thigh and the bullet which had entered the abdomen had gone through the liver, through the diaphragm and on into the chest where it had entered the bottom of the heart. By the time Dr Marks saw Duplessis, septicaemia had set in and the chest had to be drained. The treatment was of no avail and septicaemia had finally proved to be the cause of death.

Charles' only defence was that this was a case of mistaken identity. He had not left his room at the hotel and the murder weapon was not found in his room. Of course, the only person who confirmed this alibi was the hotel manager, Robert Watson and he could easily have missed Charles going back out to commit the crime. It was perhaps highly significant that on January 17th, a young schoolboy had found a rusty revolver near some railway arches. There were six empty cartridge cases in the gun and forensic tests showed that the bullets found at the crime scene and in Duplessis' body, were fired from that gun. The weapon had been found along a direct route from Albermarle Street to the hotel in Dean Street.

The jury took two hours to decide that Charles was guilty as charged. On March 11th, two murder appeals were heard before the Lord Chief Justice and Justices Sellers and Croom-Johnson. The appeals of Arthur Charles and James Palmer, who had been convicted at Chester for the murder of Maureen Branagan, were both dismissed. In due course, Palmer had been reprieved, but there was no such escape for Charles.

On Tuesday, March 26th, 1946, 34-year-old Arthur Charles was hanged at Durham prison by Steve Wade. It was already the seventh execution carried out in that year, and the second at Durham.

CHAPTER TWENTY-FOUR

FOOTSTEPS

BENJAMIN VALENTINE HEDLEY lived in one of the rooms on the ground floor of 26 King Street, North Shields. The entire house was divided up into six or seven single-roomed bedsits and over the time he had lived there with his wife, Elizabeth, Benjamin Hedley had seen many tenants come and go.

It was on January 17th, 1950, that someone new moved into the room directly above the Hedleys, who came to know the new occupants as 23-year-old Mary Victoria Longhurst and her four-year-old daughter, Patricia.

In fact, Mary Longhurst did not live alone with her daughter for very long. In fairly quick succession, two men came to stay with her but each of them remained there for only a few days. In February, however, a third man arrived. This was George Finlay Brown and he stayed there for weeks rather than days. Even this relationship did not last too long, however, and during the first week in March, Brown, too, moved out of Mary Longhurst's flat.

Brown had not wanted the relationship to end but Mary had moved on and was now seeing another man, Frank Dougal Boucher. Brown, though, was not one to allow another man to usurp him and so he began to pester Mary to return to him until finally, at 12.10pm on Friday, March 10th, she walked into the Central police station where she told policewoman Mabel Ashley that she wished to make a complaint about the way Brown was behaving towards her.

It was this complaint which led Constable Gordon Cowie to call at Brown's lodgings, in his mother's house at 52 Princes Street, at 3.30pm that same day. Constable Cowie told Brown that Mary Longhurst had claimed that he had been following her around, accosting her in the street and generally making a nuisance of himself. He warned Brown that if this behaviour continued, Mary could take out a summons against him and he would probably be bound over to keep the peace. Brown replied that he understood and was sorry if he had caused any trouble. Cowie ended by saying that it might be better if Brown stayed away from Mary altogether, and Brown had said that in future he would. There, for the time being, the matter was allowed to rest.

At 9.30pm that same evening, Benjamin Hedley left 26 King Street. His wife had earlier gone to visit a friend who lived in Norfolk Street, and Hedley had arranged to call for her. By the time they got back to their flat, it was about 9.45pm. The hallways and stairs in number 26 were not carpeted and so footsteps and conversations could easily be heard, especially since Benjamin was also in the habit of leaving his window open to let in some fresh air. It was not unusual then that, when at 10.00pm, someone came into the house, Benjamin was not only able to hear them, but could also distinguish that there were two people and both were women. The women went up into Mary's room where they stayed until 10.30pm. Benjamin also caught snatches of conversation and this confirmed that one of the people he had heard was Mary, the other he presumed was a friend of hers.

Some 20 minutes after Mary and her friend had left, the front door opened again and Benjamin heard heavy footsteps moving rapidly up the stairs. The door to Mary's room opened and the Hedleys heard those same heavy steps walking across their ceiling, Mary's floor. Not only that, but it seemed to be a tread that Benjamin recognised.

It was 10.55pm, only five minutes after the last visitor arrived, when Benjamin heard lighter steps going up the bare boards of the stairway. These steps stopped outside Mary's room, the door opened and Benjamin heard Mary's voice cry, "Oh!" This was followed immediately by a man's voice shouting, "Come here, I want to see you." The voice was one Benjamin knew well and confirmed what he had already suspected. Mary's visitor was none other than George Brown.

The visit was most certainly unwelcome for now Mary shouted, "There's the door. Get out of here and leave me alone." A loud conversation followed during which Mary said that she had been to see a Mr Ridley at the National Assistance Board and he had told her that her money would be stopped if Brown lived there again. Brown said that he did not believe her, whereupon Mary challenged him to go with her to see Ridley the next morning and discover the truth for himself. The argument increased in volume until Brown was heard to shout, "No, I'd rather swing for you." This was followed by a cry of, "Don't George," and then came the sounds of a scuffle, with furniture being thrown about and Mary screaming, "Murder! Will somebody come here?" Finally, the unmistakable sound of an hysterical Patricia crying, "Leave my Mammy alone." filtered down through the rest of the cacophony.

Benjamin Hedley had heard enough. It was time to call the police. As he pulled on his coat, all went quiet upstairs but this was perhaps even more ominous after what had just passed. By midnight, Hedley was telling his story at the police station and by 12.06am he and Constable John William Dowey Atkinson were heading back to King Street.

Hedley returned to his own room to ensure that his wife was alright, while Constable Atkinson went upstairs and knocked on the door of Mary's room. All was still quiet and no one answered. This, of course, was long before the days of police officers having their own radios and Atkinson, realising that he might need assistance to get into the room, had no alternative but to telephone his station from the nearest public call box. Calling briefly on the Hedleys to tell them what he was doing, Constable Atkinson walked to the box at the corner of King Street and Tynemouth Road. Meanwhile, only a minute or so after the police officer had left, someone had opened the door of Mary's room. Heavy footsteps now ran down the stairs and out into the street. Hedley ventured out of his room at this point but by the time he reached the front door, there was no one to be seen in the street.

It was 12.12am on March 11th when Detective Constable Thomas Edward Baikie received the report from Constable Atkinson. Baikie went by car to the scene of the disturbance and within minutes, he and Atkinson were back outside the door to Mary's room. "Is there anyone in there?" shouted Baikie. A child's voice shouted something, although neither policeman could distinguish exactly what was said. It was enough, however, to confirm that someone inside the room might need assistance so Baikie shoulder-charged the door and smashed it open. The room was in total darkness but Baikie soon found the light switch and snapped it on.

Little Patricia Longhurst was hiding underneath the bedclothes. At the other end of the bed lay her mother. Mary's legs were apart, her knickers around the ankle of one foot. She had her head pressed close against the wooden board which formed the bottom of the bed and when the police officers took a closer look they could see that string had been tied tightly around her throat and had then been used to tie her to the bed board. Though medical assistance was summoned, Mary Longhurst was quite obviously dead.

Constable Baikie also contacted his superior, Detective Inspector Anthony Graham, who was at home at the time. He was soon on the scene and having made a quick examination of the damaged furniture, the rucked back carpets and the smashed ornaments in the room, and having spoken to the Hedleys, Inspector Graham took Constable Baikie with him to call on George Finlay Brown.

It was 1.05am when Brown's mother opened the door to the two plain clothes officers. Inspector Graham told Brown that they were investigating the death of Mary Longhurst, and wished to interview him at the station. Brown, who had been asleep in bed, alongside his brother Norman, when the police arrived, made no objection.

Brown said that he was more than happy to make a statement and was now given paper so that he could write it out himself. He wrote, "At 6.10pm, I left home and went to the Hope Inn, and stayed there till 7.45pm and left with a mate named Bob Elrick. From here we went to the Alnwick Castle. Left here 9.05pm, then to the Uncle Tom's. Came out 9.20pm and back to the Hope Inn. Bob left me at 9.45pm. At closing time I went along the street. I saw James Mason. Left him at 10.25pm to go and talk to a girl I knew, Mary. Then we went to the New Quay. I left about 11.10pm came back up the street. Left Boro corner about 11.25pm and came along home which I reckon took ten minutes so that's all I know till the police came for me in the morning."

At 7.30am that same morning, while Brown was writing his statement, Inspector Graham noticed a light coloured thread on Brown's trousers, close to the right turn-up. Graham took this, sealed it in an evidence envelope and gave it to Detective Sergeant William Darling. He, in turn, would forward it to Dr Lewis Charles Nickolls at the Forensic Science Laboratory at Wakefield. Meanwhile, at 11.20am, Brown was charged with the murder of Mary Longhurst. He made no reply.

The trial of George Brown opened at Newcastle on May 30th, 1950, before Mr Justice Morris, the prosecution case being led by Mr E.G. Robey, who was assisted by Mr F.B.H. Hylton-Foster, while Brown was defended by Mr H.R.B. Shepherd. The proceedings lasted for two days.

Frank Boucher, who lived at 51 Church Street, North Shields, testified that he had known Mary all his life, although they had been keeping company together for only about a week before her death. On March 3rd, she had called at his house for a cup of tea, leaving Brown, who was still living with her at the time, to take care of Patricia. She had been there for no more than 15 minutes when Brown had appeared and asked Mary if she would return home as the child was crying. Mary returned but told Boucher she would see him the next day.

The next incident of significance took place on March 6th. Boucher was standing at the corner of Camden Street with Mary and two friends of theirs, Dorothy Waugh and Eddie Saunders. They all started walking towards West End together when they noticed Brown on the other side of the street but walking in the opposite direction. Brown crossed the street, grabbed Mary by the arm and pulled her back, saying that he wanted a word with her. The other three had walked on a few steps and although Boucher did not hear the entire conversation between Brown and Mary, he did hear Brown say that he would 'get her' if she was seen with anyone else. By then, of course, Mary had thrown Brown out of 26 King Street, and he was now living at his mother's house.

Elizabeth Evelyn Crammen had been to the Plaza Dance Hall on the night of March 9th, leaving there at about 11.00pm. On her way home, she walked along King Street, by which time it was close to 11.15pm. She knew Mary by her maiden name of Mary McVelia, and had seen her talking to Brown in King Street. Elizabeth said, "Goodnight" but Mary did not reply. At the time she seemed to be rather heavily involved in a fairly heated argument with Brown.

Although Mary and Brown had split up, it seems that Brown did spend that night of March 9th in her room. Benjamin Hedley had heard them returning and also the sounds of raised voices. At one stage Brown had shouted something about Mary seeing a man named Dougal. This was the name by which most people knew Frank Boucher. The argument had continued until 1.00am and the following morning, Hedley had heard Mary and Brown coming downstairs.

Benjamin Hedley and his wife, Elizabeth, also gave evidence of having picked out Brown at an identification parade at the police station on March 11th. The defence objected strongly to this, saying that such evidence was of no value whatsoever since both the Hedleys were identifying a man they knew well. After all, Brown had lived above them for some six weeks.

Margaret Jean Ritchie lived at 5 George Street, North Shields, and she was one of Mary's closest friends. Margaret detailed what she knew of Mary's movements on the evening of March 10th. At 8.30pm Mary had called at Margaret's house and after enjoying a cup of tea, they had returned to Mary's flat at 9.15pm where they stayed together until 10.00pm. Mary had gone out for no more than ten minutes but she was soon back. They finally left together at 10.30pm, which, of course, fitted in with the evidence of Benjamin Hedley, who heard two women leaving at about that time.

When Margaret and Mary left her flat, Patricia was asleep in the bed. Mary had called in on a neighbour, Mrs Bryson, telling her that Patricia was alone in the room, left her key in the lock on the outside of the door and gone out with Margaret to find Frank Boucher.

The two women found that Boucher was not at home, so they now visited Dolly Waugh's house in Limehill Street, where more tea was consumed. They stayed there until 11.10pm when Mary and Margaret again called on Boucher to find that he was still out. Mary saw Margaret to her house at George Street, said her goodnights and returned home. These later times did not quite agree with what Benjamin Hedley had said but the prosecution were claiming that in the intervening period, Brown had arrived at Mary's room, found the key in the lock, let himself in and waited for Mary to return.

Florence May Okhegwai had spent the night of March 10th with her friend, Marion Bruce, in a public house in Saville Street West, where they stayed until closing time at 10.00pm. As they were standing outside the pub, a man passed and looked intently at her. Later, as Florence walked home down Borough Bank, this same man, who she subsequently identified as Brown, approached her and asked her for sex. She refused, but this at least indicated what was on Brown's mind. Florence put the time of this last encounter somewhere between 10.30pm and 10.45pm.

A pathologist, George Edward Stephenson, testified that Mary Longhurst had been a healthy woman, 5ft 1¾ins in height and weighing 8st 7lbs. The cause of death was asphyxia due to strangulation by a double ligature around the neck. He also produced photographs showing that when the ligature had been cut off, a deep track remained around Mary's throat so considerable force had been used to hold her down and tie the knots.

Dr Nickolls of the Forensic Science Laboratory gave evidence that the fibre sent to him by Sergeant Darling and found on Brown's trousers matched the fibres of the quilt in the murder room. Dr Nickolls had also examined the clothing Brown had been wearing at the time of his arrest. On the right leg of the trousers, he found another fibre which was dyed a yellowish-green, the same colour as the tablecloth found in Mary's room. Finally, he had found a small tuft of fibres which again were similar threads to the quilt.

The only witness for the defence was Brown himself. He claimed that after leaving the Hope Inn at closing time and talking to James Mason he had then met a girl named Mary who said she came from Coventry. He denied seeing Mary Longhurst at any time on the night she died and said that he had not mentioned this other Mary before because he attached no special consequence to it.

The police, of course, had tried to trace this mysterious

Mary, but she had never come forward. The prosecution claimed that there was a very simple reason for this: the other Mary did not exist and the evidence of the witnesses, the fibres found on Brown which linked him directly to the murder scene and the history of his relationship with Mary, meant that he was the man who had been in her room on that fateful night.

The jury were out considering their verdict for just over half an hour. Having adjudged Brown guilty they saw Mr Justice Morris don the black cap and tell him, "You have been convicted of a dreadful crime for which the law knows only one penalty." He then sentenced Brown to death, the prisoner hearing those dread words without showing any emotion. At the back of the public gallery, though, Brown's mother started to sob loudly and had to be assisted out of the court. A woman juror was also seen to be in tears.

Brown's appeal was heard in June, and dismissed. On July 10th, the Home Secretary announced that a 21-year-old labourer, Francis McClean, who had been sentenced to hang at the Old Bailey for the murder of his landlady, was to be reprieved. On that same day, though, he announced that the sentence on Brown would stand.

The next morning, Tuesday, July 11th, 1950, George Finlay Brown was hanged at Durham jail. He was still only 23 years old.

CHAPTER TWENTY-FIVE

MISTAKEN IDENTITY?

FOR MORE THAN five years, 25-year-old Evelyn McDonald had lived with a Bengali seaman named Montez Ullah. They had lived together in South Shields, but due to Ullah's employment, Evelyn was left alone quite often. It was during one of these long absences that she moved in with her lover's cousin, a Pakistani named Tahir Ali, who at 39, was 14 years her senior. When they first set up home together, the couple lived in Birmingham but in due course, they returned to South Shields and eventually moved into rooms at 32 Saville Street.

Tahir was also a seaman, who worked as a ship's fireman, and when he next went to sea, he naturally expected Evelyn to be waiting for him when he returned. After all, he had paid out a good deal of money, giving her a fortnightly allowance of £5 and in total, spending somewhere between £500 and £600 on keeping her happy while they had been together. However, when Tahir Ali did return to South Shields, in November 1951, he found to his dismay that Evelyn was no longer living at Saville Street. She had gone back to Ullah and they were once more living together at 62 Adelaide Street. A friend of Evelyn's, Mary Lucas, was apparently also living with them at that address.

In mid-November, there was a serious argument between Tahir Ali and Evelyn. He had visited her at 62 Adelaide Street and asked her if he could take her out again. At one stage during the conversation, Ali apparently tapped Evelyn playfully on the back with his hand but she took it the wrong way, leapt to her feet and slapped Ali quite hard, to which he retaliated. The argument escalated and so violent did Ali become that Mary Lucas felt she had to intervene.

At one stage she had to step between them and physically separate the couple. Ali, having been pushed away, shouted that he would finish Evelyn off and if Mary Lucas got in the way again, he would finish her off too. He had walked out of the house at this point and had not attempted to see Evelyn again until the night of Tuesday, November 20th, 1951.

At 7.30pm that evening, Evelyn McDonald, Mary Lucas and Evelyn's mother, Katherine, were drinking in a public house in Market Street. There was one other person present at the time and that was Tahir Ali. The group stayed together until closing time at 10.00pm, when they all left the pub and boarded a bus, riding as far as the Town Hall at South Shields. Here Evelyn and Mary, alighted, followed by Ali. Mrs McDonald continued her journey alone.

Ali, Evelyn McDonald and Mary Lucas walked back towards Adelaide Street and on that stroll, Ali made several more attempts to get Evelyn to return to him, or at least to go out with him again. Evelyn was not to be persuaded, though, and at one stage, Ali dragged her into a small side lane and a brief struggle followed. As Mary Lucas watched, Ali pulled out a flick knife and brandished it towards her friend. Far from being frightened into submission, Evelyn was heard to say, "If you want to fight, put away the knife and fight clean."

This comment seemed to bring Ali to his senses for he allowed Evelyn and Mary to continue to walk on towards their home, he following a few paces behind. However, as they reached the Pavilion Cinema in Adelaide Street, Ali rushed forward again and stabbed Evelyn three times. Two of these wounds, to her back, penetrated Evelyn's lungs but the one that caused her death within one minute of the attack was the one which struck her in the chest and went through her pulmonary artery. Mary ran forward and caught her friend in her arms as she fell. Evelyn looked up and cried, "Mary, he has stabbed me."

Ali had run away after the attack but he was picked up 20 minutes later in Albermarle Street. He made his first appearance at the South Shields magistrates' court on November 21st, when the proceedings lasted just eight minutes. The prosecution case was handled by Mr A.G. Brown, and only evidence of arrest was given, Detective Inspector Welbury stating that he had interviewed Ali at the police station and charged him at 11.30pm. In reply, Ali had said, "I am here. Please yourself what you do."

On the same day, the inquest on the dead woman was opened before the deputy coroner, Mr E.C. Glenton. Evidence of identification was given by Evelyn's mother, a widow, who lived at 100 Portland Road, Humbledon, Sunderland. She said that Evelyn, who had given birth to a child when she was just 17, had left home soon afterwards, although she had remained on good terms with her family and Katherine McDonald had seen her at regular intervals. She had last seen her daughter alive when she got off the bus at the Town Hall at around 10.35pm on November 20th.

In due course, Tahir Ali was sent for trial. The proceedings against him opened at Durham on January 31st, 1952, before Mr Justice Hallett. The case for the Crown was led by Mr H.R.B. Shephard, assisted by Mr Gordon Smith, while Ali was defended by Mr G.S. Waller and Mr W. Johnson. The trial continued into the following day, before a jury of seven men and five women. All the evidence was translated for the benefit of the prisoner.

The prosecution opened their case by giving the past history of Evelyn McDonald, what they called 'a very sordid story'. They went on to claim that the crime had arisen out of jealousy and, referring to Ali, added, "The fact that he is a foreigner, and of a different upbringing, is no excuse for his using violence here."

The entire focus of the defence was that the man who had stabbed Evelyn McDonald was not the man now standing in the dock accused of her murder. Someone else had caused Evelyn's death and this was a case of mistaken identity. The prosecution had simply to concentrate on showing that Ali was indeed the man who had wielded the knife.

Mary Lucas told the court how, at one point in the struggle which had taken place before Evelyn was stabbed, the dead woman had managed to pin Ali's arms behind his back and had asked Mary to take the knife out of his pocket. Mary had refused, saying that she was frightened. As for the weapon itself, Mary described it as being one which had a button which had to be pressed to release the blade. Under cross-examination, she admitted that she met a lot of coloured seamen and took money from them. She denied, however, that she had confused one with another and was absolutely sure that the man who had stabbed Evelyn McDonald was Tahir Ali, a man with whom she was well acquainted.

Katherine McDonald also swore to the court that the man who had been with them in the public house and who had later travelled on the bus with her daughter, was Ali. She broke down as she gave her evidence but said that she could not possibly be mistaken. Another witness, though, did confuse matters a little. Mary Clark had been close to the scene of the attack and had seen a coloured man strike out at Evelyn McDonald. Mrs Clark had attended an identification parade after Ali had been arrested but she had picked out another man from the line-up.

No trace of blood had been found on any of Ali's clothing but Dr George Edward Stephenson, the pathologist who had examined Evelyn's body, and described her wounds to the court, also testified that it was possible that her assailant might have made good his escape without having any of her blood upon him.

No knife had been found on Ali, or at his home. Detective Sergeant Ferguson had searched Ali at the police station and at the time he had remarked, "Me not got knife." However, later at the police station, when Ali was being questioned about the attack, he had also said, "She make a fool of me — get my money." This, the prosecution held, was the motive for the attack and was tantamount to an admission that Ali had been involved.

Ali spent over an hour in the witness box during which time he claimed that he was somewhere else at the time of the attack upon Evelyn and that there were two witnesses who could prove it. The first was a man he did not know, while the other was a woman, who he knew quite well. The police, though, had been unable to trace either witness and so the case came down to being the word of Tahir Ali against Mary Lucas. Ali told the court, through his interpreter, that he had not threatened Evelyn at any stage and was not interested in her coming back to him. He admitted that he had been in the public house with her that night but said that he had parted from them immediately after they left the pub and had not even boarded the bus. As for the murder weapon, he had not disposed of it, for he had never owned a flick knife in his life. He believed that another man was responsible, that Mary Lucas knew who that man was but that she had chosen instead to identify him as the assailant.

The jury took only 35 minutes to decide that Ali was guilty as charged. Asked if he wished to say anything, Ali replied, "What can I say?" The death sentence was passed and after hearing it, Ali turned around in the dock and spoke briefly to his sister before being taken down to the cells below the court.

The local Moslem community now rallied around their countryman. Mr Sayed Gulam Shah, the president of the Moslem League of Great Britain said that he had received many offers of help from local Moslems and other communities around the country and that every effort would be made to save Ali's life. Meanwhile, his defence team announced that they would appeal against the sentence.

That appeal was heard on March 6th, before the Lord Chief Justice, Lord Goddard, and Justices Ormerod and Parker. Ali's counsel asked the court's permission to call Mrs Mary Jane Laws, who would tell the court that she had seen Ali at the time he was supposedly stabbing Evelyn McDonald. She was the witness the police had, until now, been unable to trace.

In addition to this, the defence believed that the evidence of certain witnesses had been wrongly admitted and they objected to prosecution evidence which tended to support the identification made by Mary Lucas as to the identity of the assailant. Giving their judgement, the appeal court judges said that not only had Mary Lucas said that Ali was the man involved, but the evidence of other witnesses who heard the words used, backed up Mary's testimony. Leave to call Mary Laws was refused, as was permission to introduce further evidence. The appeal was dismissed.

Telegrams were sent by the local Moslem community to the Prime Minister of Pakistan, asking him to intervene on behalf of the condemned man, but it was all to no avail. On Friday, March 21st, 1952, Tahir Ali was hanged at Durham prison. He never admitted his involvement in the death of Evelyn McDonald.

CHAPTER TWENTY-SIX

A NONSENSE
IN THE LAW

IN MARCH 1957, the British Parliament passed the Homicide Act which limited capital punishment for murder to five possible categories. From that time on, a killer could only be executed for the following crimes: murder in the course or furtherance of theft; murder by shooting or causing an explosion; murder while resisting arrest or during an escape; murder of a policeman or prison officer; two murders committed on different occasions. This somewhat ludicrous state of affairs meant that a burglar who killed while stealing from a shop, for instance, would face the death penalty, while someone who poisoned all the members of his family at the same time would face a life sentence. It was this idiosyncrasy in the law which was, in 1958, to cost a man his life for the sake of a cheap purse.

Linda Violet Ash was a 75-year-old widow who lived in a house in Marlborough Avenue, Gosforth, Newcastle upon Tyne. She lived on the ground floor while the upstairs portion was let out to Mrs Sybil Mary Tate and her husband. Mrs Ash did not let out rooms for financial reasons, but rather because she was afraid to be alone in the house at night. Although she was getting on in years, she was still sprightly enough to lead a full and active life, but the upkeep of the garden of the property was largely beyond her and this was why she placed an advertisement in a nearby newsagent's window, offering payment to anyone interested in helping out.

On the morning of Monday, April 14th, 1958, Sybil Tate was downstairs talking to Violet Ash when someone knocked on the front door. It was a man whom neither lady had ever seen before and he announced that he had seen the advertisement for a jobbing gardener and was interested in discussing terms. As Mrs Tate left, Violet and the stranger were still talking on her front doorstep.

It was late afternoon, around 5.30pm after her return from work, by the time Sybil Tate called again on her downstairs neighbour, but now she received no reply to her knocking. It was unusual for Violet to be out at this time and so, thinking that her neighbour might be at the back of the house, Mrs Tate walked to the kitchen door at the rear. The door was unlocked but when Sybil Tate pushed it open she saw immediately why Violet Ash had not answered her call. Mrs Ash lay on the kitchen floor, her head a mass of blood. She was barely alive.

Rushed to the Royal Victoria Infirmary, Violet Ash died from her injuries the following day without ever regaining consciousness. A murder hunt was under way.

Detectives interviewed Sybil Tate and other neighbours who reported a man who had knocked on their doors and asked for directions to Mrs Ash's home. A description was pieced together and on the day that Mrs Ash died, the police announced that they were satisfied that the man who had called about the gardening job was almost certainly the same man who had battered her to death. He was described as being 40 to 50 years old, 5ft 10ins tall, with fair hair and light coloured eyes. He was also described as being thin featured, clean shaven and had a pallid complexion and a somewhat arrogant manner.

It was also on April 15th that the officers in charge of the case announced that they believed that robbery was not the motive. Mrs Ash's daughter, Joyce Marion Pantridge, who lived at Broadway West, also in Gosforth, had been over the house at the request of the police and said that not only had nothing apparently been taken, but that nothing even seemed to have been disturbed. The police were also able to say that the attack appeared to have been a sudden one. A household hammer had been used to inflict the injuries and since there was no evidence of bruising to Violet Ash's arms or hands, it was unlikely that she had had time to defend herself.

By April 16th, a medical examination of the body had revealed that Violet Ash had been struck from behind and had received four separate blows. The fatal blow had hit her behind the ear and towards the back of her head and it appeared that this, and, indeed the other blows, had been inflicted by a right-handed man. Two hammers had been found in the house and the larger of these showed evidence of bloodstaining and fitted the wounds on Violet's skull. That same evening, the officer in charge of the case, Detective Superintendent John Patterson, head of the Northumberland CID, announced that a request for assistance had been made to Scotland Yard. That night he briefed two detectives who had travelled up from London, Superintendent Leslie Davies and Sergeant Sydney Gentle.

The investigation was widespread and late on the evening of April 16th, police in north Cumberland picked up a man who fitted closely the description pieced together by Sybil Tate and the other neighbours. He had been spotted in a café at Brampton and after he left, the police were called and the man was detained at Warwick Bridge. He identified himself as 43-year-old William Sharpe, a man who was a keen gardener and known to travel throughout the north of England doing odd gardening jobs to earn his living. He was questioned for five and a half hours before the police were satisfied that he had nothing to do with the murder of Mrs Ash and released him.

By April 17th, inquiries had revealed that they wished to trace a lorry driver who might be able to offer them assis-

tance. At 7.00am on April 14th, the day of the attack at
Gosforth, a lorry had been stopped by the police as part of a
routine patrol, close to Haggerston which was south of
Berwick. The lorry had carried a passenger who again closely
resembled the wanted man and they now wished to speak to
the lorry driver in order to find out what had happened to
that passenger.

On this same day, April 17th, the case took a new turn when
it was revealed that after a second inspection of the murder
scene, it had become apparent that cash may have been taken
and that robbery was after all the motive. If this could be
proved, then the case would become a capital one and the
perpetrator, once he was found, would face a sentence of death
by hanging.

On April 18th, Violet Ash was buried in Gosforth after a
service at All Saints' Church. That same day, the lorry driver
who the police had been looking for reported to a police station
at Dalkeith. Thomas Kane lived in Main Street, Salsburgh,
Lanarkshire, and told the police that he had given a lift to a man
who said he was a jobbing gardener looking for work. This man
had been picked up at Haddington, near Dunbar, and had been
dropped off on the outskirts of Newcastle.

By April 24th, the police had drawn up a list of 50 or more
jobbing gardeners and promised that every one would be
traced and checked out. When the breakthrough came,
though, it was not in the north of England, but in London.

At 1.00am on April 25th, 44-year-old Frank Stokes walked
into Cannon Row police station and told the officer on the
desk that he wished to give himself up for the murder of a
woman. Stokes went on to say that he was the man the police
were looking for in connection with the murder of Mrs Violet
Ash in Newcastle. At 4.00am that same day Superintendent
Davies and Sergeant Gentle returned to London and
questioned Stokes. Again he admitted that he had killed Violet
Ash.

According to Stokes' story, he had seen the advertisement in the newsagent's window and, after asking directions, had knocked on Mrs Ash's front door. After discussing what the job involved, Stokes had said that he wanted 4s 0d an hour for his labour. Mrs Ash had said that this was too high a figure so he left the house but stopped on the corner and thought things over. In due course, Stokes returned to the house and told Mrs Ash that he would accept her offer, which had been 6d less, at 3s 6d per hour.

Mrs Ash went into the kitchen and began to remove some tools from underneath her sink. Throughout this time she was muttering something about people not being able to make up their minds. She passed a hammer to Stokes and as she continued complaining, Stokes had said, "You agreed 3s 6d an hour, why bring it up again? Why keep going on about it?" He claimed that Violet Ash had persisted in mumbling about people chopping and changing until finally, in a temper, he lashed out with the hammer and struck her on the back of the head. Stokes said that he had removed nothing from the house, except for the front door key which he had used to lock the door after he left. He then handed the key over to Superintendent Davies.

There was, however, a problem for Frank Stokes. When he had first walked into Cannon Row and admitted his guilt, Stokes had, as a matter of course, been searched. Amongst the property found on him was a woman's purse. It was a cheap, common purse as might be purchased in many stores throughout the country but it resembled one that Joyce Pantridge had said belonged to her mother. If Stokes had taken that single item from Violet Ash's house, then he had killed her during a theft and would be charged with the capital offence.

After Stokes had been interrogated, he and the two Scotland Yard detectives, Davies and Gentle, returned to Newcastle and it was there, on April 27th, that he was charged with murder during the furtherance of theft. Stokes made his first appearance at the West Castle Ward magistrates at the Moot Hall, Newcastle, on April 28th. In reply to the charge, he replied, "I do not wish to say anything at this stage. I reserve my defence and I make a plea for legal aid." He was then remanded until May 7th.

A further week's remand followed on May 7th but in due course Stokes was committed for trial on a charge of capital murder. The trial opened at Leeds on July 21st, 1958, before Mr Justice Edmund Davies. The Crown case was led by Mr Bernard Gillis, assisted by Mr Rawdon Smith, while Stokes' defence lay in the hands of Mr G.S. Waller, assisted by Mr W. Steer. The jury were all male and the proceedings lasted for three days.

There was, of course, no doubt that Frank Stokes had killed Mrs Violet Ash. When asked to plead to the charge, Stokes had replied, "Not guilty to capital murder but guilty to murder." The prosecution now had to show that the cheap purse found on Stokes had come from Mrs Ash's home, in order to obtain the maximum penalty under the law.

Joyce Pantridge wept in court as she reported how she had arrived to see her mother lying in a pool of blood on her kitchen floor on the evening of April 14th. The day after this she had returned to the property with two policemen and made a careful inventory of the things she found there. All her mother's jewellery was safe in a box on the dressing table but the only money in the house was a sixpenny bit and a shilling piece in a purse on the dressing table. Her mother had been in the habit of keeping money in the house and there was usually at least a few pounds in notes in a wallet. On a second, examination a day or two later, she had noticed that this purse was missing. Her husband had seen the purse a day or two before the attack and there had certainly been banknotes in it then. Joyce Pantridge believed that there might have £10 or even £15 inside the purse when it was taken.

Mrs Pantridge was not absolutely certain of the colour of her mother's purse. It may have been navy blue, or it may have been black, but it was very similar in design to the black one found on Frank Stokes when he was charged. Under cross-examination from Mr Waller, Joyce Pantridge agreed that the wallet found on Stokes was of a very common type and that the most she could say was that it was similar to her mother's. She could not positively identify it as hers.

Frank Stokes stepped into the witness box to give evidence on his own behalf. He explained that although he was a hotel porter by trade, he had done work as a gardener on previous occasions. Seeing the advertisement in the newsagent's he had gone to apply for the position. At this point, Mr Waller asked Stokes, "What was in your mind when you went to that house." To this, Stokes had replied, "Merely to seek a job."

Stokes repeated the evidence he had given in his statement to the police about the original disagreement over the fee per hour and added that when he returned to the house a few minutes later, he had said that being an old lady she might not be able to afford 4s 0d and so he would knock it down to 3s 6d. Mrs Ash agreed to this figure and then outlined what duties she expected of him. One of the jobs was the mending of a fence at the back of the property and it was for this reason that she handed him some tools, amongst which was a hammer.

Coming now to the attack itself, Stokes said, "I struck her once. Then she fell on the ground and I struck her again after." Believing that Mrs Ash was dead, Stokes had turned off the radio so that the neighbours might think she was out, and left immediately after locking the front door. He did not take any property from the house, apart from the front door key, which he said he had found in the lock.

After leaving Marlborough Avenue, Stokes had gone to Newcastle Central Station and bought himself a ticket to London. That ticket cost him some £4 8s 0d and that money was his which he had on him when he first went to Mrs Ash's house. In fact, he had had about £11 on him when he called at

Marlborough Avenue. As for the wallet which was found on him, he had stolen that on April 15th from Whitehall Court in Ewell, Surrey. Once again he had answered an advertisement for a gardener and the black wallet he had came from that location.

Having heard all the evidence, the jury decided that not only was Stokes guilty of murder, but that the wallet had come from Violet Ash's home and therefore he was guilty of murder during the furtherance of theft. There was only one sentence for that crime and Stokes listened, apparently unmoved as Mr Justice Davies sentenced him to death.

The appeal was heard on August 20th before the Lord Chief Justice, Lord Goddard, and Justices Cassels and Ashworth. In fact, this would be the last murder appeal heard by Lord Goddard before he retired on September 30th.

For the defence, Mr Waller claimed that the trial judges had not impressed upon the jury that before they could return a verdict of capital murder, they must be satisfied that Stokes had the intention to steal at the time the assault took place. Further, Mr Waller suggested that the judge prejudiced Stokes by allowing part of his voluntary statement in which Stokes admitted that he had stolen a wallet from a house in Surrey. This would surely predispose the jury to believe that a man who admitted one theft could just as well be guilty of another. The final point of the appeal was that the judge had represented to the jury that Stokes was a bogus gardener when there was evidence that he had done previous work of this kind.

In reply, Lord Goddard stated that on the first point, if the jury were satisfied that he went to the house to steal, that was enough in the eyes of the law. When it came to the statement which the defence claimed had incriminated Stokes, Lord Goddard said, "If a man chooses to say something that incriminates himself, why should it not be used as evidence? What a man says has always been admissible as evidence. In this case he was giving an explanation about a purse found in his possession, and a purse was missing from Mrs Ash's house." As for the third comment, that Stokes was a bogus gardener, Lord Goddard stated, "He might have been the most skilful gardener that ever existed, but he did not go to the house to get a gardening job. On his own confession, he went there to steal." That last sentence was of course completely at odds with what Frank Stokes had said. He had never admitted to anything of the kind, but nevertheless, the appeal was dismissed.

On Monday, September 1st, it was announced that the Home Secretary could find no grounds for recommending Her Majesty to intervene and so there would be no reprieve. At 9.00am on the morning of Wednesday, September 3rd, 1958, Frank Stokes was hanged at Durham jail. There were just 16 people outside the prison at the time, 15 women and a man who was a friend of the murdered woman's family.

Frank Stokes had been the fifth man to die on the gallows since the 1957 Homicide Act came into force. A further 24 men underwent that same penalty before this anomaly in the law was removed.

APPENDIX

Although this book contains stories in which the convicted man paid the ultimate penalty at Durham, there were other executions at that establishment during this century. Here then is a complete list of all executions at Durham prison since 1900:

John Bowes 12th December 1900
John George Thompson 10th December 1901
Thomas Nicholson 16th December 1902
Samuel Thomas Walton 16th December 1902
James Duffy 8th December 1903
George Breeze 2nd August 1904
Robert Lawman 24th March 1908
Joseph William Noble 24th March 1908
Matthew James Dodds 5th August 1908
Jeremiah O'Connor 23rd February 1909
Abel Atherton 8th December 1909
Thomas Craig 12th July 1910
Robert Upton 24th March 1914
Frank Steele 11th August 1915
Joseph Deans 20th December 1916
William Hall 23rd March 1920
James Riley 30th November 1920
James Hutton Williamson 21st March 1922
Daniel Cassidy 3rd April 1923
Hassen Mohammed 8th August 1923
Matthew Frederick Atkinson Nunn 2nd January 1924
Henry Graham 15th April 1925
Thomas Henry Shelton 15th April 1925
James Smith 10th August 1926
John Thomas Dunn 6th January 1928
Norman Elliott 10th August 1928

Charles William Conlin 4th January 1929
James Johnson 7th August 1929
Ernest Wadge Parker 6th December 1933
John Stephenson Bainbridge 9th May 1935
George Hague 16th July 1935
Christopher Jackson 16th December 1936
Robert William Hoolhouse 26th May 1938
William Parker 26th July 1938
John Daymond 8th February 1939
Vincent Ostler and
William Appleby 11th July 1940
John William Wright 10th September 1940
Edward Scollen 24th December 1940
Henry Lyndo White 6th March 1941
Edward Walter Anderson 31st July 1941
William Ambrose Collins 28th October 1942
Sidney James Delasalle 13th April 1944
Charles Edward Prescott 5th March 1946
Arthur Charles 26th March 1946
John Wilson 13th December 1949
Benjamin Roberts 13th December 1949
George Finlay Brown 11th July 1950
John Walker 13th July 1950
Patrick Turnage 14th November 1950
Tahir Ali 21st March 1952
Herbert Appleby 24th December 1952
John Vickers 23rd July 1957
Frank Stokes 3rd September 1958
Brian Chandler 17th December 1958

There were no executions at Newcastle during this time which do not appear in the main body of this book, and from the period 1868, when public executions ceased, to the year 1900, there were only four other hangings at that prison. These were:

John William Anderson 22nd December 1875
Patrick Judge 16th November 1886
William Row 12th March 1890
Samuel George Emery 11th December 1894

BIBLIOGRAPHY

NEWSPAPERS

Evening Chronicle
Illustrated Chronicle
Newcastle Weekly Chronicle
Newcastle Daily Journal and Courant
Newcastle Journal and North Mail
Shields Gazette and Shipping Telegraph
Northern Daily Mail and South Durham Herald
The Times

Public Records
ASSI 45 85/5 Shelton
ASSI 45 86/4 Smith
ASSI 45 89/5 Johnson
ASSI 45 98/8 Parker
ASSI 45 101/13 White
ASSI 45 102/3 Collins
ASSI 45 106/2 Charles
ASSI 45 110/3 Brown

INDEX